Lost in Cabbagetown

TERRY BURKE

Lost in Cabbagetown

A Memoir of Surviving Boyhood in 1960s Toronto

DUNDURN PRESS

Publisher: Kwame Scott Fraser | Acquiring editor: Kathryn Lane | Editor: Susan Fitzgerald
Cover designer: Karen Alexiou
Cover image: neighbourhood photo: rear of 622–8 Dundas Street East, corner of Sumach Street, City of Toronto Archives; sky: Unsplash.com/Omar Ram; back: Unsplash.com/Pawel Czerwinski

Library and Archives Canada Cataloguing in Publication

Title: Lost in Cabbagetown : a memoir of surviving boyhood in 1960s Toronto / Terry Burke.
Names: Burke, Terry, 1947- author.
Identifiers: Canadiana (print) 20220403031 | Canadiana (ebook) 20220403147 | ISBN 9781459750784 (softcover) | ISBN 9781459750791 (PDF) | ISBN 9781459750807 (EPUB)
Subjects: LCSH: Burke, Terry, 1947-—Childhood and youth. | LCSH: Cabbagetown (Toronto, Ont.)— Biography. | LCGFT: Autobiographies.
Classification: LCC FC3097.26.B88 A3 2023 | DDC 971.3/5410092—dc23

Canada | Canada Council for the Arts | Conseil des arts du Canada | Ontario

ONTARIO ARTS COUNCIL
CONSEIL DES ARTS DE L'ONTARIO
an Ontario government agency
un organisme du gouvernement de l'Ontario

ONTARIO CREATES

We acknowledge the support of the Canada Council for the Arts and the Ontario Arts Council for our publishing program. We also acknowledge the financial support of the Government of Ontario, through the Ontario Book Publishing Tax Credit and Ontario Creates, and the Government of Canada.

Printed and bound in Canada.

Dundurn Press
1382 Queen Street East
Toronto, Ontario, Canada M4L 1C9
dundurn.com, @dundurnpress

Having brothers and sisters is like having best friends who will never leave you. No matter the good or the bad, they will always be there for you.

Dedicated to all my brothers and sisters.

An Irish Blessing

May you have the hindsight to know where you have been,
the foresight to know where you are going,
and the insight to know when you have gone too far.

PROLOGUE

Like so many big-city neighbourhoods, Cabbagetown has gone through a great number of transitions since it first took shape in the latter half of the nineteenth century. The name *Cabbagetown* first appeared in print in the late 1880s. The area known as Cabbagetown was, in fact, a proliferation of tiny fields and squatter's shacks that had become home for the steady flow of immigrants coming from all parts of Europe and the British Isles. Through famine and war, the migration continued to grow over the next hundred years. Most of the immigrants were so poor they could survive only by growing cabbage and potatoes in their front and back gardens.

The core of the area is generally defined as being bound by Church Street in the west, Bloor and Dundas Streets to the north and south, and the Don River Valley running along the eastern edge. In the beginning it was little more than a patchwork of muddy roads, with a scattering of tiny, hastily built huts, each with a few chickens and its own vegetable plot to help sustain the inhabitants through the long cold winter. But that all changed by the beginning of the twentieth century, with the coming of the railway and Toronto's growth into an industrial hub. The new industries brought a great increase of immigrants into the area, all looking for work in the factories springing up near the mouth of the Don River and along the shoreline of Lake Ontario.

After the Great War, Cabbagetown became domain of small cheap houses, thrown together to meet the needs of the immigrant families that flooded the area. These poorly constructed houses quickly deteriorated, but with every house full, landlords had little to no incentive to make any improvements. The grim years of the Great Depression only deepened the decline and hastened the decay.

In 1948, construction began on what was to be Canada's first low-rent housing project. To make way for the new Regent Park, most of the old, dilapidated houses built between Gerrard and Dundas Streets had to be torn down. The Irish immigrant families who had inhabited the area were forced to move into the already crowded neighbourhood north of Gerrard Street. In his 1950 novel, *Cabbagetown*, Hugh Garner aptly describes the area as "the largest Anglo-Saxon slum in North America."

Irish and Italian people made up the bulk of these new arrivals, but beyond these two ethnic groups, there were hundreds more immigrants from every country in eastern and western Europe. After the Second World War, the numbers continued to increase into the thousands. Added to the mix were Poles, Hungarians, Czechs, Russians, and Jews, all eager to escape the horrors of war. They were looking for refuge and had left war-torn Europe with such hope for a brighter future. But what they found was only slightly better than what they had left behind. There was plenty of work in the factories, but it was hard labour. Most men worked for twelve hours each day, six days a week, and for all that they made barely enough money to feed their families.

Always, there was the dampness and disease to contend with. A Cabbagetown winter rarely passed without influenza and consumption taking a toll on the very young and the very old.

At the dawn of the 1960s, if you wanted evidence of just how overcrowded Cabbagetown was becoming, all you had to do was look at the schools that dotted the area. With the majority of immigrants being Catholic, the two Catholic schools were literally bursting at the seams. St. Martin's, on Winchester Street, had been designed to hold 250 to 300 students. When my brothers, sister, and I started there in the fall of 1959, the school population was well above 500 and still growing. Even with portable classrooms surrounding the property, an extension had to be added to the main building just to keep up with the never-ending influx of new immigrants.

Like so many others before us, our family came to Canada in search of a new and better life. Our family's story began on a hot summer day in the latter half of the 1950s. Having lived in the tenements near the River Liffey, in the heart of Dublin, we understood hardship. Our house in Cabbagetown wasn't much to look at. Unlike the grand Victorian homes on Carlton Street, which intersected with the north end of Dermott Place, our narrow little laneway seemed almost like an afterthought. The road was barely ten feet wide and littered with broken asphalt and so many potholes that it was impossible to walk or drive in a straight line.

Most of the houses along Dermott Place looked like they had been thrown together with leftover wood and just enough nails and tarpaper to keep them from toppling over. We could close every door and window, but that didn't stop the wind from whistling through the cracks and crevices in the walls. When the rain came, there were buckets everywhere to catch the drops seeping through the roof. My brothers and I would run from room to room, looking for any new drips coming through the ceiling.

In spite of our harsh surroundings, our family soon learned to love Cabbagetown. It had nothing to do with the rundown houses or the broken roads and sidewalks. It was the people. We had all come to Canada in search of a better life. I think when you share a common hardship, an unspoken bond begins to form. Sure, we fought among ourselves, but whether we were Irish, Italian, Polish, Gentile, or Jewish, we all stood together when it came to protecting our neighbourhood.

The Cabbagetown I knew is scarcely more than a memory. Cabbagetown still exists, but little remains of the old neighbourhood I remember so well. The strong influx of Irish, Italian, and eastern European immigrants had begun to dwindle away by the beginning of the 1970s. The new arrivals were more affluent and ready to tear down the old and turn Cabbagetown into the well-developed neighbourhood it is today.

CHAPTER 1

GROWING UP ON the south side of the River Liffey, near the heart of Dublin, in the first half of the 1950s, it's a wonder any of us survived to tell the tale. My earliest recollections of Hogan Place are full of old, rat-infested tenements and dirty streets and narrow laneways strewn with fireplace cinders and pieces of broken furniture. Years of neglect and constant rain had left the cobblestone streets and narrow lanes around Hogan Place nothing more than a great patchwork of cracks and gaping, water-filled holes.

My most vivid memories of Hogan Place are of those rare summer mornings when the sun would finally break through the gloom and give us a few hours of warmth. The clotheslines at the back of each flat would sag under the weight of newly laundered bedding. Everywhere I looked there were women carrying laundry, sweeping the steps, and draping mattresses and rugs on windowsills, trying to take advantage of the fresh air and sunshine.

My mother, Molly, who we called Mamie, always seemed happiest on days like these. With all the windows and doors open to the warm breeze, there was no need to use the fireplace. While Mamie and my sisters busied themselves cleaning our flat, my older brother Fred and I would be sent down the block to see if Granny and Grandda O'Keefe needed any help with their cleaning.

Our grandparents' flat consisted of one large room, with a four-poster bed in the far corner and an old, rickety wooden table and some mismatched chairs placed next to the front window to catch the outside light. My grandparents rarely had a shilling to put in the gas meter, so most of the cooking was done over the fireplace in the corner.

When we came through the door, my grandda would wave hallo from his armchair next to the fireplace. Mamie warned us ahead of time not to bother him. Grandda had been wounded in an artillery barrage during the Great War and still had small fragments of metal in both legs. Over the years the pain had only gotten worse. Now he rarely moved from his armchair. Mamie always told us not to be asking for anything, but after we'd dumped the ashes in the back garden and hauled a few buckets of water back up the three flights of stairs, Granny would insist we stay for some tea and a biscuit.

By the time we got back home, our flat would be scrubbed clean and the dampness could be forgotten for a little while. Mamie would tell us to go off and play while she sat on the front steps, drinking her tea and waiting for the floors to dry. On days like this, it was good to see Mamie smile. She might complain when we tracked dirt into her nice clean flat, but she enjoyed all the noise and chaos you can only find in a house full of kids.

Mamie hated when the flat was too quiet. Often we would come home to find her sitting alone, staring into the flames of the fireplace. The moment we walked in, she would busy herself, stoking the fire and pretending it was the smoke that had reddened her eyes. She would never cry in front of us, but every night before bed, she reminded us all to say a prayer for the brothers and sister we had lost.

Those days of warmth and sunshine never lasted long. By early August, the weather would begin to change. The predawn fog would come rolling up the River Liffey and blanket the entire neighbourhood. Hardly a day would pass without rain. Almost every morning from September to June, the sky would turn slate grey as another line of thunderclouds came in from the Irish Sea. For the young and old, there was no escaping the sickness brought on by the constant dampness. By midwinter, influenza and pneumonia would be taking its toll on the people of Hogan Place.

If there was one thing that Hogan Place had, it was an abundance of people. In the early morning we could listen to the women talking and shouting to each other as they leaned out over the windowsills of their flats. Just before dawn, my father, Bill, would join the steady procession of men peddling their bicycles down the street, heading for the docks along the Liffey. When we looked out the front window just before first light, the street would be filled with tiny flickers of light from bicycle lamps shining through the rain and fog. The lucky few were going to work at one of the factories that dotted the landscape along both sides of the river. Like most of the men, my da was heading for the docks to see if he could get a day's labour unloading cargo from any ships that had come in during the night.

When the dock supervisor appeared just after dawn, there was already a crush of men, all pushing and shoving as they tried desperately to be one of the few picked from the crowd. The chosen ones were in for a day of back-breaking labour. If the cargo contained fruit or vegetables, no one dared slow down. All perishable goods had to be off the ship and loaded onto waiting trucks while they were still fresh enough for sale. Rain or shine, the workday ended only when it was too dark to see.

At least these men would come home with a few shillings in their pocket. For the many left standing on the dock, it was just another day of failure. Most of them would spend the morning wandering the city streets. Anything was better than going home to face an angry wife and hungry children. By late afternoon most would be back in their usual spot on the front steps of the tenement. If someone had a Woodbine, it would be passed around until it was smoked down to the very last nub of tobacco. Always the talk turned to the feckin' government or the feckin' British or anyone else they could blame for their misfortune. My uncle Jack said that feckin' Seán T. O'Kelly, the president of Ireland, and his government would be the ruin of us all.

At the start of the month, the line at the labour exchange would form well before dawn. The dole money was barely enough to pay the rent and put a bit of food on the table, but somehow there were always a few pence left for a pint or two at Doolan's Pub, down on the corner. By nightfall we could hear the wives and mothers cursing out the windows as their men stumbled down the lane, singing rebel songs.

My da wasn't a big man, but years of heavy labour had made him strong. Before the Second World War, he had always been able to find work on the docks. After the war, he was never quite the same. He never talked about his wartime experiences, but sometimes he joked about being one of the lucky ones. He hadn't been wounded by bullets or shrapnel, but after years of fighting in the jungle of the Far East, he finally fell to malaria. He spent weeks in an army hospital in India before finally being discharged and shipped home to Ireland.

Growing up, I didn't see a lot of my da. When he was looking for work, he would leave around dawn and not return until after dark. If he'd made a few shillings unloading the boats, he might come home with a handful of carrots and potatoes in his pockets, and Mamie could make enough stew to last a week. The odd time, he would have a bag of overripe bananas that couldn't be sold. Mamie would mush them into a pulp and make sandwiches we could take to school. If he wasn't too tired after a long day's work, Da would get down on the floor and we would all dive on him, wrestling and laughing until we were out of breath. He loved to hear us roar with laughter when he rubbed his stubby whiskers against our cheeks.

My father was always a bit of a puzzle to me. He could be calm and understanding, but if we were caught lying or stealing, we were in for a walloping we wouldn't soon forget. When I was five or six, he would often use his belt across my backside. After a few whacks it would be over. By the time I turned ten, he was using his fists to beat me down to the floor.

Many times I remember curling up in a ball as his fists rained down on me. "I will teach you what happens to liars in this house!" Each word was punctuated with the blow of his fist.

All I could do was wrap my arms around my head and try to protect my face. I would cry and beg him to stop, but the punches kept coming. Many times I thought he might have actually killed me if Mamie hadn't stepped in to stop him. Da never raised a hand to my mamie or any of my sisters, but as he often told us, none of his sons would grow up to be liars or thieves.

Sometimes Da could find steady work for months, but suddenly he'd have another relapse of malaria. Day after day Mamie sat by his bed, watching him shiver under the blankets and wiping the sweat from his face. "Don't be worrying yourself about us. We will be fine," she would say every time he asked.

Sick or not, the landlord still wanted his rent and the greengrocer had to be paid. Mamie wanted Da to rest, but with the constant threat of eviction, he had no choice but to get back to work. But first he had to do something about his appearance. If he looked pale and rundown, the man in charge would simply pass him by. Smudging a little coal dust on his face and pinching some colour into his cheeks might be just enough to get picked from the crowd.

The malaria and years of heavy labour had left Da with stooped shoulders and stiffness in his all his joints. His pale complexion and thinning hair gave him the appearance of a man much older than his forties.

Even when Da was sick, Mamie made sure we didn't go to bed hungry. Somehow she managed to stretch five pounds of oatmeal into enough porridge to last a week. With so many children to care for, her life was an unending struggle. Years of child-bearing had taken a toll on her health.

Rosaleen was born in 1934, the first of twelve children. My brother Will followed two years later, and Michael two years after that. Michael was barely three pounds when he was born. Most of his early years were spent in and out of hospital with frequent bouts of pneumonia. Many times Mamie thought we were going to lose him, but each time he fought back. When he made his First Communion, at age seven, he had to be carried to the altar by one of the nuns. By age ten he had begun to put on some weight and Mamie didn't have to spend every waking minute worrying about him.

Mary Brigit came into the world a year after Michael was born. She was two months premature. She was a frail little thing who fought hard to stay alive. Just when it looked like she was going to be all right, the pneumonia set in. Mamie spent days trying to feed and comfort her and nights sleeping in a chair next to her crib. But as much as Mamie tried, Mary Brigit's health continued to deteriorate. She was just six months old when she died.

All Mamie could do was wrap her tiny body in a blanket and wait for the doctor to arrive. Death among the very young was not uncommon in those days. Sometimes it would take days for the doctor to come and sign the death certificate.

Soon after the doctor left, a small wooden box with a crucifix was delivered to the house. It was left to my father to carefully place her in the box. Late that night, once the children were asleep, he nailed the lid shut on Mary Brigit's coffin. Early the next morning, Da placed the coffin between the handlebars of his bicycle, and he and Mamie walked down to Glasnevin Cemetery. After the parish priest said a prayer over the casket, Mary Brigit was laid to rest in a secluded area of the graveyard. The priests always said it was a special place, reserved for all the babies who had gone to the angels.

A year after Mary Brigit died, Mamie gave birth to twin boys, but one died before he could even be given a name. Someone said the other boy was the spitting image of his grandfather, John O'Keefe. He was christened John, but from that day forward everyone called him Johno.

When Fred was born, some eighteen months later, barely a whimper came from his tiny body. The midwife told Mamie he probably wouldn't make it through the night, but somehow he did. Day after day, Mamie sat next to the fire, trying to feed him and keep him warm. Each day his cries became louder. The neighbours might have complained about the noise, but Mamie only smiled. She knew it was a sign that her baby was getting stronger by the day.

Soon after Fred was born, Mamie had her first heart attack. Rosaleen was twelve when she had to leave school and take over the running of the house. Not much thought was given to a girl's education in those days. Girls were expected to finish primary school and then to stay at home until it was time to get married and start having babies. Da had believed that Rosaleen could be the exception to that rule. She had always done extremely well at school, and her math skills alone could have gotten her a well-paying job as a bookkeeper. Da had hoped that his first-born child would be the one to finally break the cycle of poverty. But Mamie's heart problems stretched from weeks into months. It took Mamie almost fourteen months to recover her health after the heart attack, and by then it was too late for Rosaleen to return to school.

A year later, Thomas was born, the first in our family born in a hospital. Most newborns come into the world kicking and screaming. Thomas's skin was blue and he wasn't breathing. The nurse kept shaking him and tapping on his back, trying to force that first breath into his lungs. His first sound was barely a whimper, but at last he was breathing. When the doctors examined him, they said he had a defective heart valve and there was nothing anyone could do. Mamie stood watch over him day and night as he fought to stay alive. Thomas hung on for almost a month before dying in his sleep. Before Da took the coffin to the graveyard, Mamie made the priest promise that Thomas would be laid next to his sister Mary Brigit so he wouldn't be alone.

I was born in the fall of 1947. My sister Marie arrived roughly three years later, followed by my brothers David and Philip, each two years apart. Rosaleen was thirteen when I came along, but already she was more than capable of running the entire house, while Mamie took longer and longer to recover after each birth.

As we got older and the house got fuller, my brothers and I spent every waking hour playing in the street. By the time I was seven, my friends and I would wander the neighbourhood playing kick the can and hide-and-seek until our mothers called us inside just before dark.

On Saturday morning we would all be on the lookout for the coal man making his weekly rounds. We watched as he slowly manoeuvred his horse and cart along Hogan Place, trying to avoid the many potholes. Suddenly one of the wheels would drop, causing the whole cart to pitch sideways. The kids would cheer as the driver took the whip to his horse, trying desperately to pull the cart back to solid ground. The more we jeered, the more the driver cursed the horse and all of us for being a bunch of feckin' hooligans. We didn't care about him or his horse. We were only there to pick up the bits of coal that spilled off the cart. We might get only a few pieces, but coal was so expensive that it was good to have some extra bits to put in the fireplace.

In the afternoon, my pals Tony Murphy and Al Kennedy and I would head for the docks along the Liffey. If we got there at lunchtime, some of the dock workers would give us a penny to go to the pub and pick them up a pint of beer. If there was no money to be made, my pals and I would walk along the water's edge looking for rats. There were always a few around, feeding on the garbage. As soon as we spotted one of the big brown buggers, we attacked it with sticks or stones or anything else we could find to hurl at it. The rat catcher said he would give us two pence for every ten rats we brought to him, but we never managed to kill more than one or two.

Mamie didn't mind if I strayed from Hogan Place, as long as I was back on the street by dark. When she called me in for tea, I had best move quickly if I didn't want my brothers to eat everything and leave me with an empty plate.

I always dreaded going into the tenement late in the day. The moment the front door banged shut behind me, I was plunged into total darkness. I couldn't see anything, but I could hear the tapping of rats and mice scurrying for cover. Once in a while I would hear the sudden snap of metal as one of the many traps found a victim. Most of the mice were dead in an instant, but the rats were much harder to kill, and they would squeal as they tried desperately to escape. If the noise was loud enough, one of the neighbours would come out onto the landing and put the thing out of its misery with one quick blow from a coal shovel.

A single bulb on the second-floor landing provided just enough light to illuminate the top of the stairway and cast long shadows across the walls. Standing alone in the blackness, all I could think about were the stories Johno told me of the ghosts that haunted the tenements. I tried not to be scared, but it was hard to be brave when

I knew someone or something might be lurking in the shadows, just waiting to reach out and grab me.

As my eyes adjusted, I felt for the banister and began running up the stairs toward the light on the landing above. Now I could hear voices from our flat, but still there was one more set of stairs to climb in total darkness to reach the third floor. Sometimes Mamie would open the door of our flat, letting out a sliver of light to guide me the rest of the way.

Our flat consisted of three rooms. The largest room, at the front, was used as a kitchen and sitting area, with two small bedrooms at the back of the flat. The front room faced onto the street. My da had tried to brighten it up with wallpaper, but the paper had slowly peeled and faded from the heat and smoke of the fireplace. In the corner of the front room was a curtained-off sleeping area for my sisters, Rosaleen and Marie. David and Philip shared a crib in Mamie and Da's room. The one remaining room was just big enough to fit a dresser and two beds, with Willy and Michael in one and me, Johno, and Fred in the other.

Being the youngest in the room meant I had to go to bed first. I could hear them all talking in the front room, but the moment the door closed and I was alone in the dark, the night terrors would take over. If I cried long enough, Mamie would eventually send someone to sit with me. Johno didn't help matters by telling me all about the monster behind the dresser who would come out to get me if I didn't shut up. Michael was the only one who could get me to go to sleep. He would turn on the light and let me check everything in the room until I was satisfied that no one was there.

Michael was only eight years older than me, but for as long as I could remember, he was always the one who took care of me. When I was old enough to walk, he would often take me for long strolls along the banks of the Liffey all the way to the locks on the Grand Canal. I loved to stand on the bank of the canal and watch the barges enter and leave the locks. When the lower gate opened, I could feel the ground shake as the water came thundering down. Once the water levels were equal, the barge could continue its journey down the canal until it emerged into the mouth of the River Liffey.

One rainy Saturday in the autumn before my sixth birthday, I slipped off the steep embankment and went tumbling into the water, just below the massive wooden gate. The lock operator didn't see me, and he began cranking the huge wheel to open the lower gate. The sudden rush of water drove me straight to the bottom. I have no doubt I was only a minute away from drowning when I felt two hands pulling me out of the current and up to the surface. I would have died that day had Michael not jumped in after me and pulled me safely to shore.

When Mamie saw the two of us standing in the doorway, wet and shivering, she was angry at first. But once Michael explained, she grabbed us both in a big hug and wouldn't let us go.

That would not be the last time Michael had to jump in and save my life.

The moment my feet touched the linoleum floor in the early morning, it was a race to get dressed and run to the toilet, near the back garden wall. The hallway was still dark, but my need to pee far outweighed my fear. There was a small bucket in the corner of our bedroom, but that was usually full by early morning. The last one out of bed would be stuck with the job of carrying the overflowing bucket down the stairs and out to the toilet. Most mornings I had to stand in agony, waiting for my turn in the outhouse. Johno was never the shy one. He just peed against the garden wall. If Mamie wasn't watching, he and I would have a contest to see who could pee the highest up the wall. The old ladies hanging out the windows called us filthy little savages, but Johno just laughed as he tried even harder to arc his pee over the wall and into the next garden.

We may have called it a garden, but in reality the area behind the tenement was little more than a wasteland of old cinder and ash from every fireplace and stove in our building. On warm summer days, the pungent odour of outdoor toilets would mix with the smell of sewage coming from the river, and soon the foul air enveloped the entire neighbourhood. When the winds came up, cinder dust blew across the garden, leaving stains on any laundry left hanging on the line.

⁂

From Hogan Place, it was just a short walk to Westland Row Catholic Church. The church was the focal point for almost everything that went on in our neighbourhood. From the first Mass, at seven in the morning, through to the last, in the late evening, there was always something going on.

For those living on the south side of the Liffey, death was an almost daily occurrence. Often, on our way to school, we would stop and make the sign of the cross as yet another funeral procession came out of the church and made its way down Ringsend Road toward the cemetery.

I always dreaded having to go to confession on Saturday afternoon. There may have been a screen between me and the priest, but the barrier was far too thin to hide my identity. Kneeling in the shadows, I would go over the words again and again, hoping to get through it without making a mistake. The moment the shutter in the screen opened, the words spilled out of my mouth: "Bless me, Father, for I have sinned. It has been a week since my last confession." The next part was the worst. Telling him I'd cursed or told a fib to my mamie was one thing, but telling him I had stolen some coal or lifted an apple from one of the carts on Moore Street could lead to a long-winded sermon about ending up in hell if I continued my life of thievery.

Bright and early on Sunday morning, my brothers and I would be off and running down Pearse Street toward the church. It wasn't because we were particularly devout Catholics, but like all the kids in the neighbourhood, we didn't want to miss the eight o'clock Mass. Sunday Mass normally took forty minutes, but if we managed to catch Father Kavanagh's service, we could be in and out in about half that time. Most of the kids didn't even know his real name. To us he was simply known as Father Flash because he could rattle off all that Latin, pass out the Holy Communion, and still get us out of the church in under twenty-five minutes.

Like all my brothers and sisters, once I turned six, I started at the convent school on Baggot Street. The nuns were very strict and could be nasty at times. Rarely a day went by without some kid in our class getting whipped across the backside with a bamboo cane. But with so many kids in the class, it was easy to go unnoticed. I don't think we actually learned anything worthwhile, but if we showed up on time and knew our prayers, we could avoid the whippings for at least that day.

After we had made our First Holy Communion, the girls remained in the convent school, while the boys were sent off to St. Andrew's School on Pearse Street. I may have thought the nuns were harsh, but nothing could compare to the brutality of the priests who ran our school. They hid themselves well behind the cloak of religion. At Mass on Sunday, they spoke of faith, love, and forgiveness, but when the classroom door closed on Monday morning, we were in for another week of terror. If we hoped to make it through the morning without a whipping, we'd better know our catechism and our times tables. If someone had an ink blot on his workbook, he could expect to go home with cane bruises across his arms and legs.

I will never forget the absolute terror I felt the first time I stood staring at the chalkboard as Father McGuire loomed over me. We had been going over long division all afternoon, and I still didn't get it.

He stood right behind me, pointing at the board. "Come on, boy. What is fourteen divided into two hundred fifty-two?"

I hesitated, and he hit me across the back of the legs with his cane. When I tried to protect myself from the cane, he backhanded me in the side to the head. The blows got harder with each wrong answer, and his final blow knocked me crying to the floor. When he pulled me upright, I could feel the warm pee running down my leg.

When Mamie saw the stain on my pants and I told her what had happened, she showed little sympathy. "If the father hit ya, you must have done something to deserve it. Now get upstairs and change your pants."

I can't speak for my brothers who attended this institution longer than I did, but in my time there I learned very little other than an abiding fear of Catholic priests. Like most of the boys in our neighbourhood, I couldn't wait for school to end. If we could just hang on until our sixteenth birthday, we could finally be rid of these priests and go out to find a proper job.

Once boys turned sixteen, it was relatively easy to find work in one of the many factories along the Liffey. As far as the boys were concerned, the arrangement was perfect. The factories were looking for cheap labour and they were happy to make a few shillings a week. Unfortunately for them there was one fatal flaw in the system. According to the law, a sixteen-year-old could be hired at half the wage of an adult. That same law decreed that once a boy turned eighteen, he had to be given a man's wage. The majority of employers saved a lot of money by simply letting the eighteen-year-old go and hiring another boy to do the job at half the cost.

In Dublin alone there were hundreds, perhaps thousands, of men out of work at any given time. Once their dole payments ran out, they had little choice but to join the other desperate men trying to find a day's work on the Dublin docks.

We may have been too young to understand what the future had in store, but my da certainly knew what awaited us all if we remained in Ireland.

When the rain came in September 1956, it looked like we were going to be in for a typical Irish winter. It wasn't uncommon to get a little snow in January only to have it washed away by more rain. It was a novelty at first, but that winter the snow continued, roaring in off the Irish Sea. The prolonged poor weather all but shut down the docks in Dublin. The gale force winds and choppy seas prevented ships from coming up the Liffey. Like so many others, all Da could do was wait and hope that the weather would eventually clear and allow them to get back to work.

Rosaleen had managed to find work in a bicycle shop and Will had a job as a messenger boy. Their combined pay was barely enough to cover the rent on our flat, with just a shilling or two left to feed our family of eleven. I honestly have no idea how she managed to do it, but somehow Mamie always made sure we at least had some porridge and tea in our stomachs before we went to bed at night. We didn't have anything to eat in the morning, but at noon we would line up in the schoolyard and say grace before the priests handed each of us a jam or cheese sandwich and a small bottle of milk. There was a shelter near the back of the yard, but the big kids made us pay half a sandwich to get out of the rain. There were always plenty of leftover sandwiches, but as hungry as we all were, no one had the nerve to ask for seconds.

Just when it looked like everything was about to fall apart, our family fortune took a turn for the better. After years of trying, Da was finally taken on by the gas company. The work was hard but steady, and the pay was much better than at the docks. I remember the look of concern on Mamie's face when we heard the news. She knew why the new job paid more. The work Da would be doing required long hours in difficult and dangerous conditions.

For ten hours each day, he and another man stood at the bottom of a pit and shovelled coal into a large boxcar. Once the car was full, a steel cable pulled the eight-hundred-pound load up the track to the top of the pit. The gruelling labour was made more difficult by the incessant heat and the coal dust that filled their lungs with every breath. When Da came home at night, his face and clothing were always black with sweat and coal soot.

One day in the spring of 1957, Da was injured when one of the cables snapped and the car came crashing back down the track, brushing by him and throwing him against the back wall. He sustained some bruises and cuts. The man next to him wasn't so lucky. The car's big steel wheels literally cut him in half.

Most men lasted a few months, or at best a year, before the stress and strain of the job became too much. Da stayed at the bottom of that pit for over two years. He endured the hardship because there was simply no other choice. He worked and saved every penny he could because he knew full well that all of his boys were destined to labour in the factories, on the docks, or at the bottom of that coal pit. If any of us stood a chance for a better future, we simply had to get out of Ireland.

I can't pinpoint exactly when or why it happened, but early on I learned it was best to keep a safe distance from my da. Still, through all our troubles, I never lost respect for what he had done for us. It must have taken tremendous courage for a man already past fifty to uproot his entire family and move them halfway around the world, just to ensure his nine children had a chance at a better life.

Throughout the first half of the twentieth century, Ireland's single largest export was human beings. On a warm June day in 1959, our family became part of that sad statistic when we boarded the train in Dublin, heading for Shannon Airport and the promise of a new beginning in Canada.

CHAPTER 2

July 1959

I COULD SEE THE look of exhaustion in my mamie's eyes. It was getting late, and still the furniture had not arrived. Almost everything we'd owned back in Ireland had been sold to help pay for our tickets. Our one large steamer trunk, a few suitcases, and an odd assortment of cardboard boxes held all that remained: some clothes, blankets, pots, and dishes. They now sat in the middle of the kitchen, waiting to be unpacked. Da had managed to find some mattresses and a table and chairs at a second-hand store. All we could do now was wait for those few bits of furniture to arrive. Twice Johno had been sent to the neighbour's house to call the store, but the salesman couldn't or wouldn't give him a straight answer. So we waited, jumping up to look out the window every time we heard a car or truck passing by.

My da and three oldest brothers had been in Toronto since early March. Once they had found work and saved a little money, my mamie followed with the rest of us. We had been in Canada for only a month, and little had gone right so far.

Finding a house big enough for eleven people that we could afford to rent proved to be no easy task. The population of Toronto had been growing in leaps and bounds throughout the 1950s. In that decade alone, over half a million new immigrants had settled in Toronto, and still the number of new arrivals didn't show any signs of slowing down.

We spent our first weeks crammed into an upstairs flat on Dupont Street. Each morning at dawn, my da and older brothers would head off to work. While the rest of us slept, Mamie would struggle to make porridge on a hot plate in the tiny kitchen. Once we were up, we had to speak in whispers and walk lightly so as not to disturb the Chinese family who lived downstairs.

Finally we found a house on Dermott Place. It was nothing to look at, but at least we had the entire place to ourselves. Just being able to walk and talk as we pleased was such a relief, we hardly noticed that the house was rundown and in great need of repair. A stale, musty odour permeated the place. Dampness had warped most of the window frames, but after a great deal of effort, my older brothers managed to force them open. When the weather turned cold in the fall, we found out that the roof leaked and the wind blew in freely through the gap in the door frame.

By five o'clock on that first day in the house, we had resigned ourselves to the fact that the furniture was not coming. Fred and I were sent off to the store to pick up bread, milk, and jam. Rosaleen made sandwiches for us all while Mamie took blankets from the big trunk and spread them on the bedroom floors upstairs. No sooner had the lights gone out than we heard tapping on the floor all around us. Thankfully, it was only mice and not those big brown rats that infested the tenements back in Hogan Place.

David was only five and seemed to have no problem falling into a deep sleep as he lay squeezed between Fred and me. Based on the tossing and turning, I knew Fred was still awake, but we didn't speak. We never did. He and I rarely had a civil word to say to each other.

There was a certain pecking order in our family, and from an early age I understood my place in it. Mamie was in charge. We kids could fight among ourselves, but when Mamie spoke, we had better listen. Da didn't say a lot, but when he did step in, the result was usually a good walloping. For the boys, the unwritten rule was simple. The older ones told the younger ones what to do. Fights and arguments were an almost daily occurrence. But, regardless of the circumstances, we never hit our sisters, or any girl. Lay a hand on one of his daughters and Da would fall on you like a ton of bricks.

Rosaleen, who was now twenty-five, had gotten married just before we left Ireland, and she and her husband, Bernard, came out to Canada with us. Eventually they would get their own flat, but they stayed with us until they'd saved a little money. I knew Rosaleen had to leave and begin a life with her new husband, but still I dreaded the day she would actually walk out the door. I always thought of her as a second mother, rather than a big sister. Years of childbirth had taken its toll on Mamie's health. Each time Mamie was laid up, it was left to Rosaleen to take care of us all. As the first-born in a large family, she had little choice but to grow up in a hurry. When Mary Brigit and Thomas died, it was Rosaleen who'd had to watch over each of the babies and sit waiting with Mamie until the doctor arrived.

I have no doubt that Rosaleen loved each and every one of us, but I am sure she was happiest on the day Marie was born. Finally, after what seemed like an endless string of boys, she had a sister to take care of and spoil.

Marie was a skinny little eight-year-old when we landed in Cabbagetown. Surrounded on all sides by brothers, she could more than hold her own with any one of us. Marie was fast turning into a tomboy, but Mamie was not about to let that happen. As far as she was concerned, girls did not play rough games or wrestle on the floor with boys. Girls wore dresses and played with dolls. It was okay for boys to wander the neighbourhood and come home scruffy and dirty at the end of the day, but girls stayed home and helped their mother.

Fred was just two years older than me, but we rarely saw eye to eye on anything. If there was one thing I had learned in my early years in school, it was that no matter how hard I tried, I could never be a match for Fred. The nuns at the convent school and the priests at St. Andrew's used to say that all the good brain cells had jumped from Fred straight over my head and into Marie. I believed them.

Will was twenty when we arrived in Canada. He did manage to find a decent-paying job, but while he never said anything, we all knew he wasn't happy. He had left the love of his life, Mona, back in Ireland. Maybe he and Mona thought that distance and time would change things between them, but they never did. After a few months apart, he returned to Ireland. Mamie hoped he might return to Canada, but after he and Mona were married, they settled down in Dublin for good.

That first night in Dermott Place, it seemed like I had just closed my eyes when I suddenly felt Fred shaking me awake. The sun was barely above the horizon, but the room was flooded with the morning light.

By the time I came down, the kitchen was alive with activity. Once I passed Mamie's inspection, I helped myself to a cup of tea. Mamie ladled out bowls of porridge while the rest of us stood around the big trunk, trying to eat. The lid was rough and uneven, so Michael took the large wooden *For Rent* sign from the front window and placed it on top of the trunk, turning it into a makeshift breakfast table.

"The furniture is coming this morning, so hurry up and eat," Mamie said as she put the bowls in front of us.

Little was said as everyone busied themselves eating. Fred managed to find an old wobbly chair left by a previous tenant.

Three-year-old Philip perched on Rosaleen's lap as she fed him spoon after spoon of hot porridge. I tried to slip some of my porridge into David's bowl, but Mamie slapped my fingers with the ladle, spraying bits of porridge across the front of my shirt. I was hoping she would let me have a slice of bread, but the whole loaf had been eaten for supper the night before. Staring down at the lumpy brown paste almost made me gag. Normally, if I just had a little sugar and milk, I could stomach this stuff, but this morning there was neither. When I asked if I could have a bit of jam on my porridge, I could see I was testing her patience.

"Do you think I'm just a skivvy in this house?" Mamie often used that phrase, especially when we got on her nerves during mealtimes. Her question didn't need an answer. It meant that it was time to put my head down and start eating, if I knew what was good for me.

If there was one lesson that was drummed into us at a very young age, it was this: like it or not, we ate what was put in front of us. Mamie could be a patient woman about other things, but not when it came to eating our food. "Eat every bit of it now, and be thankful for what you've got," she'd say. And always there was the guilt-inducing reminder about poor starving babies in some faraway country who had nothing to eat: "The children in China would be glad for even a small morsel of what you have."

Those early days in Toronto couldn't have been easy for my mother. Dublin was the only home she had ever known, and now here she was, a forty-four-year-old woman starting over in a strange new world, with nine kids demanding her attention. None of the younger one knew about Mamie's heart condition, but every now and then Rosaleen would step in and take over the house. She'd tell us that Mamie was a bit tired and needed to get off her feet for the day. Sometimes we would hear whispered arguments coming from the kitchen. Rosaleen would plead with her to see a doctor, while

Mamie insisted that she had neither the time nor the money for a doctor to tell her what she already knew.

Despite everything that was going on, Mamie always found time to write to her mother and father, Granny and Grandda O'Keefe. Sometimes she would ask us if we wanted to add a little note telling our grandparents how much we missed them. It would have taken less than five minutes to scribble a few words on a page, but I always found some excuse not to do it. When you're young, you think there will be a next time for everything.

The last time we saw our granny was on the platform at the Westland Row Station in Dublin. She hugged each of us, only letting go when we'd promised to write. As the train moved slowly down the track, we kept waving until her figure disappeared into the haze of smoke billowing from the train.

Granny O'Keefe passed away just five months after we left Ireland. Grandda followed less than a month later. Mamie wanted to go home for the funerals, but there simply was no money for the fare. Although the news was very upsetting, Mamie was never one to let us see her cry.

One afternoon a few days after we received the telegram telling us that our grandda had died, I came down the stairs and headed straight for the warmth of the kitchen. An old Irish song was playing on the radio as Mamie sat quietly sipping her tea at the kitchen table. It took me a moment to realize that she was crying. The song on the radio was a sad old tune, "Dublin in the Rare Old Times," sung by the Dubliners.

As soon as Mamie saw me, she got up and walked to the stove, wiping her eyes on her apron. "Go get your brothers and sister for dinner," she said.

When I returned, the radio had been turned off and the kitchen was filled with noise and talk. No one else seemed to notice the redness in Mamie's eyes. She looked at me and smiled.

Nothing had ever come easy for my da, and certainly starting over in a new country at the age of fifty-four must have been exceptionally difficult. He had managed to find a job working for the city, but only with the understanding that he would not be eligible for any type of pension when he reached sixty-five.

Those early days in Canada, he came home long after we had gone to bed. Most nights, he was far too tired to even climb the stairs. Through the floor vent, I could hear him and Mamie talking in the kitchen, and the subject always seemed to be money. We were getting by, but just barely.

My parents came from a time and place where men worked and women stayed at home. My older brothers and sister had grown up in a country where expectations were relativity simple. Boys finished school at sixteen and then went to work for the rest of their lives. Girls finished grammar school and stayed at home to help their mothers until it was time to marry and raise their own families. High school and college were far too costly for working-class families.

We may have been in a new country, but it would take some time before any of us understood that the old rules no longer applied. It was already too late for my older brothers and sister, but for the rest of us, the changes were about to begin.

CHAPTER 3

THAT FIRST SUMMER in Canada was a difficult adjustment for all of us. Unlike in Ireland, it never seemed to rain. Life on Dermott Place settled into a series of hot summer days. Even with all the windows open, the stagnant air kept us awake long into the night. Lying there, unable to sleep, I thought about our home in Ireland and wondered if I would ever see my friends again.

Everything was so different here. Kids would give us an odd look when they heard our accent. The first day I played outside, I was jeered by the bigger boys because I wore short pants. Back in Ireland boys wore shorts all the time. When they left school at age sixteen, they would get their first pair of long pants in order to find a proper job. That afternoon I literally begged my mamie to buy me a pair of blue jeans.

We spent those early days and weeks exploring our strange new world. There wasn't much to see on Dermott Place. The roadway was just a single band of asphalt, barely wide enough to accommodate a car. Any vehicle stopping on the road would block traffic in both directions.

Our house was the first in a series of row houses that stretched all the way down the lane. The front steps of each house butted up against the sidewalk, with no room left over for any type of garden.

With the exception of the odd flower in a pot, there was nothing growing anywhere on our side of the street. Our slightly more affluent neighbours on the other side of the lane at least had their own tiny gardens at the front of each house. Sometimes I thought that Dermott Place must have been an afterthought that some builder had thrown together from leftover materials. Most of the wood-frame houses looked old and dilapidated. When the wind howled late at night, the wood creaked and the house seemed to sway on its foundation.

Every time I walked by the big, bright Victorian homes that lined both sides of Carlton Street, just up the road from us, I could only wonder at how marvellous it would have been to live in one of them. The moment I turned from the top of Dermott Place onto Carlton, it was like entering another world. The homes were large brick structures, with brightly coloured doors and huge front windows. From the street, I could see parlour rooms full of furniture, with huge ceiling lights reflecting off the wallpaper. The kids playing in this street wore proper new pants and shirts. Their clothes did not look like hand-me-downs from their brothers and sisters.

As far as we were concerned, the people on Carlton were rich. Only by looking at the people of Dermott Place could one get a true reflection of what Cabbagetown was really all about. All along the lane there were Jewish and Italian families who had come over as refugees at the end of the war. Two doors down from us lived a family of five who had arrived in 1956 after barely escaping the Hungarian Uprising. Aside from us, there were three other Irish families on our street. There were families from almost every country in eastern Europe, but the Italians and the Irish made up the largest portions, by far, of immigrants in our neighbourhood and throughout Cabbagetown.

Each evening at suppertime, the entire street would be filled with an odd assortment of odours. As soon as I turned onto Dermott

Place, I could pick up the smells of everything from cabbage and boiled potatoes to corned-beef hash and onions. Farther down the street, the pungent odour of garlic wafted from the windows.

Irish and Italian people alike heard racial slurs every day. As a kid, it was difficult to understand why other kids talked about the "drunken micks" and the "wops" stealing jobs by working for less money. Mamie told me to ignore them, but that could be hard to do when some big kid was trying to start a fight just because we were Irish.

One would think that the Irish and Italians could find some sort of bond in all the prejudice we encountered, but aside from a common religion, the only thing we seemed to share was a complete dislike of each other. Whether it was at the Saturday matinee or on the playground after school, we could count on a least one shoving match, which often turned into a fist fight. At Mass the next morning, we could look down the aisle and see the very people we had been fighting with just the day before. Now, all the combatants knelt together, with their heads bowed in prayer. But Sunday Mass provided only a brief truce. The next day the vicious cycle of violence would begin anew.

Behind our house sat what looked to be an abandoned brick factory. The tall wooden fence surrounding the property gave it the appearance of the kind of cavalry forts we saw in the movies. The main gate was secured with a chain and padlock, but a quick walk around the outside soon revealed a couple of loose boards I could just squeeze between. I saw the *No Trespassing* sign, but didn't give it a second thought. Peering through the gap in the fence, I could see the whole compound. A small one-room building sat just inside the main entrance. The windows were all broken, with bits of glass strewn about. The only noise came from a wooden door flapping back and forth in the breeze.

Once I was satisfied that the compound was deserted, I began to push my way through the gap. At that very moment, I heard voices behind me and fell backward with fright. My first instinct was to make a run for it, but one of my legs was still tangled in the fence. In my panic to pull it out, all I managed to do was lose my shoe. I lay on the ground, knowing I was caught. Any second now I would be handcuffed and taken off to jail.

It took me a moment to realize that my capturers were standing over me, laughing loudly. "You okay there, Mac? You look like you're about to shit your pants." They were both still laughing as the taller of the two reached down to help me up. "Come on. Get your shoe on, and I'll show you an easier way to get inside."

These two, Wayne Boland and Jimmy Duncan, were the first friends I made in the neighbourhood. Wayne was just a year older than me, but his cocky, self-assured attitude always made him seem much older.

He lived just around the corner on Spruce Street. The first time he invited me inside his house, I couldn't get over how still and quiet it was. I started to take off my dirty shoes, but he told me not to bother. We were the only ones in the house. Wayne put a big bag of cookies on the kitchen table and we began to eat. After devouring a half-dozen, I hesitated to take more, but he insisted.

"Don't worry. My mom doesn't care what I eat," he said.

Hearing this, I felt truly envious. With no brothers or sisters, he had this big house all to himself. He could eat what he wanted and stay out as long as he liked.

Wayne had trouble keeping friends, and it didn't take me long to discover why. By the time I came along, he had pretty much alienated every other kid in the neighbourhood except Jimmy. Wayne was not a very likeable person, but as he always had money and cigarettes to share, all the kids would pretend to be his friends. He could be mean and nasty if he didn't get his way. He was bigger and fatter than most kids, and he seemed to enjoy throwing his weight around when we played soccer or hockey in the street. Everything would start out fine, but within minutes some skinny little kid would be lying on the ground crying after being run over by Wayne.

Wayne and Jimmy and I were practically inseparable that first summer in Cabbagetown. Looking back on that time, it is hard to imagine how such vastly different people could have been friends at all. I was the youngest by six months and knew practically nothing about life. Wayne may have been a bragger and a bully, but he did seem to know a lot about sex. Jimmy and I were never quite sure if what he said was true, but it was fascinating to listen to him explain all the things adults would never talk about. In our house, if we were bold enough to even mention the word *sex* to our mamie or da, we were sure to got a slap we wouldn't soon forget. Mary Hughes lived near the bottom of the lane, and for a nickel she would lift her dress and let us look. At least we understood our parts were different, but it was left to Wayne to explain how everything worked. Jimmy and I just sat there spellbound as Wayne told us how the parts came together to make babies.

Jimmy was the strongest one in our little group. Wayne might be able to push the rest of us around, but Jimmy could knock him flat on his back with a single punch. Jimmy never talked much, but he had a temper. If anyone dared mention his mother, Jimmy would be on top of him in an instant, kicking and punching until the kid took the words back.

Jimmy's family had come over from Ireland soon after the war. He was the second of three children and the first one born in Canada. Those early years in Cabbagetown had been difficult for his family. His mother suffered from depression and often took to her bed for days at a time. His father got the odd bit of work as a day labourer, but never anything permanent. When he did make a little money, he usually spent it on drink at the Winchester Hotel. Soon the family was surviving on a tiny amount of welfare money and food parcels from the Saint Vincent de Paul, a Catholic service organization.

Jimmy was eleven years old when his father left. He said he was going to the store to pick up a pack of cigarettes, but he never came home. His family waited all that day and into the next before calling the police. They checked the hospitals and searched every street and alleyway, but he was nowhere to be found. After weeks of searching, the police gave up.

When they told Mrs. Duncan they had seen this happen many times before, she simply refused to accept the fact that her husband had abandoned them. Jimmy's mother had always been sickly, but when her husband disappeared, she lost her sanity. Many months passed and still she couldn't let go of the idea that her husband would return. Every time I passed their house, near the bottom of the lane, I saw her sitting there, staring out the window. Day after day, she watched and waited for a husband who was never coming home.

The one time I called on Jimmy, she began shouting the moment she opened the door. "Jimmy's not here. Now get away with ya before I call the police!" After a while, none of the kids on our street dared knock on the door.

Sometimes I'd hear some of the women gossiping about the crazy lady who lived down the lane. When I mentioned it to Mamie, she scolded me for eavesdropping.

"Besides," she said, "that poor woman has enough problems of her own."

Mamie liked Jimmy and would often invite him in for a glass of Kool-Aid on those hot summer days. She liked Wayne at first — until the day she saw the cigarettes in his shirt pocket. She didn't say anything to him, but she warned me that if she ever caught me smoking, she would wallop me into next week.

That summer was a long succession of sweltering days. Once in a while someone might bring out a ball to kick around, but most of the time we picked a tin can out of the garbage and used it to play soccer. Sometimes I would ask Fred to join in, but he seemed more content to sit on the front steps, reading one of his library books. Sometimes Mamie would force me to include David in our game. At first he would be very enthusiastic and ready to go, but he was no match for the much bigger kids. I have to say he was much tougher than I thought. Even when he was knocked to the ground and his nose started to bleed, he didn't cry. When Mamie saw the state of him, she blamed me.

Between the screaming kids and the pushing and shoving, the game would last only a few minutes before a fight broke out. Soon one of the women would stick her head out her window and order us to get the hell away from her front door. Every woman on the block knew us all by name, and if we were bold enough to talk back, we'd be called cheeky buggers and threatened with everything from a soup ladle to a broom if we didn't mind our manners. The game would start at the top of the street, but by the time we were called in for tea, we were down at the far end of the lane.

After Sunday Mass, I could always find Wayne and Jimmy hanging around the back of Woolworths, watching the older men pitch pennies against the wall. If we were lucky, the winner might give us fifteen cents to take to the corner store to buy cigarettes for him. Five loose cigarettes cost a dime, leaving us a nickel to buy a big piece of toffee to split between ourselves. Sometimes, while the clerk was busy counting out the cigarettes, Jimmy would swipe a bar of chocolate and stick it down the front of his pants. We knew it was a sin to steal, but Jimmy said it wasn't really wrong if you were stealing food to feed your little sister.

If we wanted to make some quick money, Wayne, Jimmy, and I would head up Parliament and hang around the Winchester Tavern. Friday afternoon was always the best time to stake out a spot near the front door. For the men who had a job, it was payday, and for the unemployed, it was the day they collected their dole. By late afternoon the bar was crowded with men trying to quench their thirst. If we hung around the door long enough, a few drunk men would stumble out, looking for something to eat. The chip wagon sat in an empty lot just a few blocks up the street, but after an afternoon of heavy drinking, these men were far too wobbly to make the trip. An order of fish and chips cost fifty cents, but if we ran all the way there and back, most men would let us keep whatever change was left over.

All day long the bars would be packed with thirsty men, but at nightfall, when their money had run out, they would pour onto the street. It never took long for the trouble to start and the squad cars to arrive. Most men were smart enough to quiet down and head home. The rowdy few who refused to listen would find themselves hauled away in the paddy wagon and would spend the rest of their weekend in the drunk tank at the Queen Street police station.

Whenever my friends and I managed to scrape a little money together, we'd pick up some day-old biscuits at Christie's Bakery. We could smell the bakery from well down the block. The freshly baked bread and all the trays of cake in the window were enough to get my stomach grumbling. The smile from the lady behind the counter turned to disdain as soon as we asked if she had any day-old biscuits. Mamie had taught us to always be polite, but it was hard to do when the lady mumbled about us being a scruffy lot, even as she was taking our money.

The bakery was not far away, but getting there and back could be a problem. Once we passed the corner of Parliament and Gerrard, we were liable to run into the gangs that hung around the Regent Park housing project. We may have told each other that we weren't afraid, but we steered clear of the apartment buildings where the gangs hung out, ready to pounce on anyone entering their turf.

In spite of my caution, I did get jumped one Saturday afternoon during that first summer in Cabbagetown. Mamie had sent me to pick up a loaf of day-old bread. The bakery was crowded that day, and by the time I left the store, it was getting late. I foolishly decided to save time by cutting between the apartment buildings. I was less than a block from the corner of Gerrard and Parliament when my luck ran out. I tried to ignore the four boys blocking my path, but they didn't move. I was trying to skirt around them when one of them suddenly grabbed my shirt and spun me around, knocking the bread out of my hand. Before I could get my balance, the biggest kid punched me in the side of the head and knocked me to the ground. Now all four of them were standing over me, laughing.

"Let's see some money, kid," one of them said as he kicked me in the ribs.

I really wished I had something to give them, but I had spent all the money on the bread that now lay scattered on the ground. Telling them I had nothing only made them angrier, and the kicks and blows continued to rain down on me. One of them began stomping on the bread and squashing it into the ground with both feet.

The ringleader finally reached down and pulled me up by the shirt. "This is what happens to little mick bastards when they don't give us money!"

Someone told me later that I had been hit by a bottle. All I remember was the ringing in my ears and the blood dripping through my hair and down my forehead. Through the haze, I could feel myself being loaded into the back seat of a car and hear someone telling me that I was going to the hospital.

When I came to my senses I was lying on a table in the hospital clinic. By the time Da showed up, I was already stitched and bandaged and wanted nothing more than to get out of there before they could stick another needle in me. Standing on the white tile floor in his dirty work overalls, Da looked completely out of place. I could see the look of disapproval on the nurse's face when he leaned down next to me, leaving a small dark hand stain on the white sheet. I thought Da would be angry at me because he'd had to leave work early or for all the blood and vomit stains on my shirt. Da didn't like it when any of his boys cried, but with the pain in my head and the thought of getting a good walloping when I arrived home with no bread, it was hard to hold back the tears. But all the way home in the streetcar he never let go of my hand.

I was relieved to see that Mamie wasn't upset over the state of my clothes. All I wanted to do was lie down, but Mamie insisted on calling the police. When the squad car arrived, every kid on the street crowded around, trying to find out what was going on.

I had rarely seen Mamie as angry as she was that day. "He could have been killed!" she said, pointing at the bandage on my head as if to emphasize the point.

The police officer just shrugged and said there was nothing he could do. The boys who'd done this were long gone, and I couldn't tell him who they were.

It took Mamie a long time to calm down. I wasn't very hungry, but she insisted I eat a piece of bread and butter and drink some tea before she sent me off to bed. It must have been well after midnight when I was startled awake from a dream in which I was unable to move as a huge boot slowly descended toward my head. For a moment I lay there not knowing where I was. Then I felt Mamie's hand stroking my hair as she told me everything was all right. Just before dawn, she shook me awake. As soon as I opened my eyes, she smiled and told me to go back to sleep. I didn't realize it at the time, but Mamie was terrified that I wouldn't wake up. She still had vivid memories of that night long ago when my sister Mary Brigit had died in her sleep.

When I woke up in the morning, I felt much better. Mamie looked so relieved when I told her my headache was gone. I wanted to go outside and play, but she wouldn't hear of it. I didn't like staying in bed, but at least it was nice to have Mamie all to myself for a few hours. When I was finally let out to play, with that big white bandage around my head, I was the talk of the whole street.

There is no doubt that Cabbagetown was a tough place to grow up. People there always said that if you managed to survive your youth, you would grow up to become either a priest or an axe murderer. Early on it seemed to me that most of the kids in Regent Park were inclined toward the latter.

As soon as Johno heard what had happened, he wanted to take me down to Regent Park so I could point out the kids who had attacked me. I was glad when Mamie told him to stop talking so foolish. Johno had grown into a strapping sixteen-year-old, and I was sure he'd have no problem dealing with the entire gang. But for now I didn't want to go anywhere near Regent Park. Besides, my pals and I had already figured out how to get even. Only Wayne and Jimmy knew I had lied to the police officer. I didn't know the boys' names, but I'd seen two of them at the movie matinee on Saturday afternoon. We would wait for the right time and place to get my revenge.

If I wanted to see the Saturday matinee, there was only one way to scrape the money together. Wayne had a wagon he never used, and he'd let me borrow it for twenty-five cents a day. As long as Mamie was satisfied with my jobs in the house and in the garden, I could pick up the wagon by ten in the morning and head for Power Supermarket, which was full of women doing their weekly shopping. Most women didn't drive in those days, and they were always looking for someone to help them home with their groceries. Once there, I'd join the line of kids with their wagons parked out front. Slowly but surely the line of wagons would move forward until I'd finally made it to the front. Not everyone wanted help. All I could do was look enthusiastic and ask each woman as she came out the door, "Can I carry your groceries, missus?" Once I had a customer, I loaded the bags into the wagon and followed her home, hoping that the woman was generous and didn't live too far away. Most would give me ten or fifteen cents, depending on the distance I had to travel. On a busy Saturday morning, I could make just enough money to pay off Wayne and still have a quarter for the movies. Jimmy and I never had money to buy candy, but if one of us distracted the saleswoman in Woolworths, the other one could easily slip a chocolate bar into a coat pocket.

Regardless of what movie was showing, the matinee was always packed with screaming kids. Gangster movies or westerns were very popular, but as long as there was lots of action, we loved it. If Roy Rogers's or Gene Autry's name appeared on the screen, the theatre would immediately erupt into a chorus of boos and jeers. Show us the Lone Ranger or the Cisco Kid galloping across the screen or James Cagney shooting it out with the cops and we would cheer all afternoon.

The dialogue didn't matter much because we could never hear it. But prolonged talking made the crowd restless. "Come on, get to the good part!" someone would shout at the people on the big screen, as more and more kids joined in the mayhem. If things really got out of hand, the movie would suddenly stop and the house lights would come on. An uneasy silence descended over the theatre as the manager made his way down to the front. The message was always the same: "You're all a bunch of hooligans, and if you don't pipe down, I'll kick you out on the street!" No one spoke as he moved back up the aisle, mumbling to himself. His threats worked for a few minutes, but once the lights went down, the spitballs, popcorn, and empty Cracker Jack boxes would again begin to fly.

On a Saturday in late July 1959, my movie-going days came to an abrupt end, at least for the next couple of months. Jimmy couldn't make it to the matinee that day, and I wasn't looking forward to spending an entire afternoon watching Wayne stuff his face with candy while I had nothing. If Jimmy had been there, we could have easily lifted a chocolate bar from Woolworths, but I never should have tried it alone. I was halfway to the door with a bar in my pocket when I felt a hand grab me from behind.

Thankfully, Da was still at work when the cop brought me to our door. Maybe it would have been better if Da had been there. At least it would have been over quickly. Instead, I spent an endless afternoon dreading what would happen when he came home.

If there was one thing my da would never tolerate, it was having a thief in the family. When he beat me that day, I thought he was going to kill me. He kept punching me until Mamie pulled him off. As he was leaving the room, he warned me to stay out of his sight if I knew what was good for me. It took him a long time to calm down, and for days I had to leave the room anytime he entered. And for the next month, I was allowed to leave the house only to attend confession and Mass. It would be late September before I regained some level of freedom. I could go to the Saturday matinee, but had to take Marie and David with me, to make sure I didn't do any more shoplifting.

Saturday night was never my favourite time of the week. Mamie made us eat our dinner early to make sure we fasted the full twelve hours before going to Communion on Sunday morning. After Fred and I did the dishes, it was time for a bath. I didn't mind the washing and scrubbing — it was what came after that I truly dreaded. Mamie would have us sit at the table and lean forward over a sheet of old newspaper spread out on the table. With our hair still wet, she would take a wire brush and slowly run it from the back of our heads to the front. It was hard not to cry when those tight wire bristles dug right into my scalp. It felt like every hair on my head was being pulled out by the root.

During the school year, we had to endure this torture at least twice each week. Every Monday morning, before the first class, the nuns would line us up and inspect our heads for lice and fleas. Rarely a week went by without someone being sent home with a curt note telling their mother that her child was dirty and in need of a good wash. We could squirm and cry as much as we liked, but Mamie was bound and determined that the nuns would never say any of her kids were dirty.

Early on Sunday morning, Mamie would shout up the stairs to wake us all and tell us to get ready for Mass. By the time we came downstairs, she was already busy making porridge for her three youngest, who hadn't yet made their First Communion, while the rest of us would have to starve until we came home from Mass and Holy Communion.

Before we headed out the door, we had to pass inspection. Marie would fidget as Mamie tried to comb the tangles from her hair. I always felt sorry for poor David. He had a persistent infection that required him to wear a patch over one eye. I knew it bothered him when kids made fun of his patch, but he never talked about it. Once Mamie was satisfied with our appearance, she would add a final touch by licking her fingers and flattening every hair on our heads.

Philip was just three years old, and keeping him clean on Sunday morning could be a real challenge. Mamie had tried leaving him home with one of the older siblings babysitting, but as soon as he realized he was being left behind, he would grab on to Mamie's leg and start crying and begging to go along. She could never say no to Philip. Mamie loved us all, but Philip would always be her special baby. She was forty-two when he was born. It was a long and difficult birth that caused even more stress on her already weakened heart. The doctors told her what she already knew. Philip would be the last child she'd ever have.

I really don't know what the rest of my siblings got out of it, but for me, Sunday Mass was just something I had to endure each week. The whole family went together, so there no choice but to go. But even if I had been alone, I still would have gone because I was afraid of what might happen if I missed Mass. From as far back as I could remember, the priests and nuns had warned us about the mortal sin that those who failed to keep the Sabbath were committing and the fiery punishment that awaited them.

My mind often goes back to those endless hours spent listening to priests through Masses, novenas, confessions, First Communion, and confirmation. I learned how to put on a pious face that made it look like I was paying attention to what was being said. There I would sit each Sunday morning, stomach growling, pretending to listen as the priest droned on in Latin.

When it was time to go to the altar for Communion, I would try to remember everything the nuns had beaten into to us back at the Convent School in Dublin: "March forward slowly, like a good little Catholic. Keep your hands together in prayer and keep your back straight and upright as you kneel down at the altar." Keeping your balance while kneeling down was always the tricky part. For most of us it took two or three good whacks with the cane before we finally got the hang of it.

"When the priest gets to you, close your eyes, open your mouth, and stick out your tongue. Once he places the Communion wafer on your tongue, just close your mouth and swallow." Back in the convent, we practised for weeks, using small peppermint candies. The nuns would watch us closely as we marched back to our seat. It is hard to swallow a whole peppermint, but any sign of chewing was met with a stiff slap to the back of the head.

Sometimes after Mass, Da would load us down with blankets, towels, and a big basket of sandwiches and Kool-Aid. Mamie carried Philip in her arms as she herded us all aboard the Parliament streetcar. My younger brothers and sister could ride for free, while Fred and I tried scrunching down below the height line on the bar. If the driver wasn't paying attention, we could quickly skip by and hope he didn't call us back to drop in the ten-cent fare. We would transfer to the Queen streetcar and ride it east to the old Woodbine Racetrack. From there, it was just a short walk down to Kew Beach.

We all looked forward to those Sunday excursions to the beach because they gave us a chance to catch up with our cousins. Our two families had come to Canada together, but we hadn't seen them since they moved to the west end of Toronto.

People would often stop and stare at the whole mob of us as we sat around talking and played on the beach. Mamie looked so happy and relaxed. Her week was filled with cleaning and cooking, but now she had a little time to just sit on her blanket and chat with her sister, Kitty.

All the young ones got together and built a massive sand castle. Johno was always willing to lie down and let the kids bury him under a mountain of sand. Fred was never one to mix in. He preferred sitting on the edge of the boardwalk, quietly reading one of his books. He was skinny and pale, as we all were, but regardless of how hot it was, he refused to take off his shirt.

My cousin Patrick and I were about the same age, and we didn't waste any time stripping down to our bathing suits and heading straight for the water. Lake Ontario wasn't particularly clean, so we had to be careful to avoid the many dead fish that floated in on the waves and settled on the shoreline. Soon Patrick and I would be called out for something to eat. We ate standing up, wet and shivering, and nothing ever tasted quite as good as those jam sandwiches washed down with a big cup of orange Kool-Aid. As we ate, Uncle Peter would fire up his Coleman stove and boil up a big kettle of tea. Our family never went anywhere without a large bag of loose-leaf tea.

Once all the food and drink were out of the way, Da used some rocks to set up goalposts on the grassy area near the back of the beach. My uncle then divided us into teams for the family soccer match. Mamie and Aunt Kitty sat watching and cheering us on.

At five o'clock, it was time to pack up and head home. Again, people would stare at us, the gaggle of kids filing down the aisle of the streetcar.

Da was never shy about striking up a conversation with anyone on the streetcar. "This is only half the clan," he would say, beaming with pride.

Mamie could only sit there looking embarrassed. Soon the stranger would be looking at the accordion folder of pictures Da carried in his wallet. My father could be a brutal man at times, but when we saw him bragging about us to some stranger, we knew we were loved.

As Michael drove down the street one morning in August 1959, we all waited on the front doorstep. It may not have been much to look at, but to us that 1954 Chevy station wagon was a gorgeous sight to behold. The two-tone blue paint was starting to peel and there was some rust on the bumper and around the doors, but none of that mattered. This was the first car our family had ever owned, and we stood there together, taking in the moment.

After Michael had taken all the kids for a spin around the block, the car was moved into the alley behind the house. Marie, David, and I would spend the next few mornings just sitting in the car, trying to imagine what it would be like when we took our first big excursion. The car wasn't even moving and already we were arguing about who could sit next to the window.

Da had promised to take us all on a trip, but weeks went by and the car never moved from its back-alley parking spot. Michael and

Johno were the only ones with a licence, but neither one could get time away from their new jobs. Da kept talking about getting his driver's licence, but after years of riding a bicycle or taking a streetcar, he wasn't quite ready to get behind the wheel of a car.

It took the rest of the summer, but when Da finally got his licence, we all knew exactly where we wanted to go. One cool September morning after Mass, we piled into the station wagon and headed for Niagara Falls.

Mamie had us put the cushions from the chesterfield into the back cargo compartment for the younger ones to sit on. With the entire family stuffed into the car, there was barely room to move. At the time I didn't know what shock absorbers were, but if our car had them, I don't think they were working very well. Every time the car hit a bump in the road, all of us in the back would bounce straight up and bang our heads on the roof. It was funny at first, but soon we had to stop to stretch our legs and try to get the numbness out of our backsides.

When we reached the Burlington Skyway, there was a momentary panic — nobody could find a dime to pay the toll. We were only supposed to slow down and throw a dime into the basket, but when Da got to the barrier, he just stopped. Mamie was desperately searching through her purse, trying to find the right change, while the rest of the adults rummaged through their pockets. Within seconds, a long line of cars had formed behind us. Horns were blowing; people were cursing and shouting. All of us in the back hunkered low, trying to hide from the hostile stares. Thank God we were able to scrape together ten pennies to pay the toll.

By the time we reached Niagara Falls, the day had turned cool and rainy. We found a parking spot and all of us scrambled out of the car and lined up next to the railing for a few photos. The combination of cool temperatures, rain, and the mist coming off the falls made it difficult to stay outside for more than a few minutes.

All told, we spent roughly ten minutes looking at the waterfalls before jumping in the car and heading home.

My da was good at many things, but I'm afraid driving was not one of them. It wasn't that he was a *bad* driver. It was just that, regardless of whether we were on a side street or a highway, he drove far too slowly and with an abundance of caution. Cars would come up behind us, the drivers honking their horns, impatient to get by. Da seemed completely oblivious to the noise and rude gestures as yet another car sped by us. None of us criticized his driving, but we were all silently thankful when he decided to let Michael or Johno take the wheel.

CHAPTER 4

WHEN I WOKE up on the first Tuesday of September 1959, I briefly considered faking an illness. Each time I pulled the blanket over my head, Fred just pulled it back.

I could ignore Fred — he would eventually go away — but then I heard Mamie's voice. "Don't make me come up there!" she yelled from the bottom of the stairs.

It was time to move. Even with my shirt and socks on, I felt a chill when my feet touched the floor, and the dampness of the linoleum made me shiver. Fred was already dressed, and he laughed as I jumped up and down trying to get my pants on.

"Don't forget your job" was all he said before heading down the stairs.

I guess old habits were hard to break. Even though we had an indoor toilet in this house, we still had a pee bucket in the boys' room at night. It was particularly useful in the early morning, when all of us needed to get into our tiny bathroom at the same time. Being the last one out of the room, it was my job to empty the bucket. On warm days, the smell was so bad that I would try to hold the bucket well out in front of me, but the weight of it would make my arms shake, causing the pee to spill onto my hands and splash to the floor. Once the pot had been dumped down the toilet, I had to take a rag from under the sink and wipe up the trail of pee I'd left in the hallway. I hated the tingling feeling I got when cleaning my hands with lye soap and cold water, but I knew Mamie would check as soon as I went downstairs. No matter how tightly I squeezed my eyes shut, that lye soap seemed to burn right through my eyeballs.

Before we could sit down to eat, Mamie had to give us the once over. "It looks like all you gave yourself was a lick and a promise," she would say as she pulled down the back of our collars to inspect our necks. If the skin on our hands and faces wasn't cold and red, we were sent back upstairs to wash again.

By the time I came down the stairs that morning, everyone had eaten and they were already putting on their shoes. Mamie was brushing Marie's hair, while David refused to sit still long enough for Fred to tie his shoelaces. When I complained to Mamie that I was hungry, she handed me a brown paper bag and told me to eat my jam sandwich on the way to school.

The day I had been dreading was here. For as long as I could remember, school had been a terrifying place. It had only been a few months since we'd left Dublin, so the memories of St. Andrew's School were still fresh in my mind.

Fred seemed especially quiet as he walked ahead of us that first morning. Marie chattered away about something, but I was hardly listening. David was excited about his first day in kindergarten, but still upset over the eye patch he had to wear under his glasses.

As the four of us headed up Carlton Street and turned onto Sackville, I couldn't help but feel that same old sense of dread. I could at least take some small comfort in knowing that there were no priests teaching at this new school. Still, there would be a lot of nuns. I hadn't forgotten how nasty they could be, but at least they couldn't hit us quite as hard as a priest.

St. Martin's School faced onto Winchester Street, just a block away from Riverdale Park. A black wrought-iron fence stretched across the front of the property, and the brownstone building was surrounded on three sides by an asphalt playground. The school had been built in the early 1920s, when the area's population was relatively small. Now with Cabbagetown literally teeming with new immigrants, a double row of portable classrooms had been added along the back fence.

I envied my friend Wayne because he was a Protestant and got to go to the public school on Spruce Street. Compared to St. Martin's, his school was huge. The property was spread over three city blocks, with a big grassy playground and two baseball diamonds. Of course, the part I envied the most that there were no priests or nuns to make life miserable.

As we got closer to St. Martin's that morning, I briefly considered taking off for the park. I could spend the day hiding out; with all those kids to look after, the nuns would never miss me. But the sound of Fred's voice brought me back to reality. He stood holding the door, waiting for me to get inside. When the big double doors closed behind us, all outside noise disappeared. The only sound came from the echo of our footsteps, and as we walked down the tiled hallway, my thoughts of escape quickly faded.

We didn't have to look far for the main office. Fifteen or more new kids stood in line along the wall, all waiting to hear where they were to go. The first time I saw Sister Alphonse she was coming out of her office. She was a short and stocky woman, with a ruddy complexion. The starched white collar she wore underneath her veil looked tight and uncomfortable. Her long black habit seemed to flow around her as she walked briskly down the hallway. At first she seemed to ignore our little group, but just as she was about to pass us by, she stopped suddenly and turned around.

She peered at us over her glasses. No one moved. "You there, stop leaning against the wall and stand up straight," she said.

We had no idea who she was talking to, so we all jumped at once. Although none of us knew her, we had heard stories from kids on the street. Sister Alphonse had a way of looking right through us. It was said she could detect a lie in an instant, and God help the kid who tried to put anything past her. She may have looked old and slow, but when she grabbed on to a kid, there was no getting loose.

Thankfully, that first morning, she seemed pleased when we all jumped to her command. In a moment she was gone down the hall and out the back door.

At precisely nine o'clock we watched as she stood in the open doorway and began swinging a big brass bell back and forth. At first the sound of the bell was too low to be heard over the noise of playing children, but as the clanging grew louder, a collective groan spread throughout the yard. Playtime was over and the first day of school was about to begin. The sound of screaming kids was replaced by adult voices shouting orders for everyone to line up. It took only a few minutes for the lines to file through the door and down the hallway. Teachers stood by their classroom doors, counting heads. When the last door closed, our little group looked quite disheartened. We had hoped this process would be over by now, but here we all stood, still waiting. Now we would each have to go through the embarrassment of entering a classroom already full of kids. The teacher would make us stand at the front of the class and introduce ourselves. All of the good desks near the back would be gone and we would be forced to sit in the front row, right under the teacher's nose.

Finally, a rather frazzled looking woman came out of the office, clutching a stack of papers. Thankfully, Mamie had already registered us at the school weeks earlier, so all we had to do was wait for our names to be called and then we were led to our respective classrooms. Fred looked calm and confident, as he always did. He and I didn't get along, but that day I would have been more than happy to stay with him through the entire ordeal.

When the lady finally called my name and told me where I was to go, I was absolutely mortified. I was just a month away from my twelfth birthday, but they were putting me in grade five.

The lady said something about needing to find out where I stood, but I wasn't listening. All I could think about was being stuck among all those ten-year-old kids. I wanted to say something, but I was far too scared to speak up. The lady seemed nice, but she might have a cane nearby, ready to use on boys who spoke out of turn.

The portable classroom sat against the back fence. The wood-frame exterior appeared old and weather beaten. It looked like a fresh coat of paint had been added to brighten it up, but already there were signs of fading from the hot summer sun. The roof looked sturdy enough, but later in the fall we would have to place buckets around the room to catch the raindrops.

At least the inside looked bright and clean and was just wide enough to accommodate four rows of desks. Once all the windows were open, the September breeze kept the room cool and comfortable. A small pot-bellied stove sat nestled in the back corner, but when winter came, our little heating system didn't prove very efficient. Those sitting in the backs row were toasty and warm, while those near the front of the class shivered in the cold.

As I stepped through the classroom door that first morning, it felt like all of my worst fears were being realized. The entire room stopped and turned to stare at the new kid. I had no idea what to say or do. I just stood there, nervous and very self-conscious. I was thankful Mamie had let me wear blue jeans that morning instead of shorts so no one could see my legs shaking.

I didn't think things could get much worse, but I was wrong. As the teacher stood up, I felt an immediate sense of dread. All of the teachers in St. Martin's were women, but only four of them were nuns. It is hard to describe the letdown I felt as Sister Mary Joseph stared back at me.

The murmuring started as I made my way to the front of the class. All I could do was stand there pretending to smile while she introduced me to the class. Thankfully, once I'd found a desk, she moved on to other things and left me alone for the morning.

Most of the morning was devoted to grammar. Sister Mary Joseph wrote a sentence on the board and then called someone up to underline the noun or the verb. To me, the exercise was rather basic, but many of my classmates seemed to find it difficult. In the afternoon we worked on addition and subtraction problems in our arithmetic books. When I looked around, I was surprised to see that I was among the first to finish.

Sister Mary Joseph said very little as she moved up and down the rows. Sometimes she would stop at a pupil's desk and point out an error and then move on to the next person. The first time she glided past my desk, I stole a glance at her long, flowing robes. I felt sure that somewhere under that black habit she must be hiding a cane, ready to strike. At one point I saw her pick up a ruler, and as she moved down the aisle I thought one of us was about to be rapped across the knuckles. Nothing happened. Sister Mary Joseph was the strangest nun I had ever met. She smiled through most of the day and didn't raise a hand to any of us.

Walking home that afternoon, I felt a great sense of relief, but I was not about to let my guard down. After all, this was just the first day. There was still lots of time for the whippings to begin.

Those first few months in Cabbagetown were some of the happiest I can remember. The school work was generally easy, and Sister Mary Joseph was nothing like those nasty nuns we had at the convent back in Dublin. Still, she could be very strict at times, especially if she caught someone using bad language. We had one kid in our class named Mike Malone. We all called him Specks because of the thick black glasses he wore. One day during a particularly rough game of soccer, one of the bigger boys threw Specks up against a wall, sending his glasses flying across the schoolyard. Sister Mary Joseph would let us get away with the odd curse, but as soon as the F-word flew out of Specks's mouth, she grabbed him by the collar and marched him straight to the washroom. I am sure he didn't find it funny, but for the rest of us, it was hard not to laugh when we came in from recess and saw poor Specks standing in the doorway with a big orange bar of Lifebuoy soap protruding from his mouth.

By late fall the old factory behind our house had been pulled down and turned into a parking lot for Power Supermarket. With the factory gone, we now had a shortcut to the back alleys leading to Parliament Street. Once we were well clear of our house, we would take a look around to make sure the coast was clear. Wayne always had a couple of cigarettes in his pocket. He tried to tell me they were his, but we knew he lifted them from his mother's purse. His ability to inhale and blow smoke out through his nose was quite impressive. I usually had just a puff or two. The first time I smoked a whole cigarette, I didn't pay enough attention. Just as I was about to take another drag, I saw old Mrs. Baxter coming through the back alley toward us. As soon as she spotted us, she began shaking her head in disgust. When she walked past without saying anything, I thought she might keep it to herself.

But when I came through the door that evening and saw the look on Da's face, I knew I was done for. I hardly had time to move before he hit me on the side of the head and knocked me to the floor. I was ready for more, but he just stopped.

I felt his hand grab my shirt and he pulled me upright. "That was for lying to your mother."

I wasn't sure what he meant, but I kept nodding. I would have agreed to anything to keep him from hitting me again. I don't know why I got off so easy that day, but maybe it had something to do with the fact he had been smoking for most of his life.

❧

The winter weather of 1959 was a completely new experience for our family. The incessant rain of an Irish winter had been bad enough, but it couldn't compare to the snow and freezing temperatures we endured during our first Canadian winter. The locals seemed to take it in stride, but for immigrants like us, the cold seemed to reach right down into our bones.

As soon as there was enough snow on the ground, my siblings and I set to work building our first snowman. Marie and David formed the first small ball of snow and began rolling it back and forth through the backyard. Fred and I made one big ball for the base. Philip wanted to help, but the poor kid was having difficulty just staying upright. Between his bulky snowsuit, boots, and mitts, he could hardly move his arms or walk without falling on his face. He looked like a little round robot as he tried desperately to make his own ball of snow. As soon as he was ready, Fred lifted him up to place the head on our snowman.

Late at night, I would wake to the sound of Da shovelling coal in the basement. The furnace looked like a giant octopus, with long metal arms stretching in all directions. Da referred to shovelling coal as feeding the beast. Mamie always said that with the high cost of coal, it was like watching our money go up in flames. But, regardless of how much coal Da fed the ancient furnace, it barely gave off enough heat to reach the bedrooms upstairs. Most mornings we would get dressed under the covers. Even with thick socks on, I could still feel the dampness when my feet touched the cold linoleum floor.

When we entered our portable classroom in the morning, we could see our breath. For those first few minutes, the air was filled with the cracks and groans of expanding metal as our pot-bellied stove tried to warm the space. By mid-morning, the combination of the stove and our body heat made our classroom just warm enough to work without our coats on.

If it was too cold to go out at recess, Sister Mary Joseph would have us stand up and run on the spot. We even tried doing jumping jacks, but there wasn't enough room between the rows of desks. We tried not to laugh when the good sister gave us a demonstration of the exercise. She just looked so funny jumping around in her long black robes.

After a week of exams, we were all looking forward to the Christmas holidays. As the hours ticked by on the twenty-second of December, every eye was on the clock, just waiting for that final bell to ring.

I was already in the crush of kids trying to get our coats on and get out when I heard Sister Mary Joseph call my name. She told me to go to the office to see Sister Alphonse. As I crossed the schoolyard and entered the back door of the building, I just couldn't stop shaking. I couldn't for the life of me think what I had done, but I knew that being sent to the office was never a good thing.

I though the secretary might give me some hint, but she barely looked up when I came into the office. I could just see the outline of Sister Alphonse through the glazed glass of the inner office. Every kid in the school knew she kept a leather strap in her desk. As I stood there waiting, I rubbed my hands together, trying to warm them up. If I was going to get the strap, it would hurt all the more if my hands were cold.

When my name was finally called, I almost ran into her office. If I was going to be punished, I thought it best to get it over with as quickly as possible. I stood in front of her big desk, trying not to shake. At first she said nothing. She barely glanced at me as she rooted around in her desk drawer. When she finally found what she was looking for, she stepped toward me.

Instead of a leather strap, she held an envelope in her hand. "Sister Mary Joseph tells me you are doing very well, and we have decided to put you into grade six right after Christmas. Give this to your parents and tell them to contact me if they have any questions."

Between my stealing, my smoking, and my lying, I knew I wasn't a very good son. In the past few months, Da had walloped the hide off of me more than once. But that evening when I showed him the letter, he actually said he was proud of me. That would be the first and last time he ever said those words to me.

CHAPTER 5

ONCE, DURING OUR first few weeks in Canada, when we lived upstairs in the Chinese family's house on Dupont Street, we had been invited downstairs to see a television for the very first time. I sat on the floor watching in fascination as the grainy black-and-white picture filled the tiny screen.

When our first television arrived just before Christmas, we all just sat there staring at the blank fourteen-inch screen. We could never afford a new television, but Johno had found a second-hand set for just ten dollars. The problem was that it didn't work. Finally, after an hour of tinkering around in the back and changing the tubes, we suddenly saw a tiny light appear in the centre of the screen. It seemed to take forever for the set to warm up, but slowly the light began to expand until the screen was filled with a black-and-white test pattern. A steady hum filled the room, and we waited, transfixed, for something to happen. None of us knew that most television stations didn't begin broadcasting until four o'clock in the afternoon.

It only took a week or so for the novelty to wear off and the arguments to start about which of the three stations we would watch. As soon as the shouting began, Mamie would walk in, turn off the TV, and tell us to get outside and play.

One Saturday morning in December, Mamie and Da took all of us downtown for the first time. My friend Wayne Boland had bragged to me about how he could go to the stores on Yonge Street whenever he wanted, but every time I asked Mamie, her answer was no. Today, when we got off the streetcar at Queen and Yonge, I could see why Mamie had refused to let me go alone. Even O'Connell Street in downtown Dublin was never this busy.

Philip and David were more than happy to be carried in Da arms. Mamie clung tight to Marie's hand, while Fred and I fought our way through the crowd. It took some time to worm our way through to the front of Simpson's department store, but the effort was worth it. All the display windows were decked out with scenes of Christmas. Little toy children skated on a frozen pond, while a train chugged through the village. Everywhere we looked there were toy soldiers playing drums, children sliding on toboggans, and elves dancing to the sound of Christmas music. Across the road the displays in the Eaton's windows were even bigger and more elaborate. It was the most amazing thing I had ever seen. Even Da was laughing and pointing at the dancing toys. It was good to see him relax and enjoy himself for a change.

As we manoeuvred through the aisles, trying to find Santa, shoppers pushed and shoved in every direction. David and Philip jumped with excitement when we finally found Santa, but I was long past believing in any of that. All I wanted to do was get up to the toy department to look at the wagons. I had already mentioned a wagon to Mamie at least forty times, but reminding her again couldn't hurt.

It was almost one o'clock when we'd finished fighting the crowds and emerged back onto Yonge Street. It had been an amazing adventure, but the best was yet to come. Even though there was still a week before the big day, all of us were about to get our first Christmas present of the year.

The building on Shuter Street was literally teeming with kids of all ages. Da had gotten a job with the Toronto Works Department, and today was their annual Christmas party for kids of employees. All the boys got a hockey stick and all the girls were given a doll, no matter what our ages were. There was more than enough candy and chocolate for us to stuff our faces all afternoon. At one point, Da called us over to introduce us to his friends from work. As usual, he had the accordion folder of pictures out as Mamie stood there trying to hide her embarrassment.

On Christmas Eve Fred and I lay in bed listening to the voices in the kitchen. Mamie was urging Da and the older siblings to hurry up so they wouldn't be late for midnight Mass. Even after the front door closed, we stayed put to make sure the coast was clear. Then, just a few minutes before midnight, Fred and I tiptoed down the stairs and headed straight for the Christmas tree.

I was more than a little disappointed when all I found was a checkers game and some colouring books under the tree. I looked in all the closets and even down in the basement, but I didn't see any sign of the wagon I had been asking for since the end of summer.

When we woke up on Christmas morning, the bedroom was damp and cold, as usual, and the thick frost on the bedroom window made it difficult to see outside. This was one morning when Mamie didn't have to call us twice. All of us where dressed and downstairs, ready to go, by seven o'clock.

I would have given anything for a hot cup of tea and a piece of fried bread that morning. I was so hungry, I would have even settled for a bowl of porridge. But breakfast would have to wait until after Communion. It didn't matter that it was Christmas. In our house, Mass and Holy Communion came before everything else.

Fred and I wanted to hurry as we walked to church, but Marie and David were having a hard time keeping up. We knew that the church would be crowded with what Mamie called "submarine

Catholics," because they only surfaced at Christmas and Easter. As soon as we were clear of the house, I made a suggestion to Fred. He was in charge, but this was one of the rare times when we agreed on something. To get to Our Lady of Lourdes we would have to walk all the way up past Winchester to Sherbourne Street, at least a fifteen-minute walk, or longer with the little kids. Instead, we decided to go to Sacred Heart Church, or Paroisse du Sacré-Cœur, which was across from Allan Gardens, just a ten-minute walk down Carlton. The sermon would be in French, but everything else would be in Latin, just like at Our Lady of Lourdes. Mamie might not approve, but it was Christmas morning after all, and we wanted to get Mass over with as quickly as possible.

That first Christmas in Cabbagetown, it rained all day. Even Da was in a rare good mood and made a joke about how the rain reminded him of a typical Irish Christmas. He was trying to cheer Mamie up, but his little joke only served to remind her of past Christmases back home. Mamie was never one to talk about her feelings, but we knew that the loss of her mother and father was still foremost on her mind.

When Jimmy Duncan showed up at our door that afternoon, Mamie gave him a small bag of sweets. He hadn't received any toys for Christmas, so he and I cut down a few small tree branches and used some string to fashion a bow and arrow. Wayne had gotten an entire cowboy set, including a hat, vest, cap gun, and holster. Together we got soaking wet as we spent the entire afternoon running around the neighbourhood playing cowboys and Indians. Mamie wasn't upset when she saw the state of me, but she still made me strip in the hallway so I wouldn't track dirt through the house. She asked Jimmy if he wanted to come in for some dinner, but he said he had to get home and look after his baby sister.

That night was one of the few times I actually got ready for bed without being told. Just before I headed up the stairs, Mamie called me into the kitchen. She had been up since dawn and had spent most of the day cooking and cleaning up a steady stream of dishes and pots. Now she was sitting at the table with a cup of tea. It was good to see her off her feet.

"Did you enjoy your Christmas?" she asked.

I just smiled and nodded.

"I know you wanted a wagon, but maybe when things get better."

She didn't need to explain. I knew how tight the money was, especially when there were so many kids to buy presents for. I mumbled something about how much I liked the checkers game. Mamie patted me on the cheek and sent me off to bed.

On Saint Stephen's Day, or Boxing Day as my friends here called it, the entire house was alive with aunts, uncles, and cousins. I had long gotten over my homesickness, but most of the adults sat around the kitchen table talking about Ireland. The kitchen was shrouded in a curtain of smoke from my da's and my uncles' cigarettes, and Mamie kept jumping up to make pot after pot of tea.

When it came to alcohol, our family did not fit what some people considered to be the Irish stereotype. My uncles may have taken a beer from time to time, but Da didn't drink at all. Mamie did keep a fifth of whiskey in the kitchen cupboard. She always said that a teaspoon of whiskey and a little bedrest were the best cure for whatever ailed you. Sometimes I actually wished that my da would take a drink. The drunk men I saw stumbling out of the Winchester Hotel looked so happy and carefree. I thought perhaps if Da took a drink, he could relax and laugh more, like he used to back in Ireland.

Da sat at the table sipping his tea and listening to Uncle Peter go on and on about the good old days in Ireland. Uncle Nicky reminded him about the lack of work in Dublin and how we were all better off since coming to Canada. But there was no real argument.

They just seemed to enjoy being around family as they talked away the afternoon.

The conversation did get a little heated later on, when Uncle Michael O'Keefe brought up the subject of moving. Uncle Michael always had what Mamie called "the wanderlust." He and Aunt Marcella and their kids had been the first in the family to leave Ireland. His stories about the good life in Canada are what convinced my da and all the uncles to come here.

Uncle Michael had started out working in the mines in Lynn Lake, Manitoba. Now he was trying to convince my da and the uncles to go with him to the United States. "There's great money to be made in the Missouri gold mines," he promised.

Some of my uncles said it was an interesting idea, but none of the aunts wanted anything to do with it.

Some months later, Uncle Michael and his family moved to Missouri, and as I understand, they did quite well for themselves. Mamie would hear from her brother from time to time, but when Michael and Marcella passed away in the late 1960s, we never heard from that side of the family again.

The bitter cold continued all through January. No matter how much coal Da shovelled into the furnace, the heat never seemed to reach the upstairs. Even if we kept our shirts and socks on, the bedsheets always felt damp beneath us. In summer I often wished for a bed of my own, but when the cold winter wind came funnelling through the cracks in the window frame, it was nice to have all that body heat to keep us warm. In the early morning, Fred and I raced to be the first one out the door and down the stairs so the other would be stuck emptying the pee bucket. But it didn't always pay to be first. Some mornings David would show up in the kitchen in his bare feet with nothing on but a T-shirt, and Mamie would send the first one down back upstairs to get David dressed and clean up any pee that had spilled on the floor. After all that work in the morning cold, even a bowl of hot porridge tasted good.

Every day the wind and snow came roaring down through the Don Valley. By the middle of the month, the surrounding hills were covered in a deep blanket of snow.

Wayne was the only one with a proper wooden toboggan, while the rest of us had to make do with cardboard boxes or small bits of plywood we'd picked out of the garbage. I was only allowed to go sledding if I took Marie and David along, but thankfully they didn't last long. After they'd tumbled off our makeshift sled and ended up face down in the snow a few times, they both decided they'd had enough. Mamie was not very pleased when they walked through the door, red-faced and soaking wet.

Now at last I could get away from what my friends called the kiddie slide and try the steepest part of the hill, where only the big kids dared to go. The run started with a drop straight down. Then, just at the bottom, there was sharp slope up. By now the sled had picked up so much speed that both it and the rider flew straight up in the air. If the rider was light enough, they could go airborne for ten or fifteen feet before crashing back to earth.

Now that it was my turn to go I could feel the fear welling up from the pit of my stomach. If only I hadn't sent David and Marie away, I would have had the perfect excuse not to go. I might have backed out, but when Wayne called me a chicken, I had no choice but to close my eyes and push myself off the brink of the hill. I tried digging my heels into the snow to slow down, but the cardboard beneath me just skipped over the snow and soon I was flying out of control. All I could do was hang on for dear life and hope to God I didn't break my neck. When I hit the top of the second slope, the cardboard went out from under me and I flew through the air until

I finally landed face first in the snowbank. I had the wind knocked out of me and it took me a moment to recover, but with my friends watching I had to act like the whole thing was just so easy. When Wayne suggested doing it again, I suddenly remembered I had to get home early for supper.

Later on that winter, after a couple of kids had broken their arms, someone from the parks department poured ashes on that part of the hill. At least I could brag to my friends about how far we had sailed through the air. It was easy to be brave now that the hill was closed.

After Christmas break, I was actually looking forward to going back to school. I hoped Jimmy Duncan would be there that day so I had at least one friendly face in my new class. Jimmy should have been in grade seven by now, but he'd been held back a year because of his frequent absences. On the days he did show up for school, he was usually accompanied by a truant officer. Then, once the lunch bell rang, Jimmy would disappear again.

Unfortunately, after just one week in Sister Agnes's grade-six class, my old feelings of dread came back with a vengeance. All the self-confidence I had built up in Sister Mary Joseph's class was gone. All my classmates and I could hope for was to get through a day without being slapped in the head or whacked with a ruler.

Sister Agnes looked younger than the other nuns in the school, although with all those clothes, it was difficult to tell. She was a tall, skinny woman, with a pencil-thin nose and a protruding chin. In class we were all terrified to speak unless she asked a question, but behind her back we referred to her as the wicked witch of the west. Her habit looked too large on her skinny frame. She was constantly adjusting her veil and pulling at the stiff white collar that surrounded her face. In the late afternoon, when the sun reflected off the windows, the classroom could become quite warm. Between the heat and her constant need to move about the room, it didn't take long before beads of sweat formed on her forehead and slowly trickled down her cheeks. She would pull a handkerchief from her sleeve and wipe the sweat away, but some of the droplets fell from her chin, leaving tiny dark stains on her collar.

Unlike Sister Mary Joseph or Sister Alphonse, Sister Agnes never laughed — or even smiled. I don't believe she liked being around children. Math was always taught in the latter part of the afternoon. It was the most difficult subject for most of the students, as was clear from all the blank expressions around the room. Maybe if she had taken the time to answer our questions, we would have understood more, but Sister Agnes was not a patient person. As the afternoon wore on, she only became more vexed by our inability to learn. It often seemed that we had been placed in her class as a penance she had to endure in order to get through another day.

Sister Agnes used a yardstick as a pointer, and it never left her hand. Her eyes were constantly scanning over us, ready to lash out at anyone who displeased her. Every morning as we came into class, she would use her stick to measure the girls' dresses. Any girl with a hem at or above the knee was given a whack across the backside and then forced to wear brown paper wrapped around her legs for the rest of the day. At least once each week we would have to endure Sister Agnes's prodding fingers digging into our scalps, looking for any signs of dirt or lice. If she found anything, the culprit would spend the day sitting alone against the back wall, well away from the rest of the class.

Sister Agnes rarely sat at her desk, preferring instead to walk back and forth, continually tapping her yardstick across her palm. When we heard the rustling of her habit and the tapping of the stick, we knew she was coming up behind us. All we could hope for was a quick glance as she walked by. If she stopped and leaned down, we knew we were in trouble. Sloppy writing would get us a swift rap across the knuckles.

Tommy Moore was one of the smartest kids in our class, but according to Sister Agnes, he had one major flaw that could not be overlooked. Tommy had the misfortune of being born left-handed, and only frequent smacks across the hands could correct what Sister Agnes called "the devil's work." She would force him to use his right hand by jamming his fingers into position around his pencil, but as soon as she let go, the words and numbers became one long illegible scrawl. Every mistake was met with yet another rap on Tommy's hands, and having to write with a sore right hand only made things worse. Maybe if we had been better, more mature people, we would have felt sympathy for poor Tommy, but most of us just felt a sense of relief. As long as she was torturing Tommy, we could get away with all kinds of mistakes.

If Sister Agnes weren't enough to deal with, my grade-six classmates seemed to dislike me from the very first day I spoke up in class. They had been together from the start of September, and I was once again the new kid. Thinking back on it, I guess I was just trying to make a good first impression. Had I known what Sister Agnes was like, I never would have stuck my hand in the air, but in that moment, I simply couldn't believe my good luck.

Sister Agnes stood at the chalkboard explaining long division to the class. It had been two years since Father McGuire had beaten me senseless over this very subject. If there was one thing I had learned from Father McGuire, it was that fear can be a great motivator. By the time I'd left St. Andrew's, I was a master of long division. So, as soon as Sister Agnes put the first problem on the board, my hand shot straight up in the air. Sister Agnes didn't seem impressed when I gave the right answer. After she had written three more problems on the board, mine was still the only hand to go up. She began roaming the class, picking on different people to answer the question. Each incorrect response was met with the sharp smack of her ruler. Only the ringing of the bell for afternoon recess saved the class from further punishment.

By the end of that recess, I was beginning to wish I had never left grade five. Two of the older boys in my class cornered me in the schoolyard and kept pushing me backward. I could see a teacher on the far side of the yard, but she couldn't see us through the maze of kids.

Harold Garvy, one of the boys, was easily the biggest kid in the class. He was just a few months older than the rest of us, but he stood at least half a foot taller. In the schoolyard, his sidekick, Donny Lund, was never far away. Donny was rather small and scrawny, with pale, pockmarked skin.

That afternoon, Donny did most of the talking while Harold slowly circled around me. "Just who the fuck do you think you are?" he spat out. "Maybe you're just some smartass little bastard who thinks he's better than the rest of us?" Donny kept glancing around for teachers as he talked.

I stammered something about not wanting to fight, but that seemed to make him all the bolder. He suddenly stepped forward and pushed me with both arms. Somehow, in the heat of the moment, Harold had knelt down behind me, and as Donny pushed me, I fell backward over top of him. They laughed as I lay there holding my head. I wasn't really hurt, but I figured if I played this up a little, maybe they would leave me alone.

Fortunately for me, my saviour Sister Mary Joseph had seen the whole thing through her classroom window and came rushing to my aid. I had never seen her so angry, as she demanded an explanation. Donny Lund finally muttered that we were just fooling around, but the sister wasn't buying it.

"Are these two hooligans picking on you?" she asked me as I stood up.

I hesitated. I knew a yes might save me for now but get me killed later. I tried to smile and hide my scratched and bloody elbows. "No, Sister. We were just playing."

I don't think she believed me, but after giving us a long lecture about being good and staying out of trouble, she finally walked away. From that moment on, Harold Garvy, Donny Lund, and I became best friends.

Harold and his family had come to Toronto from Glace Bay, Nova Scotia, just a year earlier. He still had that distinct "down home" accent, and sometimes he and I would be mistaken for brothers. I never corrected the misconception. I thought it best to let the other schoolyard bullies believe I had this big brother watching out for me.

In Donny's case, I found that once you got past all his bravado, he was truly a nice guy. He came home with me for supper a few times, and even though he was such a skinny kid, he could pack away two or three platefuls of whatever my mamie put in front of him. Before the school bell rang in the morning, I would find him sitting against the fence, munching on a bag of chips and drinking a bottle of Coke. He never brought a lunch to school, preferring to walk over to the corner store and pick something up. I would stand next to him watching in amazement as he pulled one- and two-dollar bills from his pocket to spend on candy and potato chips.

Once in a while he would show up at school with a black eye or bruises on his face and arms. Sister Agnes would send him to see Sister Alphonse, and he would be gone for an hour or more. He didn't have to tell us where the bruises came from. Everyone in the neighbourhood knew about his father.

One afternoon earlier that year, Donny was sent to the office, and we all saw a police car parked in front of the school. When

Donny came back to the classroom, he looked like he had been crying. When I ask if he was okay, he tried to smile, but I could tell he was frightened. That afternoon in the park was the only time I saw Donny cry. He told me that Sister Alphonse had called the police, and although they had said there was nothing they could do, he was still afraid they might come to his house, ready to take him away to an orphanage.

Donny was an only child. His mother had passed away when he was five years old, leaving him alone in the care of his father. Most evenings, his father would come home from work at around six o'clock. As soon as Donny spotted him walking down the road, he knew it was time to get upstairs and pretend to be doing homework.

Sometimes his father would come upstairs to check, but most nights he just yelled up to make sure Donny was home. Soon he would settle down in front of the TV and start drinking. It might take three or four hours, but once Donny was sure his father was passed out on the couch, he could come down to the kitchen and make something to eat. If the house was chilly, he would throw a blanket over his unconscious father. Once he was sure his father wouldn't wake up, he helped himself to any loose change and small bills he could find in his father's wallet.

When Donny came downstairs in the morning, his father would already be gone. Donny would do his best to clear away the beer bottles and straighten up the house before heading off to school.

"Weekends are the hardest," he told me. His father always came home early on Saturday, and he expected the house to be spotless. If Donny had done a good job, his father might take him over to the Satellite Restaurant on Parliament Street, where they would share a big plate of pancakes.

Sunday was the day Donny feared most. The drinking would start early. Then something would set his father off, into a rage. It could be as trivial as bumping into a piece of furniture or not being able to find what he was looking for in the cupboard. All Donny could do was try to stay out of the way and hope the storm would pass quickly.

CHAPTER 6

FOR A YEAR that had started out with such promise for our family, things took a drastic turn for the worse in early April. When Da woke my older brothers up for work that morning, he didn't look well. Mamie suggest that he should stay home and rest, but Da wouldn't even consider it. To him, missing a day's work because of what he said was just a cold was nonsense.

When I got home from school that afternoon, my sister Rosaleen was in the kitchen making supper for all of us. Once the younger kids were home from school and the older ones came from work, she told us that Da had passed out at work and had been taken to St. Michael's Hospital in an ambulance.

Mamie told us later that she'd had this sense of dread all morning. When one of Da's workmates came to the door, she knew the malaria had returned. She didn't really know her way around downtown, nor did she know which streetcars to take, but the moment she heard Da was in the hospital, she headed straight out the door.

Hours went by without any word. We all just sat there, picking at our food. No one said anything. We were worried not just about Da, but also about Mamie being lost somewhere in downtown Toronto. We jumped every time a car came down the street.

Johno kept talking about going out to find Mamie. "This wouldn't be a problem if we had a bloody phone in this bloody house," he said to no one in particular.

It was well past nine o'clock when our neighbour Mr. Baxter came banging on the door with a message from Mamie. It had taken her quite a while to find the hospital, and then she'd had to wait hours before seeing the doctor. Da had suffered another relapse of malaria and would be laid up in hospital for at least a week or two.

Mamie spent every waking hour by Da's bedside. We all wanted to see him, but young children weren't allowed to visit. I don't think the nurse believed Mamie when she told her that I was fifteen, but she let me in just the same. Marie and the younger ones would have to wait until Da came home. I hardly recognized him as he lay shivering under a mountain of blankets. His hair was matted with sweat, and Mamie kept wiping his brow. Seeing Da so helpless, it was hard to fathom why he scared me so much. Now all I wanted was for him to get better and come home again.

Those first few days, he slipped in and out of delirium. It took six long days for the fever to break and another three days before he could finally come home. Da had never been a very big man, but when he came through the door, we could see he had lost weight. It took all his remaining strength just to climb the stairs. The doctor told him to stay in bed for at least a week, but after only two days, he was up and arguing with Mamie about going back to work.

Da had every right to be concerned. He had been with the city works department for just over seven months, but he had to put in a full year's work before he'd qualify to be in the union. Until that happened, there was always the possibility of his being let go.

My brother Will had returned to Ireland a few weeks earlier and was just starting a new job, working for Air Lingus in Dublin Airport. Michael and John were helping out, but with Da out of work for so long, there was barely enough money coming in to cover the rent. And aside from all the normal bills, there was still a monthly payment to be made for all the airline tickets from our move. It would take over a decade before our flight to Canada was finally paid off.

Mamie mentioned that maybe the Saint Vincent de Paul charity could help us out, but Da refused to even discuss it. Our parents never argued in front of us, and that morning was the first time I heard my father raise his voice to my mother. The very notion of taking what he called a handout was completely unacceptable to him.

When I came home from school in the afternoon, Mamie would send me to the bakery down near Parliament and Dundas. It was a fair distance to walk, especially because I had to avoid the gangs of Regent Park. The trick was to get to the bakery just before closing time. If I timed it right, I could get a loaf of leftover bread for a nickel. At the market around the corner, fifty-nine cents could buy a bag of oatmeal big enough to make a week's worth of porridge. Mamie would try to cheer us up by talking about all the wonderful things we would have once Da went back to work. Things would get better, she promised, but for now we would have to make do with a little porridge in the morning and save the rest to have with our tea in the evening.

Although our family was struggling financially, Kenny Bell's family was much worse off. Kenny and I weren't really friends at first. We were in the same class at school, but I didn't get to know him until he showed up on our street one day in late spring and asked if he could join our street hockey game. His short, skinny frame made him an easy target for Wayne's bullying. Within the first few minutes, Wayne had rolled right over him, knocking him hard to the ground. Most kids would have quit after that, but not Kenny. In an instant, he was on his feet and charging straight at Wayne, driving him backward into the pavement. I think we all heard the distinct crack when Wayne's head bounced off the curb. We expected him to jump up and beat the hell out of this skinny little kid, but instead he just lay there, crying and holding the back of his head.

It wasn't easy being Kenny's friend. He never had much to say. His quiet nature made him seem aloof and unfriendly, but I think it had more to do with all the teasing he took over the state of his clothes. There was no denying that the clothes he wore often looked dirty and worn out. When the weather got warmer, some of the kids refused to sit close to him in class because of the smell. After school most of us would head for the park, but Kenny took off as soon as the bell rang. I knew he delivered newspapers at four thirty every afternoon, but I think this was also an excuse to get away from all the unkind remarks he had to listen to every day.

Sometimes on Saturday afternoons, when the paper was thicker and heavier than during the week, I would give Kenny a hand with his deliveries. We would arrange to meet at four o'clock, but by the time I reached the corner of Parliament and Carlton, he would already be there, getting everything ready to start his deliveries. As usual, he barely said a word as he busied himself stuffing newspapers into a big canvas bag. Once the bag was full, it seemed to take all his strength just to get it off the ground and hoist the strap over his shoulder. His short, bandy legs were just long enough to keep the heavy bag from dragging along the ground.

At first he seemed very defensive when I offered to carry the extra papers. "I can't pay you anything," he said.

I told him I didn't want money, but said perhaps he could tell me how I could get my own paper route. In all the weekends we worked together, he never offered me any money, and I never asked. I already knew that every penny he made went straight to his mother.

Kenny's family lived in a laneway just off Carlton Street. From the outside, the house looked shabby and rundown. Parts of the wooden frame were rotten, and the tarpaper underneath was peeling away from the walls. The front window was covered with what looked like an old white bedsheet.

The first time I called on him, his mother let me in. As soon as I stepped through the door I could smell a damp, musty odour. The window cover blocked most of the sunlight from coming in, and from the hallway I could see only bits and pieces of furniture scattered about the living room.

The moment I saw Kenny's face, I regretted being there. He hadn't known I was coming, and now he looked very embarrassed. He couldn't seem to get his coat and shoes on fast enough. His mother said something to him, but he was already out the door. He barely spoke a word to me all afternoon, but I could tell he didn't want me to call on him again.

The majority of people in Cabbagetown were poor, but Kenny's family was practically destitute. His father had been out of work for a very long time, and the family of six was barely getting by on welfare.

When I met up with him one day near the end of May, he seemed much more talkative than normal. He told me that when he'd come home from his paper route on the previous Friday afternoon, he'd found Sister Alphonse sitting in the kitchen and talking to his mother. He thought he was in some kind of trouble, but rather than punish him, his mother told him to go outside and play. Poor Kenny paced back and forth in the laneway, trying to think of what he had done wrong. When Sister Alphonse finally came out, she just smiled at him and hurried up the lane toward the school. When he asked his mother what was wrong, she rubbed his hair and told him everything was all right.

On Saturday morning, a man had come by the house and dropped off two brown paper bags full of groceries and a used wringer washing machine. The kids still teased Kenny about his old, torn clothes, but nobody complained about the smell anymore.

Earlier that spring, when I'd brought up the idea of getting a paper route to Mamie, in order to help with the family's bills while Da wasn't working, her answer was an unequivocal no. She had already gone through this experience with Fred, and she was not about to make the same mistake with me. Fred had gotten a job delivering the *Toronto Telegram*, but when he went out to collect the weekly payment, some people couldn't pay and others just didn't answer the door. After a month of deliveries without a penny to show for his work, Mamie made him quit.

Aside from the money issue, we all knew that it was not a good idea to mention the *Toronto Telegram* in front of Mamie. She refused to read that particular newspaper after the lies they had printed about her on the day we landed in Canada.

About a week before we arrived, Da had met a man who turned out to be a reporter for the *Toronto Telegram*. When Da mentioned that his family and our cousins, the Tracys, were all due to arrive in Toronto the following week, the reporter thought it would make an excellent human-interest story for the paper. So when we stepped off the plane, my da and the reporter were waiting on the tarmac. The reporter talked to all of us and took numerous pictures of both families. Everyone was tired and just wanted to leave, but he convinced my mamie to take one final photograph with our family and the Tracy kids lined up on the aircraft stairs.

The story and the photograph appeared on the front page of the next day's *Telegram*. There Mamie stood at the top of the stairway holding our baby brother, Philip, in her arms. The rest of the Burke and Tracy children were lined up from the top to the bottom step.

According to the caption under the photo, all fifteen children belonged to my mother.

Mamie was horrified that someone could write such blatant lies. Needless to say, she and Aunt Kitty were not pleased, and from that day forward, neither one would trust anything she read in a newspaper.

Thankfully, by May, our house had returned to normal. We knew that Da's malaria would eventually return, but as Mamie often said, that was a worry for another day. Mamie always put on a brave face in front of us, but Da's health was a constant source of concern for her. After his return to work, he took every hour of overtime he could get. Most work weeks were sixty hours long, and the strain was beginning to show.

Normally, being allowed to leave school at lunchtime would have been a great treat, but on one late spring afternoon I would have gladly stayed at school all day and night if it meant I could have avoided the pain and suffering that awaited me.

For a couple of weeks or more, my back teeth on one side had been hurting, but I found that if I chewed on the other side of my mouth, it didn't bother me. Still, Mamie made an appointment at the School of Dentistry for me. Our family could not afford a regular dentist, but you could get teeth pulled for free at the School of Dentistry on Bloor Street, as long as you were willing to let a student do the work. With all the poverty in Cabbagetown, there was always an ample supply of guinea pigs willing to put themselves in the hands of some inexperienced student holding a set of pliers.

I had never seen a dentist before, so I hoped that talking to Johno might reassure me. Rather than help, Johno seemed to take an almost sadistic delight in telling me about the needles and drills and pliers I was about to have shoved into my mouth. When he got to the part about the pliers ripping into me and all the blood I would be spitting up, I couldn't stop shaking.

I tried not to tremble as I climbed into the big chair, but as soon as I saw the long metal probe coming toward me, I shut my eyes and prayed it would be over soon. When the student dentist touched the sore spot with the probe, I flinched. An older man watching from the side said something I didn't understand. The teacher and the dental student never actually spoke to me, but I could tell by their demeanour that whatever it was they were discussing was not going to turn out well for me. The older man's next words confirmed my worst fears. Two of my back teeth would have to be removed.

My eyes darted in every direction as the dental student reached for a hypodermic needle. He held it up and pumped a tiny jet of liquid out through the top. I squeezed my eyes shut. The needle pierced the roof of my mouth, and then he held it in there for what seemed like thirty seconds. When he finally pulled it out, I thought the worse must be over, but he moved the needle under my teeth and stuck it in again. Once it was withdrawn, I slowly opened my eyes just as he put the needle down. I stared at the tray full of instruments, trying to figure out which one he would use for my next bit of torture.

"Don't worry," he said. "The worst part is over."

I didn't believe him.

After about ten minutes, I could no longer feel anything in my lower face. The older dentist tapped my cheek and jaw until he was satisfied that I was sufficiently numb. The two of them kept up a steady dialogue, but by then I wasn't listening. All I could do was stare at the shiny metal pliers sitting right there in the middle of the tray. As soon as the younger one reached for them, I shut my eyes again and dug my fingers into the leather arms of the chair. I could feel the edge of the pliers as they dug in around each tooth. The student dentist kept telling me to relax and keep my head still, but it was difficult not to move when I could hear the cracking as he tugged and twisted each tooth.

"You can relax now. We're all done." He seemed to take a deep breath even as he spoke. I could sense that we both felt a great deal of relief now that it was finally over.

After I'd gargled and spat into the little round bowl for a few minutes, he handed me the two teeth wrapped in a tissue. "Here you go," he said. "Take this home and maybe you'll get some money from the tooth fairy."

That evening, Mamie made me a cup of lukewarm tea and praised me for being such a brave boy. When I showed her the teeth, she gave me a dime. Later on, I threw them in the garbage. After all, I was twelve years old and far too grown up to believe in the tooth fairy.

It didn't happen very often, but some nights, after a particularly bad day at school, I would wake up in a fearful sweat. I could go for days or even weeks without thinking about Ireland, but on days when Sister Agnes was in one of her more vicious moods, memories of the convent school and St. Andrew's would come flooding back in my dreams. There was nothing distinguishable about the image I saw. It was just a black, faceless blur holding a cane above its head. Just as the cane came down to strike me, I would jump awake. Lying there in the dark, I would remind myself that these events were all in the past and I would feel a great sense of relief. We had been in Canada for almost a year now, but still I found it difficult to look at a nun or a priest without feeling some level of fear and resentment.

When Father McIsaac had first walked into our classroom that spring, I assumed we would once again be treated to a stern lecture on all the reasons we would be going straight to hell if we failed to mend our wicked ways. He was about ten minutes into his talk when it dawned on me that he had yet to mention anything about sin or repentance or even heaven or hell. In fact, in the thirty minutes he was in our class, all he spoke about was baseball. The parish was setting up a softball league. Father McIsaac even made a joke about having to play the games at the public school on Spruce Street: "I am sure we can give those Protestant kids a good run for their money."

By the end of his talk, the whole room was ready to sign up for the team. Even the always complacent Jimmy seemed a little excited about the prospect of playing baseball. One or two of the girls were upset about not being included, but the majority didn't seem to care. Even the Kiwanis Club that opened on Gerrard Street was for boys only. Fair or not, it was just the way things were. I don't believe any of us gave it a second thought at the time.

As the weather improved through the spring, Jimmy's absences from school become more frequent. Sometimes I would see him on the street in the evening. We never talked about where he had been all day, but once in a while, if there was no one else around, he would pull a handful of coins out of his pocket. I didn't ask him where the money came from. I assumed that he and his older brother had spent the day downtown. Most kids would have taken those coins straight to the corner store and filled their pockets with candy. When Jimmy went shopping, he usually came back with a bottle of milk, a loaf of bread, or a bag of potatoes.

When he did show up at school, he always had a note from his mother. Sister Alphonse tried calling on his mother, but couldn't get past the front door. Regardless of how hard she tried, Sister Alphonse could never seem to get through to Jimmy. On any given day, there were a number of boys who failed to show up for classes, but Sister Alphonse considered Jimmy a special case. He was one of the smartest students in the entire school, and Sister Alphonse knew he had the ability to do so much in life if he could only apply himself. She wasn't one to give up, but no matter what she tried, nothing seemed to get through to Jimmy.

Now the threat of not being able to play baseball finally got Jimmy's attention. His attendance was still spotty at best, but when we had a game, he had to be in class for the entire day if he wanted to play baseball after school.

The first time Father McIsaac showed up at one of our baseball games, we were all a little stunned. We had never seen a priest in "civilian" clothing before.

Even Sister Alphonse and Sister Mary Joseph showed up at a game from time to time. They, of course, remained in their usual black garb, which must have been rather uncomfortable on such warm spring afternoons. In spite of the heat, they both seemed to enjoy themselves. The normally reserved Sister Alphonse even cheered and applauded when one of the boys smacked a ball over the fence. No one had the heart to tell her that it was just a foul ball.

I would like to say that I was a good ball player, but I wasn't. The only reason I got to play in every game was because Father McIsaac insisted that everyone get a chance. With as many as twenty boys on the team, each of us had at least a couple of innings to show our worth to the team. I never hit a ball over the fence, but I did manage to get a few hits, and I could run fast enough to get on base. My biggest problem was playing outfield. They say that most good players want the ball to be played to them. When I stood out in the field, I prayed that no fly ball would come my way. Even if I managed to get a glove on the ball, nine times out of ten I would drop it. When you're on a team of twelve-year-old boys, you'd better be able to catch a fly ball. Making excuses like the sun being in your eyes just won't cut it when the game is on the line. No one would hassle me when Father McIsaac was around, but later on there were enough jeers and laughter to make me wish I had never stepped foot on a baseball diamond. Thankfully, Jimmy was there to stick up for me. When you're friends with the best player on the team, who also happens to be the toughest kid on the block, the bullies leave you alone.

Sometimes, when nobody was around, Jimmy would go to the ball diamond and bat fly balls into the air while I stood in the outfield trying to catch them.

"Just keep your eye on the ball and look it right into your glove." He repeated the same thing over and over until eventually I began to get the hang of it.

I would never become what anyone would consider a good player, but hearing our team cheer when I actually managed to catch the ball did wonders for my confidence. I only wished Jimmy had been there to see it all. By late May, just when all the final tests were about to begin, Jimmy was missing once again.

The notes from his mother may have fooled the teachers, but like most of his friends, I now knew where he was going when he disappeared in the afternoon. For weeks now, there had been a rumour going around that Jimmy's father had been spotted in Allan Gardens. Most of us didn't believe it was true, but every day, Jimmy and his brother, Bill, would spend hours searching the park and the alleys, looking for any sign of their missing father. Even after his brother was jailed for shoplifting, Jimmy refused to stop looking.

I have to admit I was more than a little frightened the first time Jimmy asked me to go with him, one Saturday afternoon. I didn't want to go, but Jimmy kept begging me to come with him. Bill would be free on Monday, but Jimmy didn't want to waste an entire weekend waiting. If there was any chance of finding his father, he simply had to go right now.

Allan Gardens was relatively small compared to most of the parks in Toronto. During the day, most of the foot traffic came from people using the park as a shortcut to get downtown. There might be the odd person walking their dog or some old men feeding the pigeons. Or you might see a scruffy old bum rooting through a garbage can or curled up on a bench, trying to sleep. They mostly kept to themselves, only wanting to be left alone. Still, there were plenty of stories about the crazy old men who inhabited the park. The stories were probably untrue, but they were enough to keep most women and children away, even during daylight. Jimmy was about the bravest person I knew, but even he was unwilling to enter the park alone.

Jimmy and I had been wandering the park for almost an hour before he finally worked up the nerve to approach an old man sleeping on a bench. As soon as Jimmy lifted the man's coat to get a look, the man jumped up and grabbed Jimmy's arm. Jimmy managed to pull himself free, and we both ran as far and as fast as we could. We could hear the man shout after us. "You little fuckin' bastards. Come back here and try to rob me and see what you get!"

We were both scared and shaking, but I could see how desperate Jimmy was to give it one more try. At least our first encounter taught us that we could certainly outrun any of these men. Still, Jimmy hesitated before approaching anyone. It was sheer luck when we spotted a familiar figure from our neighbourhood. We stood back at first, not wanting to get to close until we were sure he recognized us.

Johnny Forty Coats was almost a daily fixture on Parliament Street. Judging by his thinning grey hair, he was probably well past middle age. People called him Johnny Forty Coats because of all the clothes he wore. It didn't matter whether it was the depth of winter or a hot summer day; Johnny never had less than three or four layers of clothes on. No one knew where he came from. He just showed up in our laneway one morning and never left. Johnny never asked for a handout, but every now and again one of the old ladies in the neighbourhood would leave a slice of bread or a boiled potato on the porch for him.

On hot sunny days, he often took shade in the alley next to our house. Mamie didn't mind if I took him a slice of bread or a cup of cold water, as long as I didn't get too close. He never said please or thank you, but judging by the way he gulped it down, it was obvious he really needed it. After a while he began calling me kiddo whenever we saw each other in the street.

Most mornings we would see him wandering the alleys off Parliament Street, talking to himself as he picked through the garbage looking for food or a bit of cardboard he could sleep on. Johnny didn't take kindly to anyone trying to invade what he considered his territory. He may have looked old and worn out, but he was always ready to fight with any bum he caught going through what he called his garbage cans. By late afternoon, he'd be plodding along Carlton Street with a knapsack on his shoulder and a few sheets of cardboard under his arm. We always wondered where he was going so late in the day, but when Jimmy and I saw him sitting on a bench in Allan Gardens, we had our answer.

When we saw Johnny on the street, we could never be quite sure how he would react. When we spotted him in the park that afternoon, we knew it was best to approach him very carefully.

Jimmy and I kept smiling and talking as we inched closer. Johnny seemed friendly enough, but even though we told him our names, he didn't seem to recognize us. He kept looking around, trying to make sure no one was getting too close to his bench. "You're not with the police are ya?" he said.

Jimmy told him we were from Parliament Street, but still he seemed suspicious. "You can stay if ya like, but you have to find your own bench. This is mine," he said, stretching his arms out so we couldn't sit down.

Eventually he realized we weren't a threat. Jimmy took a small photo out of his pocket and held it out in front of Johnny. It was all Jimmy had of his father, and he didn't want to let it go. When

Johnny snatched the photo from his fingers, I thought Jimmy was going to jump on him to get it back. Thankfully he held his temper long enough to see that Johnny was just trying to get a better look at the photo. Soon there were other men leaning over, trying to see the picture. Those who came too close to Johnny were given a look that told them to back off.

I had forgotten about the man who had chased us out of the park earlier. Now we saw him coming straight for us, mumbling about what would happen to people who tried to steal his coat. There was no time to explain. In a matter of seconds, he was right there, ready to let fly with both fists. But when he saw Johnny, he stopped dead in his tracks.

I was beginning to understand that this was not the same Johnny we knew from our neighbourhood. On Dermott Place he was the quiet old bum who wandered the street alone and was ignored by almost everyone. In the park he was a whole different person. Maybe it was respect, or maybe it was just fear. Either way, it didn't matter to Jimmy and me. As long as we stayed close to Johnny, no one would dare touch us.

By now Jimmy was starting to get worried, as his tiny photo made its way through the dirty fingers of each man. It was all he had of his father and he wanted it back in one piece. Some men look closely at the picture, while others barely glanced at it before passing it on. We were both beginning to realize that these men didn't understand what we were asking or why we were there. Most of them had just drifted over out of curiosity.

Suddenly, there was a faint glimmer of hope when someone said they knew the man in the picture. All we had to do was give him a packet of smokes and he would bring him right over. For a second, Jimmy looked so hopeful, but then he realized the man was just making fun of us. Johnny stood up, and the man took off down the path.

Once Jimmy had his picture back, we knew it was time to leave. Someone less cruel suggested we come back after dark, when there would be more men in the park. Jimmy didn't answer. He wiped the smudges off the photo and stuck it back in his pocket. As we walked out of the park, I looked back. Johnny was settling down on his bench, while the others had moved off to find a resting place for the night.

Jimmy and I hardly spoke on the walk home. As we were passing Sacred Heart Church, I made an offhand remark about how his brother could help him look once he was out of jail.

I thought it would make him smile, but it only seemed to upset him more. His response surprised me. "After what he has done, I don't want my father back," he said. "I just need to warn him to get away from here, as far as he can. Bill hates him and will probably kill him the first chance he gets."

Once the words were out of his mouth, Jimmy looked strangely relieved. It was like he had finally released this big dark secret he could no longer keep inside. But when he realized what he had said, he began making excuses for his brother. "Don't worry, my brother has always been a hothead, blowing off stream."

Even as he spoke, I wasn't sure whether Jimmy believed his own words. We didn't speak for a while, but just before we turned onto Dermott Place, Jimmy made me swear never to repeat anything he had told me.

In the days that followed, I thought about it all the time. When I heard that Jimmy and Bill were out searching the city again, I prayed that they didn't find their father. As time passed, I began to relax. I even managed to convinced myself that the threat wasn't real. Still, weeks later I was relieved to hear that Jimmy and his brother had more or less given up the search.

My hopes of getting a wagon of my own for Christmas had been dashed, but several months later, an opportunity arose from an unlikely source, a kid named Alex Delchuk. Alex and I didn't like each other. We'd never had a fight or even an argument. But something about his demeanour rubbed me the wrong way, and instinct told me that the feeling was mutual. He was a grade ahead of us, and whenever we saw him at recess or lunchtime, he was always by himself.

Like so many families in our neighbourhood, Alex's family had come to Canada as refugees, soon after the end of the war. Alex had been just a baby when they escaped from Poland. Sometime before his tenth birthday, Alex's mother had disappeared one day, leaving his father alone to raise their two young boys. There were different rumours about where his mother had gone. Some people said that she had simply left with another man, while crueller people said that she was in the mental hospital up in Orillia. Whatever the truth was, Alex never spoke of it. One day some kid in the schoolyard said something to Alex about his mother being in the loony bin. In an instant, Alex threw him to the ground and began pummelling him with both fists. When the teacher pulled them apart and demanded to know what had caused the fight, Alex just stood there, looking defiant and refusing to speak.

One morning in early June, I spotted Alex in his usual spot by the fence. Normally we just ignored each other, but that morning he called my name and walked toward me. I have to admit that I was more than a little intimidated. After we had seen him fight, even the biggest kids knew it was best to leave him alone.

"I heard you were looking for a wagon," he said. "How much would you give me for mine?"

His question took a moment to register. I had seen him at Power Supermarket a few times and knew he had a very nice-looking Red

Flyer wagon. Before I could answer, he told me his family was moving north of the city and he no longer needed it.

Not knowing what to answer, I blurted out, "Five dollars."

He mulled it over for a few seconds before saying yes. For a moment I was caught up in the excitement of actually owning my own wagon, but then it dawned on me that I didn't have anywhere near that kind of money. I thought he might get upset when I stammered that I needed to check at home, but he finally agreed to give me until the end of the week to sort it out.

All the way home I thought about what words I could possibly use to convince Mamie to give me the money. By the time I opened the door, I had come up with a plan. Now I just had to find the right time to spring it on Mamie.

I always thought Mamie had some kind of sixth sense when it came to things like this. Maybe she knew I was up to something when I did the dishes without being told. I don't know how she figured it out, but the moment I finished speaking, she came back with a surprising answer: "I won't give you the money, but I will loan you the five dollars if you can tell me how you plan to pay it back."

Like all my brothers and sisters, I never assumed my parents would just give me money. We may not have had much, but very early on, we all learned the same valuable lesson. No one in this world was going to hand us anything for free. Hard work and perseverance were the only ways of achieving our goals.

My plan was simple. If I worked at Power Supermarket every Friday night and Saturday morning, I could pay the five dollars back within a month. Mamie agreed.

Every Saturday afternoon without fail, I would hand over all the money I had made. I never asked, but sometimes Mamie would hand me back a quarter and send me off to meet my friends at the Saturday matinee. Arrangement or not, Mamie could still be a real softy at times.

At school Alex was sullen, but when I went to his house to pick up the wagon, he seemed like a different person. It was the first time I had ever seen him smile.

I had planned to get the wagon and be on my way, but Alex insisted I come in and sit down in the kitchen. Then he disappeared up the stairs and left me sitting across the table from his father. I realized right away that his father spoke little or no English. At first we just sat there in awkward silence, but then Mr. Delchuk suddenly jumped up and began pointing at the cases of bottles against the wall. It didn't take long to figure out that he was offering me a bottle of soda pop. As soon as I had a bottle of ginger ale in front of me, he began making another series of gestures. Judging by the number of pop bottles stacked against the wall, I assumed he was trying to tell me that this was what he did for a living.

"Sherbourne Street," I blurted.

"Yes, yes," he said, still pointing at the bottles. He seemed pleased that I had managed to figure it out.

The big Canada Dry bottling plant was on Sherbourne, just across the street from Our Lady of Lourdes Church. We would often stop there on the way to Mass on Sunday. Through the large front window, we could watch as the long line of bottles travelled on the conveyor belt. It was fascinating to watch — each bottle came in empty, and by the time it reached the far end of the line, it was filled and capped.

Thankfully, Alex finally arrived in the kitchen with a big box of hockey cards. I could see that he knew a lot about hockey, but didn't often get the chance to talk about it. Soon he had spread all the cards across the table, as he went on and on about the teams and his favourite players. I was suitably impressed when he showed me some of his hockey equipment. His father had promised him he could join a league once they settled into their new house. Alex told me that the five dollars I had paid him for the wagon would go toward the cost of a new pair of skates.

Alex and I became friends in the space of just a few days. One warm night near the end of June, he and I camped out in his backyard. When I said I had never slept outside before, he laughed and told me how he loved sleeping under the stars. I told him all about the deal I had made with my mamie to get the wagon. My story must have reminded him about his mother. Before that night, I had always been careful not to mention it, but lying there in the dark, he told me what had happened. She had abandoned them and run off with another man. He thought she was somewhere in the United States, but he had no idea where. All he knew for sure was that she wasn't ever coming back. He tried to pretend that he no longer cared, but the break in his voice told me otherwise.

That night would be the last time I ever saw Alex. A few days later, he and his family were gone. He promised to send me his address as soon as he was settled, but I never heard from him again.

The weeks turned to months and I had more or less forgotten about Alex when one day, soon after Christmas break of the next school year, Kenny Bell told me about something he had read in the newspaper. According to the article, Alex and his father had been killed in a head-on collision on the highway, somewhere around Lindsay, Ontario. They had been on their way to the local arena for hockey practice. Who knows what could have happened if Alex had lived to fulfill his dream? Perhaps he could have been the next great player in the National Hockey League. Alex was just thirteen years old when he died.

❧

As the school year drew to a close in June, Jimmy would often disappear for days at a time. If he showed up at all, it was only because he was trying to avoid being kept back in grade six for yet another year. When I did see Jimmy, he never strayed too far from his house. His mother didn't sit and watch out the window anymore. Now she spent most of her days in bed, while Jimmy and his brother took turns watching over her.

I wouldn't see him for days, and then suddenly he would show up and beg me and Wayne to go downtown with him. "Come on, come on," Jimmy would say. "Your ma will think you're at the movies and you'll still be home by five o'clock."

I knew exactly where he wanted to go. I also knew that if Da ever found out, he would wallop the life out of me. But I always found it difficult to say no to Jimmy.

For some reason, he just loved riding the subway. I think the strain on him was becoming too much, and sometimes he simply wanted to get away. For him, the subway was a refuge, a place where he could have some fun and forget about the problems that awaited him at home. Even as the time to go home approached, Jimmy would plead with me to stay just a little longer. I think if Jimmy had his way, he would never leave the train.

College Station was only busy on the evenings when there was a hockey game at Maple Leaf Gardens. On a Saturday afternoon, it was generally quiet. All we had to do was wait until the man in the ticket booth was busy with a customer and then we could easily sneak under the turnstiles and onto the platform before anyone noticed. In the time between trains, the only noise we could hear was the sound of our footsteps echoing along the tiled walls. If we crept up to the edge of the platform and stayed completely quiet, we could hear the rats scurrying around the steel tracks. They were difficult to see in the dark, but if we threw a stone or a tin can right at the tracks, the noise would send them darting in every direction.

We could hear the train long before we saw it. The moment it emerged from the tunnel, the wind came rushing in a great burst of air down the platform. We tried to pick the car with the smallest number of passengers so we could move about without drawing too much suspicion. Most people were friendly enough, but after one strange encounter, we decided it was best not to speak to anyone on the train.

I don't think any of us had ever heard the word *pedophile*, but we did know about perverts. My friends at school talked about how these dirty old men liked to hang around the school and the park, looking for kids they could lure into the bushes so they could try to put their hands down the kids' pants. Based on what I'd heard in the schoolyard, I knew exactly what a pervert would look like. He would be an older man, probably a bum, with dirty clothes and a scruffy beard.

The man on the train was none of those things. He looked to be in his twenties, clean shaven and well-dressed. He seemed friendly as we talked about how much fun it was to ride the train. It wasn't often we met an adult who was interested in what we had to say.

Then, just as we were about to enter King Station, his demeanour changed. Suddenly, he stood up and moved toward the door. As the train glided to a stop, he asked us if we wanted to come home with him. He said he would give us all some peanut butter and jam sandwiches and chocolate cake for lunch. Before we could answer, he offered us each a dollar so we'd be able to get back on the train afterward. I have to admit, for a split second, it sounded to me like a great idea. We could get a free sandwich and cake and even make a dollar out of the deal.

I may have been a very stupid and naive kid, but Jimmy understood what was really going on. "Fuck you" was all he said.

The man seemed startled by Jimmy's loud words. He glanced around the car to see if anyone else was paying attention. Wayne and I just looked at each other, still not sure what was going on. The moment the door opened, the clean-cut man with the nice clothes was gone. Thank goodness Jimmy was there to explain to us what had just happened.

Once the train reached the end of the line at Union Station, it was easy to get lost in the crowd. Then we'd cross over to the northbound platform and catch the train back to College Station. With the noise and the rocking of the train as it sped through the dark tunnel, it was always an exciting way to spend an afternoon. But, like any good thing, it had to come to an end sometime. Late one afternoon we were cornered by a train inspector just as we were crossing the concourse in Union Station. When we couldn't produce either a transfer ticket or any money, he told us get the hell out of the station before he called the cops.

It was a relief to get away, but now we had to really hurry if we were going to make it home before anyone found out. The more I thought about my da's fists raining down on me, the faster I ran. Still, it was after six o'clock when I reached the front door. My only hope was that Da was late getting home from work. Just as I touched the handle the door swung open, and there was Da. I tried to say I was sorry, but he grabbed me by the shirt collar and struck me in the side of the head with his fist. As I was falling down, I wrapped both arms around my head, trying to lessen the force of the blows.

Thankfully, Mamie was there once again to step in front of him and save me from further punches. "Okay, Billy, that's enough," she said as I lay there crying, hoping it was over. Even when Da was at his worst, Mamie had a way of calming him down. As soon as he dropped his fists, she turned to me. "You get yourself up those stairs and stay there!"

It would be a very long time before I saw the light of day. When Da was at work, I could come downstairs, but if we did run into each other, he just ignored me. Going to and from school and Sunday Mass was the only time I was allowed outside. Mamie warned me that if I was even one minute late getting home from school or Mass, she wouldn't be there to protect me. She didn't have to say any more.

Every month more and more families moved into the neighbourhood. By the spring of 1960, the school was literally bursting at the seams. More students meant more portable classrooms. Even recess time had to be staggered because the schoolyard was too small to accommodate everyone at once.

After Easter, it had been announced that a new extension was to be built onto the existing building. The added classrooms would take up most of the remaining property and stretch all the way back to the boundary fence along Salisbury Avenue.

Although the actual construction would not begin until early July, much of the preliminary work had to be done while school was still in session. With all the building materials and scaffolding surrounding the school, the whole property became a large construction site. Three of the portables had to be removed, forcing at least ninety students to move inside the building for the last month of the school year. With forty or more kids now in every classroom, there was barely room to move. The addition of twenty grade-four students to our grade-six classroom had at least brought one positive benefit: Sister Agnes couldn't easily get at the kids whose desks were in the middle of the room. The extra work made her nastier than ever, but with so many new kids to terrorize, she paid less attention to the rest of us. Sometimes the classroom felt like a pressure cooker ready to explode. Morning roll call was utter chaos. After a day or two, most of the nuns didn't bother to count heads.

Donny Lund was the first to disappear, and after we saw him get away with it, Harold and I joined him for a morning of wandering around the Don Valley. At first it felt great to be free of St. Martin's. It was a glorious sunny morning in June. Harold came up with the idea to catch some garter snakes we could take home for pets, so we made our way down to the banks of the Don River. After an hour of turning over rocks and finding nothing, Donny and I were ready to quit.

That's when all the what-ifs began to creep into my thoughts. What if Sister Agnes had noticed us missing and she was standing by the school gate, ready to whip us with her yardstick? What if we were caught by a truant officer and dragged into Sister Alphonse's office to be beaten with her leather strap? Worst of all, what if Mamie found out and sent me upstairs to wait for Da?

When I told Harold and Donny I was going back, they both laughed and called me a chicken. Regardless of what they said, I was not about to change my mind. I could see by the expression on his face that Harold was beginning to have some doubts as well. Soon Donny was the only holdout. He called us a couple of babies for being so frightened. Harold just laughed, but I was getting a little angry with being called names.

"It's easy for you," I said, pushing Donny backward. "Your old man doesn't give a shit about ya, but mine will kick the hell out of me if he finds out I took off from school!" The moment I said the words, I regretted them, but it was too late.

Just the mention of his father was enough to send Donny charging at me. Both of us rolled on the ground, arms flailing, trying to land a punch on the other's face. It was more like a wrestling match than a fist fight, with neither one of us inflicting any real damage. It only lasted a minute before Harold pulled us apart. He laughed as Donny and I stood bent over, trying to catch our breath.

I don't know if it was because of our little fight or simply the prospect of being left alone, but after a few minutes, all three of us started back up the hill toward the school. By the time we'd reached the edge of the park, we were all talking again. Harold was relatively clean, but Donny and I had mud stains on our pants from rolling around in the weeds. I was surprised when Donny suggested we go to his house to clean ourselves up a bit. Donny was never allowed to bring his friends in the house. He insisted we use the back door so we couldn't be seen from the street.

After cleaning our shoes and brushing the mud off our pants, we looked a little more presentable. Donny said his father wouldn't be home before dark, but he still seemed nervous just having us there. Although we were running short on time, Donny insisted on wiping out the sink and mopping up any telltale marks we'd left on the floor.

I had managed to wipe all the mud from my pants, but the dark wet stain it had left made it look like I'd peed myself. It was a warm day, so I hoped my pants would dry before we got back to the schoolyard.

When we turned onto Winchester Street, it looked like our plan to get back into the school was working out perfectly. The lunch break was almost over, but the yard was still full of screaming kids. The back gate on Salisbury Avenue was open, and with a little luck we could sneak in and be swallowed up by the crowd before anyone knew the difference.

We were literally ten steps from the gate when we heard Sister Mary Joseph's voice booming across the yard. "You three! Stop right where you are!"

In that moment I knew we were as good as dead. All the horrors I had conjured up in my mind were about to come true. As she approached, Harold muttered something about making a run for it, but it was too late. She knew exactly who we were and where we all lived. The only option left was to tell the truth and take the beating that would follow. At least it was Sister Mary Joseph who'd caught us. She did use the strap from time to time, but she was never as cruel as the other nuns.

"How many times have you boys been told you're not allowed to leave the yard at lunchtime?" she said.

We just stood there, dumbfounded. We had just been given a way out of our dilemma. It is amazing how fast your mind works when you're terrified. All we had to do was lie to a nun. The priest at Mass always said that a lie would send us to purgatory. I could only assume that telling a big lie, especially to a nun, would surely send us straight to hell. But then again, if I could just stay alive until Saturday, I could go to confession and save my soul from certain damnation.

"Well, what do you have to say for yourselves?" Sister Mary Joseph looked rather impatient as she stared at us, waiting for an answer. In an instant, the words came to me. "Sorry, Sister. We were just playing hide-and-seek behind the cars."

Then I realized she was staring at the stain on my pants. I knew that the question was coming and that I was about to compound my problem by telling another lie.

Normally the sound of the bell ringing was met by a collective groan through the schoolyard. For the three of us standing there, the bell could not have come at a better time. Would she let us go? All the students were starting to line up, ready to march inside, yet we still stood there, under her knowing gaze. It was like she could see right into us and was trying to decide if we were telling the truth.

"Okay," she finally said. "Get yourselves back inside and don't let me catch any of you outside the fence again."

As the end of the school year drew closer, the chaos within the school only grew worse. More and more construction material was brought onto the site. Bricks and boards and mounds of sand were placed next to the fence, while cans of paint and bags of cement lined the inner hallway. Sister Alphonse had a stern warning for us all. Anyone caught playing around the construction material, either inside or outside, would be strapped so hard they would be sore for a week. Some mornings it was difficult to pay attention in class when all we could see and hear were trucks backing into the yard to offload equipment. At first it was exciting to watch, but when we were told it was not safe to go out for recess, the novelty quickly wore off. Some days felt endless. I am sure the teachers felt as trapped as the students did. Even the normally mild-mannered Sister Mary Joseph could sometimes be heard shouting at kids in the hallway. Sister Alphonse tried to maintain some level of calm through it all, but there was no mistaking the look of relief on her face when the bell rang and we were all set free at the end of each day.

By mid-June, we could almost feel the excitement in the air. Even Sister Agnes appeared to be in a better mood. I am sure she was thinking the same thing we all were. School was almost over for the summer and soon she could say good riddance to us all.

My only real concern was what I would say when I finally saw Jimmy. No one had seen him in over a week, but we all knew he wouldn't be moving on to grade seven with the rest of us. I knew he would be unhappy about it, but no one could have predicted what happened the day that Jimmy's mother found out her son had failed.

Our exams were over, and we thought it was going to be just another boring afternoon of putting in time while we waited for the bell to ring at three o'clock. But then Mrs. Duncan showed up, and her angry voice carrying down the hallway caught our attention. Sister Alphonse tried to calm her down and guide her into the office, but she had no intention of sitting down. Poor Sister Alphonse could hardly keep up with her as she marched down the hall, demanding to see Sister Agnes. When she came banging on our classroom door, Sister Agnes told us to sit quietly at our desks and read our catechism books. Then she went out into the hall.

Again Sister Alphonse tried to move the discussion to her office, but Jimmy's mother refused to budge. The moment the door closed, the shouting began. Everyone in our class looked stunned. We had all heard the men in our neighbourhood cursing, but we had never heard such language from a woman. We tried to stay quiet, but it was difficult not to laugh when we heard Mrs. Duncan calling Sister Agnes an old cow.

The moment the door opened again, every head in the room shot straight down, pretending to read our books. Sister Agnes never said a word, but we knew she was watching us. No one dared look up. She was clearly upset and no one wanted to give her an excuse to turn on us.

I don't think there was a single person in the entire school who didn't enjoy hearing the wicked witch of the west being finally put in her place. We only wished it would have turned out better for Jimmy. Unfortunately, Mrs. Duncan's anger did not change his fate. Jimmy would have to spend another year in grade six.

One morning when school had been out for almost a week, Jimmy and Wayne came knocking on our door. It was the first sunny morning after days of rain, and Mamie was only too happy to get us kids outside so she could relax in the quiet of her kitchen. Fred was sent off to Power Supermarket to pick up a bag of potatoes. Thankfully, Marie was now considered old enough to watch over David and Philip. At first Philip whined that he wanted to go with me and my friends. I only had ten cents in my pocket, but I gave it to Marie to buy some Popsicles at the corner store. I didn't like being completely broke, but it was the price I had to pay to get away from babysitting and be with my friends.

As soon as we were clear of the neighbourhood, Wayne lit a cigarette and we passed it around. By the time it got back to me, the butt was so short that I had to drop it before it burned my fingertips. As usual, Wayne was doing most of the talking. Normally I found Wayne's constant chatter a real annoyance, but at least today we weren't talking about school.

Maybe it was my fault for bringing up the subject of money, but when I mentioned that I had no money for the movie matinee, Wayne pulled a crisp, new five-dollar bill out of his pocket. He went on and on about the money he'd received from his father for having such a good report card. Jimmy just kept walking. He didn't say a word, but judging by the look on his face, I guessed Wayne was just seconds away from a punch in the mouth.

I told him twice to shut up before it finally dawned on him. If he had just stopped talking, that would have been the end of it. Instead, he prattled on about how sorry he was that Jimmy's father was missing and how he didn't think it was right for Jimmy to have to go back into grade six.

I had never seen Wayne look so afraid as he did when Jimmy grabbed him by the shirt. A lot of kids, including me, would have enjoyed watching Wayne get knocked to the ground with a bloody nose, but Jimmy didn't hit him. Jimmy finally released his grip and began to walk away. Wayne took a deep breath and almost smiled once he realized he wasn't going to get punched in the face. We both called after Jimmy, asking him to stay, but he just kept walking.

Then he turned around, an odd smile on his face. "Don't worry about me," he yelled over his shoulder. "Those nuns are never going to get their hands on me again."

I yelled back that I would call on him later, but I never did. Months would pass before I laid eyes on Jimmy again.

CHAPTER 7

THE ONE BIG drawback to the warm July weather was that it cut into my ability to make money at the grocery store. When the sun was shining and the sidewalks were clear, women were much more inclined to carry their own groceries. Sometimes I would spend hours sitting on my wagon in front of Power Supermarket and not have a penny to show for it. But there was still a little money to be made if you knew where to look. On Friday nights, most of the stores along Parliament Street put out their garbage just before they closed their doors at nine o'clock. Mamie insisted that I be home by nine thirty, which gave me just enough time to scour through all the garbage bins, looking for pop bottles. I could usually find enough empties to cash in for the twenty-five cents I would need for the Saturday matinee.

Once school was out, there were plenty of jobs to do at home every morning before we were allowed to go anywhere. There were dishes to be done, floors to be swept and mopped, and furniture to be dusted. Mamie could always find something for idle hands to do, but Saturday mornings were the worst. That was the day, year-round, that Mamie cleaned the house from top to bottom — and no one was going anywhere until the work was done.

As usual Fred was the good son who never complained, but during the colder months there was one job that we both hated. At 8:00 a.m. every second Saturday, the coal man would make his delivery. It would have been nice if he brought the coal down to the basement, but he dropped the sacks at the back door and hurried away to his next stop. It was left to Fred and me to get it all down to the basement. It took both of us to lift each of the forty-pound burlap sacks, carry them down the narrow stairway and across the cement floor, and then dump the contents into the coal bin next to the furnace. We tried to empty each bag slowly, but still a cloud of coal dust steadily built up all around us. Once the bin was full, we had to gather up all the pieces that had missed the bin and sweep away the thick coating of coal dust that had settled on the floor. Regardless of how careful we were, our faces and arms ended up black with dust and soot. As soon as we came up the stairs, Mamie filled a basin full of water and sent us to the back porch to wash ourselves clean.

Normally I hated to go shopping, but it was certainly better than making beds, cleaning the toilet, or peeling the ten pounds of potatoes we always needed for dinner. The moment Mamie reached for her purse, I was right there, ready to get anything she needed. The Becker's store was farther away than Power Supermarket, but Mamie liked the gallon milk jugs we could get there for forty-nine cents. If I took my time and checked all the alleys for pop bottles, I could make a little money, and with any luck most of the housework would be done before I reached home. It didn't take long for Mamie to catch on to my little scheme, and she made sure to save at least one dirty job just for me. At first I tried protesting my innocence, but she just gave me that look that said she'd heard it all before. All I could do now was get the work done quickly and hope Mamie was satisfied enough to let me out in time for the matinee.

By late spring, there was no need for coal, but once the snow had disappeared and the ground had thawed, we set about digging a vegetable garden. Our backyard wasn't nearly as big as the one back in Ireland, but it still took three weeks of shovelling the hard, stony ground before Mamie was satisfied with our efforts.

The jobs were hard enough as it was, but having Fred boss me around all the time only made it worse. If Mamie wasn't there to hear, I would tell him to bugger off and leave me alone. Sometimes I would fantasize about what it would be like if he weren't there to torment me all the time. Maybe, I thought, when his back was turned I could whack him in the back of the head with my shovel. I could try to make it look like an accident so Da wouldn't wallop the hell out of me. Later on at confession, I could tell the priest all about my big sin, knowing he had to keep my secret. He might have me say the rosary three or four times, but that would absolve me of my mortal sin and keep from going to hell. Of course I would never do it, but thinking about it helped a long day of digging go a little faster.

Mamie tried planting all manner of vegetables in her new garden, but the soil was so poor that almost nothing seemed to grow. When everything else failed, we were left with only potatoes. Even in the poorest soil, they always seemed to thrive. By early summer we would have more potatoes than even our big family could eat.

Once Mass was out of the way on Sunday, we could finally look forward to a peaceful afternoon. Mamie would sit in the kitchen, enjoying her tea and listening to the Irish show on the radio. If it was a pay week, Da and my older brothers might walk down to Varsity Stadium and watch a football game. If Fred and I did a good job cleaning the dinner dishes, I might be allowed outside until it got dark at nine o'clock.

That Sunday evening in July started out like any other. Some of the boys on the street got up a game of road hockey at the bottom of

Dermott Place, where the asphalt wasn't quite so rough. It was just past seven o'clock when someone noticed a cloud of black smoke rising above the houses to the north. We all ran up the street, expecting to see someone's house on fire. When we turned off Carlton onto Sackville Street, we could just hear the sound of sirens wailing in the distance. By the time we reached Winchester, we were all out of breath. That's when we saw the dense cloud of black smoke hanging over St. Martin's. There must have been fifty or more kids lining the street, directly across from the school. From our vantage point, it looked like the old part of the school, which faced onto Winchester Street, was generally intact, but the new part of the school, which backed onto Salisbury, was engulfed in flames. By now the firefighters were pouring water onto the back of the building, trying to contain the fire before it reached the portable classrooms along the fence line.

Later we heard that it had taken long into the night before the fire was finally brought under control. Early the next morning, Fred and I, along with Marie and David, headed back to the school to survey the damage. Most of our classmates were already there. The windows along both sides of the building were gone, and the brown brick walls were black with soot. Someone said that the cans of paint and sheets of plywood had added greatly to the intensity of the fire. Water still dripped from the roof, forming large pools on the asphalt playground. We weren't allowed to get close to the building, but from what we could see, the interior looked completely gutted.

We didn't see any of the teachers, but most of the adults who were there stood around looking sad and dejected. For us, it was like a dream come true. There was only a little over a month left until September. Surely the school would never be ready in time? It might be many months, or even a year, before we had to go back to school!

The first reports in Monday's *Toronto Star* said that the fire had been deemed suspicious and a full investigation would be launched. Like most kids on our street, I had rarely read the newspaper before that week. Now, whenever we got together on the street, all we talked about was the fire. We weren't interested in the investigations. We just wanted to know when we could expect to go back to school. It was the Thursday edition of the *Telegram* that first reported that a witness had seen two people breaking into the school early on Sunday evening.

The following afternoon, a whole gang of us were playing hockey in the street when we saw a squad car turning onto Dermott Place. Seeing a police car in our lane was not unusual, but then a second car followed. At about the same time a third car moved into position to block off the roadway at the bottom of the lane.

Our street hockey game forgotten, we all gathered down near the bottom of the street, curious to see what was happening. Even as the cops converged on Jimmy's house, we didn't think much of it. Rarely a week went by without the cops showing up to talk to Bill about a robbery or to his mother because she'd gotten into another shouting match with a neighbour. Then we saw Jimmy and his brother being brought out in handcuffs. Neither of the boys said a word, but Mrs. Duncan had to be restrained by one of the officers.

"You're nothing but a bunch of filthy thugs!" she screamed at the cops, demanding that her boys be let go. As the cars drove away, she was still yelling after them. Her daughter finally coaxed her back into the house, but not before Mrs. Duncan had called us all a bunch of nosy bastards who should be minding their own business.

I don't know who was the first to suggest that the arrest had something to do with the fire. Someone else said they were daft to think such nonsense. Knowing the history of the family, there were numerous reasons why Jimmy and his brother might be arrested.

In the days that followed, there was nothing in the newspapers. The cops came to talk to Mrs. Duncan a few days later, but otherwise their house was quiet. Wayne and I decided that the whole thing was just some huge misunderstanding. Any day now, we would see Jimmy and Bill walk up the lane and everything would return to normal. My brother Johno laughed when I asked him if it was over. He told me I shouldn't expect to see my friend Jimmy for a very long time.

Johno was right about that. It was already into August when Bill was taken before a judge in the courthouse behind city hall. According to the papers, he pleaded guilty and tried to convince the court that he was the one who had started the fire and that, although Jimmy had been there, he had done nothing wrong. Bill was sentenced to four years in jail. Whether the judge believed Bill or took Jimmy's age into consideration, he did drop the arson charge against Jimmy. Jimmy pleaded guilty to the charge of breaking and entering, which could have put him away for three years if not for the character witness who stepped forward to speak on his behalf.

In spite of all that had happened, Sister Alphonse told the court that Jimmy was really a good boy who deserved a second chance. I think everyone was relieved when Jimmy was sent to reform school until his sixteenth birthday. Two years seemed like a long time, but at least he had a chance for a better future.

The Pine Ridge Training School for Boys was only fifty miles east of Toronto, but no one was allowed to visit. The inmates were housed in three barracks-like buildings, each capable of holding up to fifty boys. There were a number of workshops and a small administrative office spread around the compound. At the time, Pine Ridge was considered the ideal facility to train delinquent boys and get them back into society.

With Jimmy and his brother gone, their house at the end of the lane grew quiet. We saw Jimmy's sister playing on the porch from time to time, but her mother would not let her go out to play with the rest of the kids on the street. The only person allowed past the front door was the man from the Saint Vincent de Paul Society, who showed up near the end of each month.

Mamie had me drop off a bowl of leftover boiled potatoes once. I didn't want to knock on the door, so I just left it on the porch and took off as quickly as I could. When I went back the next morning, the bowl was sitting empty on the top step. Soon some of the other women in the lane started dropping off food. It was always taken, but they were never given any thanks for their efforts. We would wave hello to the girl from time to time, but her mother forbade her from talking to "the hooligans in the street." By now all the kids referred to her as the crazy old lady who lived down the lane. Mamie told me never to talk like that. As far as Mamie was concerned, she was just a lonely and poor old woman who desperately wanted her sons back.

In the summer all I wanted to do was forget about everything bad and spend every waking minute outside in the sun. Whether it was making beds, mopping floors, emptying buckets, weeding the gardens, or peeling potatoes, I hated it all. Still, it was best to keep my mouth shut and just keep working until Mamie set me free.

Sometimes Wayne and I would meet up with Donny and Harold and head down into the Don Valley. We followed the narrow trail along the bank of the river all the way north to the Bloor Viaduct. With a little effort, we could shimmy up onto the massive cement footings and sit there listening to the sound of traffic high above on Danforth Avenue. If we managed to get there at the right time of day, we could actually feel the vibration as a long freight train thundered through the valley. The noise from the train passing under the bridge would echo through the girders and down the valley floor, making it impossible to hear anything over the deafening roar. After a few minutes, when the last car had passed under the bridge and the train had vanished behind the hills to the north, the noise was gone with it.

I think it was Harold who first came up with the idea of catching muskrats. He had read somewhere that the city parks department would pay us a ten-dollar bounty on every dead muskrat we brought in. Harold bragged about how many times he had done it back in Nova Scotia.

People always said that the Don River was easy to find — all you had to do was follow your nose. Even before we reached the valley floor, we could pick up the pungent odour of raw sewage and dead fish. Sometimes, in the late fall when the wind blew in from the east, the smell would envelop the neighbourhood, all the way over to Parliament Street.

We didn't realize it then, but this would be the last time that we would be able to move freely through the Don Valley. Within a few months, the familiar landscape would be changed forever. The construction we were seeing now on the far side of the river was the beginning of what would become the Don Valley Parkway. To the south of us, construction of the Gardiner Expressway was well underway. Once these two massive projects linked up just east of the Don, traffic could easily traverse across the bottom of the city and all the way north to Highway 401.

Moving along the river bank was not as easy we had expected. In some spots the bank was quite steep and eroded by the fast-flowing water. If we got too close to the edge, where the ground was very unstable, the smallest weight could collapse the bank and send us all tumbling into the river.

We continued our trek north for the better part of an hour, but never saw a single living creature. One by one, we discarded the rocks and the sharpened sticks we had hoped would help us catch muskrats. We were more interested in using our hands to swat away the swarms of flies and mosquitoes buzzing all around us.

At least we didn't go home empty handed. Just as we were climbing back up the hill near the south end of the valley, we spotted a snake slithering under a pile of loose rocks. When we pulled the rock away, we found an entire nest of garter snakes. Harold thought it was stupid, but I didn't want to go home with nothing, so I stuck a couple of the snakes into my bag.

All the way home we argued about whose fault it was that we hadn't caught any muskrats. Harold blamed all of us for making too much noise when we walked through the bush. Of course Wayne, Donny, and I knew that Harold was just a big blowhard who probably knew next to nothing about catching muskrats.

Maybe it was the bag of snakes, or perhaps it was the fact that I was filthy and smelling of fish, but Mamie was more than a little upset when I walked into the kitchen. At least the snakes saved me from getting smacked with a soup ladle. Mamie wouldn't come near me as long as I held on to the bag. She made me hand it over to Johno and told him to take them someplace far away from the house. Meanwhile I was ordered to strip down and get upstairs to the bathtub.

"If you don't do a proper job, I'll come up there and scrub you myself," Mamie threatened as I ran up the stairs.

When Da came home from work, I thought I might be in for a walloping, but he just told me not to be upsetting Mamie so much. He actually seemed amused by the whole incident. I think it reminded him of his own wild childhood.

I was so relieved not to get hit that I didn't even mind when Mamie made me stay in the house for the next few days. But just because I was confined to the house didn't mean I couldn't do a little work. Mamie kept me busy throughout the mornings, but oddly enough, I kind of enjoyed our afternoons together. The house was always quiet in the middle of the day. Philip would be playing around on the floor while Mamie and I sat drinking tea at the kitchen table. We never talked about much, but it was nice to have her to myself, if only for a few minutes each day. At the time I knew nothing about her heart condition, but still I worried because she always looked so tired.

Once we finished our tea, it was time for me to start peeling potatoes as Mamie got started on another meal. By six in the evening, the house would once again be filled with the noise of our big family sitting down for dinner.

CHAPTER 8

BY AUGUST, IT began to look like our family had finally turned a corner. Da was back to work, and Michael and Johno had both found full-time jobs. Fred had managed to find a summer job working part-time at the Laura Secord candy shop on Yonge Street. He only made a few dollars a week, but when he tried to give it to Mamie, she said no. Instead, she insisted he put it all in a bank account. Fred was just one year away from starting high school. When that day arrived, he would need every penny just to pay for the mountain of textbooks he would need for his first year.

It had been almost thirteen months since we moved into that dilapidated old house on Dermott Place. There never was enough money to repair all the problems, but once the landlord agreed to fix the leaks in the roof and Da sealed all the cracks, at least the house was warm and dry. It took months for my brothers and me to paint and wallpaper most of downstairs rooms, but when it was all done, the house finally felt like home. At one point, the landlord actually offered to sell us the house for five thousand dollars. It sounded exciting at first, but with Da making about three hundred dollars a month, the whole idea was simply out of the question.

If we couldn't afford to buy a home of our own, at least we had a warm and comfortable house to live in. When we went to bed that night in August, it seemed that everything was finally going our way.

It was a hot and sticky night, with barely a breeze in the air. Fred and I had managed to pry up the bedroom window and jam a stick under the frame to keep it from sliding back down. We wedged a shoe under the door to hold it open, in the hope of creating a little draft through the room. It was past eleven o'clock when we finally fell asleep.

Sometime after 1:00 a.m., both of us were awakened by the sound of screaming coming from downstairs. Before we could even react, Mamie was standing in our doorway with little Philip clutched tightly in her arms and Marie hanging on to the hem of her nightgown.

"Take David and get outside!" Mamie yelled as she headed for the stairway.

When we reached the bottom of the stairs, it was difficult to breathe, as smoke filled the hallway. In a moment we were standing out on the street, staring at the front of the house, not knowing what to do next. Mamie sent Fred to wake the neighbours and call the fire department. Then she told the rest of us to stay together and ran to the back of the house, searching frantically for Da and Johno, who were both still inside. A plume of smoke rose above the back of the house. It looked like the fire was concentrated in the kitchen. Da and Johno were doing everything they could to beat down the fire and keep the flames from spreading any farther.

When the firefighters arrived, they didn't waste any time. They broke down the back door and dowsed the kitchen with their hose. The force of the water knocked over the cupboard, breaking almost every dish we owned. By the time they'd finished, the kitchen was flooded in ankle-deep water.

The whole thing was over in under fifteen minutes. The whole family just stood there watching as the firefighters went about the business of rolling up the hose and putting their equipment back on the truck. After a few words with my da, they were gone, leaving us to clean up the damage. The kitchen window was gone and the walls were black, with long scorch marks extending across the ceiling. Some of the linoleum had melted away, exposing the wooden floor underneath. Large droplets of water fell from the ceiling, adding to the flood on the floor. The water damage had knocked out all the power to the house, meaning that the cleanup would have to wait until morning.

When we came down to the kitchen just after daylight, Rosaleen was just coming in the door with a loaf of bread under her arm. She and Bernard lived all the way over on Davenport Road. Rosaleen had wanted to come as soon as she heard about the fire, but she had to wait until the streetcar started running at 6:00 a.m. All of us were hungry after the long night, but it would take a few days before the gas and electricity were turned back on. Until then, bread and jam would have to do.

At least the fire damage didn't look that bad in the full light of day. With some scrubbing and a little paint, the wall would look as good as new. The real problem was all the water they had used to extinguish the fire. The floor, the broken furniture, and especially the electric wiring would take days or perhaps weeks to repair. My da and older brothers could do most of the work, but the materials would cost more money than we could possibly afford. For those of us who were poor and living in Cabbagetown, there was never enough money left over to even consider buying fire insurance.

We would never determine the exact cause of the fire, but perhaps there was still a cigarette butt burning when the ashtray had been dumped into the garbage can. Needless to say, our landlord was not very pleased. Still, he did agree to buy the necessary materials and hire a handyman. It would take months before our house was back to normal and another two years to pay back the money we owed the landlord.

I think the most upsetting part for Mamie was the loss of the tea set and some other treasured mementoes she had brought all the way from Ireland. But we all knew that things could have been so much worse, if not for some good luck and Johno's quick action. If he had not woken up that night and gone downstairs for a glass of water, God only knows what might have happened to all of us.

In the days following the fire, Mamie wasn't quite herself. We all knew Mamie loved us, although she rarely said it. She was never one to shower us with affection, but now, suddenly, she would hug and squeeze us so tight that we could hardly breathe. When my pals called on me, I would run out the door as quick as I could. I certainly liked Mamie's attention, but being hugged and kissed in front of my friends was just too embarrassing.

At breakfast one morning about a week after the fire, Mamie hit me in the knuckles with the porridge ladle and told me to start eating. She was back to her regular self. I think it had taken her a while to get over the shock and realize that we were going to be just fine.

Sometimes, when I walked down the lane and saw Jimmy's house, I wondered if I would ever see him again. I might catch a glimpse of his little sister playing on the porch, but mostly the house was dark and uninviting, with the curtains drawn all day. When the old ladies left food on the front porch, Jimmy's mother might take it inside, but often it would sit there until the alley cats came sniffing around. Even when the man from Saint Vincent de Paul dropped of a parcel, it might sit outside until it was dark enough for Mrs. Duncan to sneak out and retrieve it without being seen.

I continued to take my wagon to the supermarket during August, and if I stuck with it until closing time on Friday night, I could usually make just enough money to get me into the Saturday matinee. I could always tell how good a movie was by the length of the line. One day there was a double feature of John Wayne movies, so by the time I arrived, the queue already stretched at least two blocks down Parliament Street. The usher didn't look very happy, and he kept shouting at the kids in line to move against the wall to make room for people passing by on the narrow sidewalk. Then, as soon as the crowd did so, one of the store owners would come out to complain because the line was blocking his doorway.

I hadn't seen any of my friends in days, and I was hoping to spot a familiar face who might let me butt into the lineup. I saw lots of kids I knew from the lane, but if anyone even looked like they were trying to cut in, the jeers and threats would start from all those waiting behind.

Then one mouthy kid spoke up. "Get lost, before you lose your teeth!"

The smart thing would have been to just keep walking down the line, but I couldn't take my eyes off the kid with the big mouth. It was obvious he didn't remember me, but I recognized him the second he spoke. He was definitely one of the four kids who had beaten me up the previous year in Regent Park.

I honestly don't know what came over me, but in that instant, it all came back to me. I could see him laughing with delight as his friends kicked and punched me while he stomped on the loaf of bread he'd knocked from my arm, mashing the slices into the ground.

I didn't stop to think. I leapt straight at him with both fists flying. My first and only punch landed right on the bridge of his nose. The force knocked him backward into a door. I could hear the thud as the back of his head broke the glass near the bottom of the door.

He looked stunned, but I was right on top of him, trying to land another punch while I still had the upper hand. But before I could get another swing in, all the kids around us came piling on. For a second I thought I might smother under their weight.

In hindsight, I was lucky that the usher was there to pull us all apart before the kid's friends beat me senseless. Even as he was hauled me up by the collar, my arms and legs were still flailing as I tried to land one more blow. As the usher reached down to help the other kid to his feet, I could see the blood and broken glass on the sidewalk.

The store owner came running outside, screaming blue murder over his broken door. I was still dazed, but as the usher loosened his grip on me, I knew I had to get out of there before the cops showed up. I took off up the street and didn't stop running until I reached the corner of Gerrard Street. Once I was sure no one was following me, I finally stopped to catch my breath and consider what to do next. A lot of kids in that line knew me, but maybe if I could stay out of sight for a few days, the whole thing would blow over.

I was all the way up Parliament Street and just turning up the alley behind Power Supermarket when it dawned on me that I couldn't go home. It was far too early for the matinee to be over, and showing up at the house now would only draw a lot of questions I didn't want to answer. At least I didn't look like I had been in a fight. My knuckles were red and swollen and there was scrapes on both my elbows, but they could be easily hidden.

I pondered where to go. Mamie always insisted we go to confession on Saturday afternoon. It was earlier than normal, but if I walked down to Sacred Heart Church, I could go to confession and kill a little time before going home.

At least this time I had something to confess other than the usual venial sins. I was pleased to see a lineup for the confessional. Fortunately for me, the priest was a French Canadian I had been to before. All I had to do was talk fast and slide the fight into the middle of my usual confession of fibbing to my mother, smoking, and cursing. He hardly seemed to notice. I knew I should tell him that I'd split open the kid's head and broken the glass, but that would have gotten me at least fifty Hail Marys instead of the usual ten. Maybe I should have felt guilty about putting one over on a priest, but then I remembered back to St. Andrew's School. I wondered if any of those priests had ever confessed or even felt guilty for all the times they had beaten and terrorized the hell out of us.

By the time we came home from Sunday Mass the next day, I was beginning to feel relaxed and confident that no one knew about my fight. There was a knock on the front door in the afternoon. Dying to get outside, I ran for the door, hoping it was Harold and Donny. Harold had always been the fighter in our little group. Maybe when I told them about my fight, he wouldn't think of me as a sissy anymore.

The moment I opened the door, I knew I was done for. The grey-haired man from the store was standing there, with a police officer beside him. For a split second, I thought about making a run for it, but then I heard Mamie coming down the hall. It was too late.

Before I could speak, Mamie was standing beside me. She had been in a good mood that morning, but as soon as she saw the cops at her door, her demeanour changed.

"That's him," the old man said, pointing at me. "He's the one who broke the glass in my door."

Mamie defended me at first, not knowing what they were talking about. "I am sure you've got the wrong person. My son has not been out of my sight all day."

I should have spoken up right there so Mamie wouldn't hear all the sordid details of my fight, but I still had a faint hope that I could somehow talk my way out of this. I tried to interrupt once, when the police officer said I'd slammed the other kid's head into the door, but Mamie gave me a look that told me to shut up if I knew what was good for me.

The old man was actually waving his finger in Mamie's face. He had a thick accent, making his words difficult to understand, but his message was clear. He didn't care about the fight. All he wanted was the fifty dollars it would cost to fix the glass in his front door.

I don't ever remember Mamie looking at me quite like that before. She was both angry and upset, but there was also a look of total disappointment in her eyes. I tried telling her it was one of the boys who had beaten me up in Regent Park, but it didn't make any difference.

"Get yourself up those stairs and stay there until I decide what to do with you," she ordered.

Sitting in the bedroom waiting for Da was torture. My mind was racing, trying to think of anything I could say to lessen the blows. My only hope was that Mamie would come upstairs with him and be there to stop him if he went too far.

I heard Da come in the front door. He sounded like he was in a good mood. The minutes ticked by as I strained to listen through the heating vent in the floor. I could hear their voices, but couldn't make out the words being said. Still, he wasn't shouting, and that was always a good sign. As I heard his footsteps on the stairs, I instinctively moved to the corner farthest from the door, next to the dresser. If he lunged at me, at least I would have a few seconds to get my arms up to stave off the first blow.

The door opened. My body tensed as I tried to squeeze even farther back against the bedroom wall. As he walked toward me, I tried to gauge his level of anger. I was definitely afraid, but I was also relieved. I had been through this so many times that I knew the waiting was the worst part. If I could make it through the next few minutes, it would all be over.

He stopped in the middle of the room, catching me off guard. I could see he was angry. His arms stayed by his sides, his right hand clenched in a tight fist, ready to lash out. Still he didn't move.

"Come over here." He pointed to the floor directly in front of him.

I hesitated, not wanting to leave what little protection the dresser provided. In the middle of the room, there would be nothing to stop him pummelling me from all sides.

"Get over here!" His loud voice made me flinch.

I slowly moved toward him. I wished Mamie were there, but there was only the two of us, standing alone in the middle of the room. I considered trying to explain, but Da was never one to listen to excuses.

His first blow to the side of my head was so sudden, I had no time to raise my arms. I almost fell over, but he grabbed my shirt to keep me upright. The second punch landed on the other side of my head. Both my ears were ringing as I tried to use my arms to block his blows. Da didn't like it when we cried, but my ears hurt so much, I just couldn't stop.

It wasn't like him to let up just because of a few tears, but for some reason, he stopped hitting me. He still had a hold on my shirt. "That was for lying to your mother," he said.

"I'm sorry. I'm sorry," I repeated over and over, hoping he would loosen his grip. It took me a few seconds to realize that the punishment was over. I kept my arms wrapped firmly around my head, knowing Da was capable of beatings far worse than this.

When he spoke, his voice sounded hollow through my ringing ears. I could tell he was still very angry, but at least he had lowered his fists. "You will stop your whinging right now if you know what's good for you."

My head hurt, but I tried desperately to stop the tears.

"Put on your clean pants and shirt and be downstairs in one minute. Don't make me come back up these stairs," he said as he left, slamming the bedroom door behind him.

I had no idea why I had to change, but so long as he didn't hit me anymore, I didn't care. The long pants and shirt I had worn to Mass were still on the bed. I put them on as fast as I could.

Mamie looked upset when I came into the kitchen. Da was shouting at me from the front door, but she wouldn't let me go until she'd wiped my face in her apron and used a little spit to flatten my hair.

Da walked behind me as we made our way down Parliament Street. By now I had figured out where we were going, but when I turned to ask, he just shoved me ahead. When I tried slowing down, he threatened me with a boot to the backside if I didn't move faster. When we reached the front of Cohen's Drug Store, he finally told me to stop. The old man stood there alone, waiting for us. He never said a word. All he did was point at the door.

If there was any doubt about what I had done, now it was clear. Most of the lower pane of glass had been removed, and a small sheet of plywood covered the gaping hole. There were still a few tiny shards of glass on the ground and some sharp pieces protruding along the edges of the putty.

I thought Da might hit me again, but he just shook his head and looked at the damaged I had caused. It was almost a relief when he finally spoke. "Well, I hope it was worth it, because you are about to find out what it's like to work for a living."

CHAPTER 9

A LITTLE BEFORE SEVEN o'clock the following morning, I felt Da's hand shaking me awake. For a moment I didn't realize it was him, and I started to complain about being too tired. The sound of his voice quickly snapped me back to reality. "Get your arse out of that bed this instant if you know what's good for you!"

By the time I came downstairs a few minutes later, Da was already out the door and headed to work. If I thought I could get a little sympathy from Mamie, I was sadly mistaken. She hardly looked at me when I came into the kitchen.

"Sit down and eat," she said as she put a steaming bowl of porridge in front of me.

I was hoping for a little milk to pour over it or even a cup of tea to wash it down, but there was nothing on the table and I wasn't about to ask. All I could do was blow on every spoonful until I got the last lumpy morsel down my throat.

I wished Mamie would sit down and talk to me, but she didn't move from the kitchen counter. I just wanted to break the silence and tell her how sorry I was for upsetting her. I had said it the night before, when Da and I got back to the house, but she never replied.

Once I was finished eating, she finally spoke. "I want you to be good and do exactly what you're told. Here, take this sandwich for your lunch." It was just a small cheese sandwich wrapped in wax paper, but it would have to do me for the long day ahead.

At this hour of the morning, Dermott Place was just beginning to stir. Most men were already off to work, while their wives busied themselves with the chores of the day. Monday was the day when most women did their laundry. Already there were women hauling baskets out to the backyard clotheslines. It was always best to get the jobs done early, before it turned into another hot summer afternoon.

For me, the summer was over. From now on, I would be working from 8:00 a.m. until 4:00 p.m., six days a week, until I had paid back every penny of my fifty-dollar debt. The old store owner hadn't liked it at first. It took my da a long time to convince him that we simply couldn't afford to give him that much money all at once and my working in his store was the only way I could pay for the damage I'd caused. All I could do was stand there watching them haggle over the length of my sentence. Finally, the old man agreed to knock two dollars off my debt for every day I worked. Having to work for the better part of August seemed like a very steep price to pay for one single punch to the head, but then again, no one cared what I thought.

When I arrived at the store, I was glad to see there was a man installing a new pane of glass in the bottom of the door. There still a spattering of blood on the door frame and a larger stain on the sidewalk, which I assumed had been left there for me to clean up later.

Cohen's Drug Store wasn't much to look at. The entire block was taken up by a variety of businesses, with the pharmacy squeezed in at the centre. The small wooden sign above the entrance was well-hidden behind a larger and brighter neon sign for the restaurant next door. For anyone in a hurry, it would be easy to walk right by without even realizing there was a drug store in the middle of the block.

After my walk in the bright morning sun, the interior of the store seemed dark and gloomy. It took a few seconds for my eyes to adjust enough to see Mr. Cohen standing behind the counter. All the way down Parliament Street, I had been trying to think of something I could say or do to make this first day less frightening. Maybe if I apologized again, he wouldn't be quite so hostile toward me. I had rehearsed my words in my head, but it would have to wait. The old man had seen me come in, but he ignored me while he spoke on the telephone. I didn't know what he was saying, but I knew he was speaking Yiddish. Many of the businesses in the area were owned by Jews, so by now I had learned to recognize it.

If I'd had any doubt about how things were about to unfold, Mr. Cohen made it clear to me the moment he came around the counter. His conversation on the telephone had sounded quite pleasant, but when he spoke to me, his words were anything but nice. I would be there on time every day and do exactly as I was told. Any failure on my part and he would be only too happy to call the police and have me charged. I certainly wasn't happy about my current situation, but going to court and possibly ending up in reform school was a much more terrifying prospect.

I had no chance to ease into this job. As soon as he finished his speech, Mr. Cohen sent me down to the basement to fetch a bucket of soapy water and a large stable broom. The old man wasn't satisfied with having me just clean the bloodstains away. I was told to scrub the entire sidewalk, right out the curb. I had to really bear down with the broom, but soon those big stiff bristles were cutting right through the stain. After refilling the bucket with clean water and dumping it over the sidewalk, I swept the excess water down the sewer drain, and the whole area looked as good as new. When Mr. Cohen came out to inspect my work, he just grunted and told me to come with him.

He marched me out the back door to a large storage shed near the back of his property. He was silent as he fumbled through his pockets, looking for the key to the padlock that hung from the large wooden door. For a second I thought he might have changed his mind about the job. Maybe he was going to punish me by locking me inside and leaving me there to rot.

He swung the door open and pulled the string to illuminate the bulb dangling from the ceiling. The shed was a complete mess of cardboard boxes, rolls of wire, bits of plywood, and various lengths of wood strewn all about. An old rusty bicycle with a flat tire was partially hidden behind some boxes. Someone had left an open tool box on the cement floor, with a few cans of paint sitting nearby. There was even a push lawn mower against the back wall, which seemed oddly out of place considering the backyard consisted of nothing but dirt and crushed gravel.

"I expect this whole area to be organized and spotless when I come back to check," he said.

I had a few questions, but before I could ask, he had gone down the path and back into the store.

Within minutes I was beginning to regret wearing my good clothes. There was hardly a breeze that morning, and with the sun beating down on the corrugated tin roof, the interior of the shed felt like an oven. Even taking my shirt off didn't help, and sweat trickled down my back.

To make matters worse, I had no real idea what I was doing. I tried stacking the boxes, but some were so heavy, the bottom came out, spilling the contents all over the cement floor. Slowly but surely, I managed to clear the centre of the floor and place the heavier items against the walls. It took me well over an hour, but when I stopped to look around, I was satisfied that the place was in far better shape than I had found it.

I was just finishing up when Mr. Cohen came back out. I wasn't expecting a compliment on my work, but perhaps he would see I wasn't the shiftless little waster he thought me to be. He barely went inside to assess my efforts before turning back around. "Not good enough" was all he said before disappearing back into the store.

My immediate reaction was to throw a shovel at the wall in frustration. But as the head of the shovel clanged loudly off the side of the shed, I regretted what I had done. I didn't know if he heard the noise but, fortunately for me, he didn't come back.

It was already past noon he arrived for his second inspection. He was still not satisfied. When I heard footsteps coming up the path a while later, I could only assume my latest effort was about to be rejected. I turned to see a woman standing in the doorway smiling, with a cup of water in her outstretched hand. I had seen her earlier, watching me from the window above the back of the store, but up close she seemed an odd little figure, barely five feet tall and dressed in black from head to toe. There were a few old ladies in our neighbourhood who dressed like that all the time. Mamie said it was out of respect for someone they had lost. Her black dress stood in stark contrast to her pale, thin face. If I'd had to guess, I would have said she was around the same age as Mamie, but her hair was almost white and pulled back into a tight bun at the back of her head. Still, her piercing dark eyes and radiant smile told me she was probably a kind lady and someone I could talk to.

I was so thirsty I practically inhaled the entire cup in one gulp. She showed me an outside tap on the side the building where I could refill the cup whenever I needed to. I hoped she wouldn't leave. She was the first friendly face I had seen that morning, and I desperately wanted someone to see how hard I was trying to do a good job. But if I was hoping for a little break from my work, it was not to be. Already I could hear the old man calling her back inside.

"Don't worry," she said. "My husband is a good person. Just do your best and everything will be fine."

I didn't know if what she was saying was true or not, but so far I hadn't seen even a glimmer of hope that this day would get any better. The fact that I really needed to pee added to my discomfort. I knew there was a toilet in the basement, but as bad as it was, I just couldn't bring myself to tell a woman I had to go. I was actually glad to see the old man come back outside in the early afternoon. By now I was squirming so bad, I didn't even bother to ask. I brushed right by him and headed straight down the stairs, desperately trying to hold it in as I felt my way through the darkness, in search of the toilet.

By the time four o'clock rolled around, I had lost track of how many times I had rearranged that shed. I knew my workday was over. I was tired and hungry. I had eaten the cheese sandwich hours earlier, and now my stomach was growling for something more. The afternoon heat had sapped away what little energy I had left. I should have been eager to get out of there, but oddly enough, I didn't want to leave. It felt like the old man and I were locked into a battle of wills, and I simply couldn't give up until he finally acknowledged that I had done a good job.

As he came up the path, I scanned the shed to ensure there was nothing out of place. Every box was perfectly aligned and stacked neatly against a wall. All the plywood was arranged by size. I had even taken one of the small plywood sheets and put it on top of two sawhorses to make a table for the paint cans, the tool box, and all the loose nails. I'd hammered a few big nails into the exposed studs so I could hang the shovels and rakes neatly on the wall. There wasn't much I could do with the bicycle and lawn mower other than straighten them up and place them out of the way against the back wall.

At least this time he went inside and took a long look around. I never took my eyes off him, hoping to see something positive in his facial expression. But I didn't get even a nod of approval. It was like his face was locked into a permanent frown and there was nothing I could do to change that. "Not bad" was all he said as he swung the door shut and snapped the padlock and chain around the handle.

I thought that was the end of my day, but rather than tell me I could leave, he told me I had one more job to complete. Once again he was silent as I followed him into the store and down to the basement. As soon as he turned on the light, I could see the problem. I thought I'd done a good job by not wetting my pants, but in my haste to pee, my aim hadn't been very accurate.

Once I had cleaned and mopped the floor, he finally told me I could go. "Be back here tomorrow morning at eight, and don't be late."

When I woke up the next morning, I began to understand what my da had meant when he said I was about to find out what it was like to work for a living. As soon as I stood up, I could feel the stiffness in my legs and back. I knew better than to complain to Da. Many a night I had seen him barely able to climb the stairs after a long day of work. I was just under two months away from my thirteenth birthday, but Da still thought of me as some skinny little kid, barely able to think for myself. Complaining after just one day's work would only confirm his suspicions.

At least Mamie seemed to be over her earlier disappointment in me. She let me have some sugar on my porridge and seemed surprised when I ask for a second bowl. Having seen the state of my clothes the night before, she told me to put on my jeans and a T-shirt. Still, before going out the door, she insisted I brush my hair and tuck my shirt in. My clothes might have been old, but Mamie always said there was no reason not to look presentable.

Once I was out and moving, I began to feel better. The warm morning sun and the long walk did wonders for the stiffness in my legs, and I actually began to feel somewhat optimistic about the day ahead. After all, hadn't I shown the old man that I could work?

My optimism was short-lived. As I walked through the front door, Mr. Cohen looked at the clock. I was a full ten minutes early, but he mumbled that I was barely on time. I kept my mouth shut so I wouldn't say anything that might annoy him. I had been in the store for less than a minute when he told me to follow him out the back door. When he began to undo the padlock on the storage shed, I felt like screaming. Surely there was nothing more I could do to improve what I had done yesterday? Had he come out during the night and messed everything up, just so he could put me through another day of torture? But everything was exactly as I had left it. When he turned, I thought I saw him smile for just a second.

He pointed toward a stack of paint cans and brushes sitting in the middle of the floor. When he told me I had to paint the entire storage shed, my heart sank. When I said it would take a long time, he just shrugged. "Well, you better get started right away," he said as he walked away.

It took me three days and almost five gallons of paint to finish the job. In the days that followed, he had me do every dirty job imaginable. I spent hours weeding the vegetable garden and then putting up a chicken-wire fence to protect it from the critters that came out at night. After the shed, I'd hoped my painting days were over, but he had me repeat the entire process in the basement storage room and washroom. Every day I would have to rearrange all the boxes to make room to paint. When I told him I had a headache from all the fumes, he let me go outside for some fresh air, but after only five minutes he ordered me back downstairs.

For the first few days, I couldn't seem to get rid of the old man. All morning long, he was right there, looking over my shoulder, making sure I never slacked off. I didn't see much of him in the afternoon, when he made deliveries, but around midday Mrs. Cohen would bring me something to drink. It was only a cup of cold water, but it was so much better than drinking lukewarm water from the garden hose.

I didn't relish the idea of going inside to ask Mr. Cohen to check my work, but at least it gave me an excuse to get out of the hot sun for a few minutes. Every so often, I could hear the sound of a customer entering the store. There was never a lot of foot traffic, but the telephone rang every few minutes. As soon as I stepped through the back door, I could feel the cooling breeze from the ceiling fan sweeping over me. I took a quick look around to make sure the customers couldn't see me. Mr. Cohen wouldn't want his customers to see this sweaty, smelly kid in the middle of his store.

One afternoon, just before quitting time, I found Mrs. Cohen just outside the front door, washing the windows. The bottom portion was already done, but even if she stood on her tiptoes, the top of the glass was just out of her reach. As soon as she saw me, that big smile of hers returned. She told me her husband was out delivering orders and should be back soon. Then the telephone rang, sending her running inside. I knew I couldn't leave without the old man's approval, so I took the wet rag and continued the job she had started. After working in the basement all day, it was so much easier to be outside, washing windows in the shade of the building.

She seemed content to let me take over the job while she stood in the open doorway, where she could hear the telephone ring. We talked about the hot weather at first. In spite of her smile, I had an impression she was lonely. She spoke with an accent, but her English was very proper. Her words were like something straight out of an English textbook.

When I asked if she had any children, she told me about her daughter, who would have been twenty this year. As she spoke, a sadness came over her. I quickly told her about my eight brothers and sisters and how we had all come over from Ireland. That seemed to bring the smile back to her face. She and I talked for quite a while, interrupted now and then by the ringing telephone. She told me all about growing up on a farm in Poland, not far from the German border. She said her name was Ella, followed by a long surname I could hardly pronounce. She laughed when she told me most people had the same problem. They'd shortened it to Cohen because it was easier to say and it fit much better on the sign above the front door. When I first called her Mrs. Cohen, she insisted I call her Ella, but I could never do that. It didn't seem right for me to be calling a woman of her age by her first name.

Her face seemed to glow as she talked about the man she had married and the daughter she'd had just before the war. I asked her what life was like in Poland during the war, but immediately knew I had made a terrible mistake. I suddenly remembered the newspaper story I had read back in May about the Israelis capturing Adolf Eichmann. For most people my age, that was the first time we heard about the concentration camps and the extermination of the Jews in Europe. It was certainly never mentioned in school.

I wished I could take back my question, but it was already too late. Her entire demeanour changed. At first she just stared off into the distance. She slowly wrapped her arms around her body, as if she were trying to protect herself from something unseen. I busied myself cleaning the window, trying to think of anything I could say to bring the smile back to her face.

When she finally spoke, she told me I reminded her of her little brother. I thought I could make some kind of a joke about how ugly he must have been, but she wasn't finished. "He is dead now," she said, before I could say something stupid. "My brother and sister, mother and father, my husband, and baby girl are all gone."

All I could think to say was how sorry I was, but I don't think she even heard me. The sudden ringing of the telephone seemed to bring her back to the present.

When she came back outside, I tried to changed the subject to the job I was doing. I took a step back to look at the windows. As far as I could see, there were no streaks or spots left to remove. The small neon *Rx* sign flashed brightly near the centre of the window and the posters, advertising everything from cigarettes to toilet paper, could be clearly seen. She hadn't said a word since coming back outside, but when she handed me a bottle of Orange Crush, I could sense that her mood had changed.

She told me that Mr. Cohen was her second husband, that they had met and married in a refugee camp, and how much better their lives had been since they came to Canada. "At least here you don't have to be afraid of being a Jew," she said.

I smiled and nodded, but in my mind I was remembering all the times I'd heard my friends making jokes and mocking the Jewish families who lived in our lane. A better person would have spoken up, but I had laughed right along with the others. After hearing her story, I realized how ignorance can make you say such cruel things. I couldn't do anything about my past actions, but one thing was certain: after talking to that kind old lady, I would never look at a Jewish person the same way again.

It was well past four o'clock when Mrs. Cohen spotted her husband's car sputtering down Parliament Street toward the store. The old Morris Minor sedan wasn't much to look at. There was rust around the baseboards and a large dent in the driver's door. Judging by the grinding noise, either the clutch was slipping or Mr. Cohen was not very good at driving a stick shift.

My job on the windows was done, but as he stepped out of the car, I busied myself going over the glass once again. The last thing I wanted was for him to see me standing around with nothing to do. He looked exhausted, and he took a moment to lean against the car before taking those final few steps into the store. I don't think he was all that pleased to see me standing out front, but when his wife pointed to the clean windows, he seemed to nod his approval.

By the end of my second week, I was finally given more jobs to do inside the store. The old man wasn't quite so gruff, but I could tell he still didn't trust me. I was never allowed to go behind the counter, and if a customer came in, Mr. Cohen told me to stay out of sight. By now I had learned to look for any job that needed doing before he had a chance to bark orders at me.

Every morning, I would watch Mr. Cohen going about his business. The short white smock he wore seemed too big for his skinny frame. One time, I happened to be by the counter just as he was changing into his smock. Wearing just a vest, he looked painfully thin. Standing out against his pale skin was a small faded number tattooed on his forearm. I only saw it for a moment as he turned to pull the smock on and button it up the side.

On Monday the smock would be glistening white and stiff with starch, but by Saturday, it would be grey and tobacco-stained from his constant smoking. The ashtrays were always full of half-finished cigarettes that he had started to smoke and then forgotten.

Sometimes when a customer came in, I would see the faintest glimpse of a smile on his face, but that would quickly disappear when the person left. When I arrived for work, he would spend a few minutes going over some task he wanted me to do, but mostly there were long periods of silence. Now and then I would hear him muttering to himself as he counted out pills to fill a prescription.

The only time he seemed truly talkative was when his wife came down from their apartment to take over the store in the afternoon. He would give me a list of the jobs he wanted done before he returned from his deliveries. When he came back late in the day, she would bring him a coffee and a sandwich. Mrs. Cohen did all she could to keep him off his feet for at least a couple of hours. They would sit in the back of the store talking in whispers. That was the only time I ever heard him laugh out loud. I could tell they cared a great deal for each other just by the way they spoke. It reminded me of the way my mamie and da would sit talking in the kitchen late in the evening.

After our initial conversation, I was careful not to upset Mrs. Cohen. She and I never talked very much, but she always took the time to ask me how I was and how my family was doing. Sometimes, on rainy afternoons, she would bring down a pot of coffee and insist I take a cup. I had never drunk coffee before I started working in the store, but I just didn't have the heart to refuse her. She would smile while I tried to swallow down the bitter black brew. Milk and sugar would have certainly helped, but she never offered, and I was too shy to ask.

After weeks of work, there was hardly a square inch of that store that hadn't been dusted, washed, swept, or completely rearranged at least three times. I even offered to wash behind the counter, but Mr. Cohen's answer was still no.

I'd had an idea floating around in my head for days now. Most afternoons when the old man returned from his deliveries, he looked utterly exhausted. He would try to sit down and rest, but always there were more orders to fill.

I think the idea that I could make the deliveries first occurred to me when I saw the old bicycle in the shed. I had never owned a bike, but back in Ireland every sixteen-year-old had to have one just to get back and forth to work. I had helped my older brothers repair their bikes so many times that I knew it would only take me a few days to get that rusty old bike back in working order. The frame looked strong and sturdy, and with a little steel wool and a bit of paint, most of the rust should disappear. There was lots of rubber on the brakes, but the chain would need some oil and grease to rotate smoothly. The tires themselves didn't look too bad, but both were completely flat. I couldn't afford new inner tubes, but for fifty cents I could buy a patch kit and have the problem fixed in no time.

If I did all the jobs the old man gave me each morning to his satisfaction, he generally left me alone to eat my sandwich. It didn't give me much time, but bit by bit, day by day, the bicycle began to take shape. Although Mr. Cohen rarely went out to the shed, I was still careful to hide the bike behind the plywood.

Now all I had to do was wait for the right time to speak to him.

One morning near the end of my third week, I noticed that Mr. Cohen was not his usual self. Usually when I arrived in the morning, he was busy working behind the counter. That morning, he was sitting down while his wife took orders over the telephone. When he tried to stand upright, he needed both arms to lift himself out of the chair. All morning long I could hear him coughing and wheezing as he stood behind the back counter, carefully doling out pills to fill a prescription. Fortunately, most of the orders did not need a prescription and could be taken right off the shelf. That day, for the first time, I was actually allowed to help fill some of the bigger orders.

After the orders were filled, I spent most of the morning rearranging the basement storeroom and lugging boxes up the stairs to restock the shelves. Poor Mrs. Cohen was not in the best of moods that morning, but through my own blissful ignorance, I did manage to get a laugh out of her.

I had just come up the stairs with an arm full of blue cardboard boxes full of what I thought were diapers. In our house we called them baby nappies, and for many years there had always been a dozen or more of those big white cloth nappies hanging on the clothesline. According to the label these were Kotex napkins, and I asked Mrs. Cohen if they were some new kind of paper nappy that didn't have to be washed. My question seemed to catch Mrs. Cohen off guard, but then she started to laugh. As sick as he was, even the old man couldn't hold back a smile.

The two of them talked back and forth while I just stood there holding the box, clueless about what was going on. It took them a few moments to gather themselves, and then Mrs. Cohen went outside, saving me from the embarrassment of having to hear Mr. Cohen's answer in front of her. I was horrified as he slowly explained things that I, as a twelve-year-old boy, was not prepared to hear. The instant I understood, I dropped that box as if my hands were on fire.

I spent the rest of the morning downstairs, rearranging all the boxes in the storeroom. When I finally got the nerve to come back upstairs, it looked like things were back to normal. The old man worked in the back counting tablets while I helped Mrs. Cohen fill the new orders.

By noon there was a line of big and small bags sitting on the counter, with a receipt stapled to the top of each one. It was plain to see that Mr. Cohen was not feeling any better, but as much as his wife pleaded with him to take a rest, he simply refused to go upstairs and lie down. The quiet concern in her voice soon changed when the old man started to get ready to make his deliveries. The language might have been foreign, but judging by the tone, Mrs. Cohen was clearly angry.

The last thing I wanted to do was put myself into the middle of their argument, but it dawned on me that this might be exactly the right time to say something. I knew I couldn't make the deliveries on my own, but perhaps if I offered to go along with the old man, I could do all the running around while he waited in the car. I could see he was annoyed the moment I brought it up, but Mrs. Cohen though it was a wonderful idea. She couldn't keep him from going, but this would at least keep him off his feet for the better part of the afternoon.

Even as we got into the car, he was still complaining. For the next few hours, I would have to listen to the same thing over and over again: "When the customer comes to the door, be polite, stand up straight, say please and thank you, and don't talk anymore than you have to."

Mr. Cohen had a small canvas pouch full of change, but I wasn't allowed to touch it. Each time someone gave me money, I had to go back to the car, get the right change, and take it back to the customer.

Our arrangement worked well at first, but as the afternoon wore on, we were falling further and further behind. He hesitated to give me the bag of change, but even he could see there was no other way. He actually looked relieved when I got back to the car, but at the end of the day, he counted every penny in the bag.

It is a terrible thing to say, but when I came in that Friday morning, I was a little sorry to see that he seemed to be fully recovered. It looked like my delivery days were coming to an end just when he and I seemed to be getting along so well. I spent the morning cleaning and mopping and doing whatever else I could do to stay busy. Mr. Cohen and I hardly spoke, so I was a little shocked when he handed me the change bag and told me to load the orders into the car.

He was in a talkative mood all afternoon. From the day I had started working for him, he had always referred to me as boy, when he spoke to me at all. Today, for the first time, he actually used my name. He even told me I was a good worker and he would be sorry to see me go. After our rocky start, this was high praise.

His kind words gave me the opening I had been waiting for. Once I started, I just kept talking. I had to get it all out before he had a chance to say no. "Maybe you could give me a part-time job doing the deliveries?"

I told him about fixing up the bike. He looked slightly annoyed, but I was quick to add that all the work had been done at lunchtime.

"I can come after school and do all the afternoon deliveries and you wouldn't have to use your car."

We still didn't know when school would start because of the fire, but even when it did begin, I could be at the store by four o'clock and make all the late deliveries.

I never took my eyes off him as I babbled on without a pause. I thought I should leave the subject of money out of it, but then I just blurted it out. "Maybe you could pay me fifty cents an hour, or whatever you think is fair?"

I could feel my chances diminishing with every passing second. He drummed his fingers on the steering wheel, like he was trying to find the words to let me down easy. When he finally spoke, it wasn't the answer I was hoping for, but at least he didn't say no. "Let me talk it over with my wife, and I'll let you know tomorrow."

The next morning, I practically ran all the way down Parliament, getting to the drug store a full half-hour before starting time. Next Monday would be my twenty-fifth day of work and my fifty-dollar debt would be paid in full. The only question remaining was whether I was finished or could return to a paying job when school started in September.

When I came through the door, the old man was busy on the telephone and there was no sign of his wife. By ten o'clock, I had settled into my usual routine of mopping, cleaning, and restocking shelves. With Saturday being the Jewish Sabbath, the store was quiet through the better part of the morning. Still, by noon business would start to pick up and the parcels would have to be prepared for the afternoon deliveries.

Just as I was about to head out back to eat my sandwich, I heard Mr. Cohen call my name. As he came from behind the counter, I tried to read the expression on his face. By all appearances, his good mood from the day before was gone.

"Come and show me what you have done to the bicycle," he said as he took the shed key from the hook next to the back door.

He walked around that bicycle three times, checking the tires, the brakes, and the chain. It seemed like he was trying to find any fault that would justify his saying no. He didn't care much for the makeshift basket I had tied to rack on the back fender. It was just a cardboard box, but it was big enough to hold the orders. When he muttered that it would need a lamp when the evenings grew darker, I took that as a positive sign that he was at least thinking in the long term. We both knew the old bike wasn't much to look at, but after repeated checks even he had to admit that it was sturdy enough to do the job.

After all of that, he finally said the words I wanted to hear. "Okay, we will give it a try for a month."

I wished he could have shown just a little enthusiasm as I kept saying thank you, but as he made quite clear, this was to be a trial, which would end the moment he heard even one complaint from any of his customers. I tried not to show my disappointment when he told me he would pay me twenty-five cents an hour for the thirty days, and if I did a good job, he might consider a raise after that.

"Do we have an agreement?" he asked, sticking his hand out to me.

I felt so mature in that moment. Saying yes and shaking hands seemed like such an adult way to close a deal.

I couldn't wait to tell Mamie when I got home that evening. More than anyone else, I needed her to know that I was at least trying to do better. She made me promise to keep up with school work, but other than that, she seemed very pleased.

When I told Da, he only shrugged. I don't know what I expected from him, but even a word of encouragement would have been nice. I tried to pretend it didn't bother me, but deep down, I was angry. Surely he saw how hard I'd been working? What had I done to make him dislike me so much? I think it was in that moment that I finally realized that the relationship between Da and me was never going to get better.

CHAPTER 10

I WAS SO BUSY working throughout the month of August that I rarely had a chance to see any of my friends. According to the kids on our street, it looked like St. Martin's was still under construction, and with any luck, it wouldn't be ready before the spring. I wanted to believe all the rumours, but I had to see it for myself.

On Sunday, when the work site was quiet, Donny, Harold, and I were able to sneak through the back gate and make our way right up to the gaping hole that would eventually become the rear entrance to the school. We may not have known anything about construction, but even we could see that, with barely a week left in August, St. Martin's couldn't possibly be ready by Labour Day. I thought about how much money I could make working all those extra hours at the drug store. I was never very good at doing math in my head, but if the school remained closed until after Christmas, surely I could make a small fortune.

My euphoria lasted less than two days. When I came home from work on Tuesday evening, Mamie showed me a letter that had arrived from the school that day. For every Catholic kid in our corner of Cabbagetown, all their hopes of freedom came to a sudden end. As of the following Tuesday, the day after Labour Day, the St. Martin's students would be divided up into two groups.

All those in kindergarten through grade four would attend the public school on Spruce Street, while the remainder of us would attend Our Lady of Lourdes School, all the way up at the top of Sherbourne Street.

Our Lady of Lourdes was much larger than St. Martin's, but like every other Catholic school of that era, they were already working at full capacity. Our unplanned arrival left them with little choice than to erect yet another row of portable classrooms.

That first week was a complete waste of time. Our portable classroom had just been installed and the electric light and heating system were still being hooked up. The first day of school was a warm September day, but the classroom felt cool and damp. Our new teacher, Mr. Burns, didn't seem particularly interested in doing anything that first day. Most of the morning he had us doing arithmetic problems straight out of our textbook while he read the newspaper. Once we saw that he wasn't paying attention, we began whispering the answers back and forth. If someone did ask a question, they almost had to shout in order to be heard over all the banging and hammering of the workmen just outside the door. If we hadn't been shivering inside the classroom, maybe we would have found the situation rather comical.

Mr. Burns didn't care where we sat. Whether at the back or front, he ignored us all. Like it or not, we were about to spend the next few months listening to a man who had absolutely no interest in getting to know any of us. After weeks in the classroom, he still didn't know most of our names. When he needed an answer to a question, he would just point in a general direction. If he said, "You there, in the second-last seat," I knew he was referring to me.

Day after day he sat behind his desk, droning on in the same dull monotone. Sometimes in the afternoon he would tell us to open our books and study, and then he settled down to read the newspaper. On the rare occasions when he did stand in front of the class, he had the most disgusting habit of picking his nose and scratching his backside at the same time.

There was one good thing about sitting near the back of the class. Harold's sister, Jeanette, sat just in front of me. Sometimes I would just sit there staring at her pretty blond hair pulled back in a ponytail. When I did manage to talk to her, all I ever got was a look of total disdain. The fact that she was a year older and a couple of inches taller than me certainly didn't help. No matter what I said or did, she would always look upon me as her brother's annoying little friend.

In the first few weeks after Jimmy was sent to reform school, I often wondered how he was doing. Once in a while when I passed by his house, I thought I might knock and ask about him, but the fear of facing his mother kept me away. She had never been in the best of health, but the loss of both her sons had only made things worse. According to the neighbours, she never came outside during the day, but sometimes late at night, she could be seen sitting on the porch, talking to herself.

As the months went by, no one talked about Jimmy anymore. I think we all just assumed that he would come home someday and everything would return to normal.

It was well past midnight on a cold October night when we awoke to the sound of a siren screaming down the lane. At first I thought our house was on fire again, but when Fred and I looked out the window, we could see the ambulance roaring past our front door. When it stopped at the bottom of the lane, we knew it could mean only one thing. There was something wrong with Jimmy's mother.

I wanted to go outside and take a look, but Mamie insisted we all go back to bed and mind our own business. "If you want to do something for Mrs. Duncan, just say a prayer for God to help the poor old woman find some peace."

The next morning we found out that Mrs. Duncan had been taken to St. Michael's after her next-door neighbour found her unconscious on the porch. Later that day, a woman from the Children's Aid Society came to the Duncan house and took the girl away. Poor Mrs. Duncan had managed to hang on through the night, but after a second massive heart attack in the early morning hours, she was pronounced dead.

For days after there were rumours about Jimmy coming home, but I didn't actually believe them until I saw him standing at our front door. I tried not to stare at the figure in front of me. It was hard to believe that someone could have changed so much in just a few months. The Jimmy I knew was a strong, wiry kid with a freckled face and a big mop of curly hair that always needed cutting. The Jimmy standing at my door was hardly recognizable. Someone had shaved all the hair off the back and sides of his head, leaving him with just enough to form a tight brush cut on top of his head. The lack of hair only made his face look thinner. Judging by his red, swollen eyes, he had been crying.

When Mamie came to the door to invite him, he gave her a half-hearted smile and said he could only stay for a few minutes. As long as I had known Jimmy, he had always been a brave and confident kid, but when Mamie reached out to check a red welt on the back of his head, he jumped back and put his arms up, as if she were going to hit him. He didn't say a word, but I could see the terror in his eyes. When Mamie asked if he was okay, he just nodded. It was obvious that something terrible had happened to Jimmy, but he was not prepared to talk about it.

He was still visibly shaken, but Mamie believed that any problem could be cured with a little food and a cup of tea. Jimmy wasn't much of a tea drinker, but by the way he devoured that sandwich, you would think he hadn't eaten in days. It took him a few minutes to relax and finally start talking. We thought he might have been allowed to come home for good, but he was only free to attend his mother's funeral. Immediately after that, he would be escorted back to Pine Ridge, where he still had about eighteen months to serve until his sixteenth birthday.

Except for a tiny obituary in the *Toronto Star*, Mrs. Duncan's funeral went completely unnoticed. With her oldest son, Bill, still serving time in the Don Jail, only Jimmy and his little sister were there to watch as the workmen lowered their mother's coffin into the ground. Jimmy knew his mother would have wanted to be buried in a Catholic cemetery, even if she hadn't been to Mass in years. But when it came to burying the poor, the city didn't care about such things. The city provided a casket and a small metal plate to mark the grave. At least they had a name to put on the plate. Some of the graves had only a number, when there was no other way to identify the remains.

When Jimmy and his sister arrived at the cemetery, there was a van parked at the front gate. After the funeral service, Children's Aid would take his sister back to a foster home and Jimmy would be driven back to Pine Ridge. That may have been the plan, but Jimmy had already made up his mind that he was never going back to that terrible place again.

Once the service was complete, the two of them were left alone to say one final goodbye to their mother. Jimmy must have known that this would be his one and only chance to get away. With his escort sitting in the van, he had less than a minute to hug his sister and say goodbye. Before anyone realized what was going on, Jimmy had disappeared into the bushes and climbed over the fence at the back of the graveyard.

A report and description were sent out that afternoon, but the police didn't give it a lot of attention. As far as they were concerned,

Jimmy was just another missing kid who would eventually show up somewhere in the city.

Later that day, there was a report of an accident at the College Station. According to the witnesses, a man had been standing near the end of the platform. No one had paid any real attention to him, but then they heard the loud screech of brakes as the train came roaring into the station. Suddenly they saw the man on the tracks. No one knew for sure how he got there. Someone said they heard a scream, but by then it was too late. The man had disappeared underneath the fast-moving train.

By the time the train came to a full stop, it was already halfway down the station. It took some time for the police to arrive and authorize the train to move just far enough forward for them to see the body on the tracks. The witnesses all said it was a man, but the body was quite mutilated, and the medical examiner soon realized the victim was just a boy.

Even when the medical report came out, it took almost seventy-two hours before the police finally confirmed that the body on the tracks of the College Station was Jimmy Duncan. The police may have had their suspicions, but with no witnesses to confirm whether he has jumped or simply fallen off the platform, the death was ruled an accident. Because his body was so badly mutilated, Jimmy's remains were cremated. A week later, his ashes were placed in the ground next to his mother.

In the days that followed, I thought about Jimmy a lot. Mamie told me it was okay to cry, but I never did. I don't know why, but the thought of him dying on the tracks just made me angry. Why hadn't he told me what was going on? Maybe I could have said or done something and he'd still be here today, sitting in our kitchen and laughing like he used to.

Soon my anger turned to guilt. My friend was dead and all I could think about was myself. It took me a very long time to get over the fact that my pal Jimmy was gone and there was nothing anyone could do to change that.

In the months after his death, his name came up from time to time. Some people still blamed him for the fire at St. Martin's. To me, it didn't really matter anymore. I preferred to think of the Jimmy who could make me laugh at his bad jokes. The Jimmy who taught me the proper way to catch a baseball. But most of all, I thought about the Jimmy who loved to ride the subway trains.

For years after, I often wondered why no one ever questioned Jimmy's death. Every once in a while we would hear some vague rumour about the Pine Ridge Training School, but no one was really paying attention. As far as the system was concerned, these were bad boys who needed to be locked up. The moment the gates of Pine Ridge closed behind them, they were forgotten. People on the outside didn't need to know about the boys being beaten or left handcuffed to a wall for hours at a time. If that didn't break them, there was solitary confinement, where a boy could spend a week in total darkness. At night, when the guards left the barracks, the younger boys could only pray for morning to come. Jimmy was a tough kid, but no match for the gangs of older boys who roamed the halls, looking for new victims to molest and abuse. Like countless boys before him, Jimmy had had to face the brutality alone.

It would take two decades and a government inquiry before all the horror stories finally came to light and Pine Ridge was shut down for good. For so many boys like Jimmy, it was twenty years too late.

The fall of 1960 and winter of 1961 were among the wettest on record. All I remember about that time were the long miserable walks to and from school every day. When the winds picked up,

I could feel the dampness seeping right through me. Those of us who arrived at school early would find a spot close to the stove before Mr. Burns arrived and ordered us to take our seats. If the janitor was late turning on the stove, Mr. Burns would allow us to keep our coats on during the morning. Still, it was hard to concentrate on school work when all I could think about was trying to stay warm.

The moment the lunch bell rang, Mr. Burns was out the door and off to the teacher's lounge, leaving us to fend for ourselves. Only the kids with boots and heavy coats could go outside, while the rest of us stood close to the stove, trying to keep warm as we ate our sandwiches. Harold and I always tried to bring a little extra food to school so we could share with our pal Donny.

Donny was still coming to school with bruises, but none of the teachers seem to notice. He never talked about it, but Harold and I knew what was going on. Donny's father had been laid off work over a month before. Donny would stay away from the house as long as possible, hoping his father would be passed out on the couch when he got home so he could make something to eat and get upstairs before his father woke up.

It is strange how your perspective on things can change over a short period of time. Only a couple of months earlier, when St. Martin's burned down, we were all relishing the freedom we thought we would have. Now here we were standing around a pot-bellied stove, wishing we could be back in a warm classroom at St. Martin's.

When the bell rang at three o'clock, I was off and running down Sherbourne, all the way to the drug store on Parliament. I always tried to save a little something from my lunch. On a good day, I could make it to the store in half an hour, leaving me a few minutes to eat whatever leftovers I had before starting my deliveries at four o'clock.

That first hour was usually the most hectic. Once I'd gathered up and sorted all the orders that had accumulated through the afternoon, I had to arrange them so that each package could be delivered in the most efficient way possible. If the bike didn't breakdown and the weather co-operated, I could normally deliver up to ten orders and be back in time to help close up the store at six o'clock. With the store open late on Friday night and all day on Saturday, I could easily double that number of deliveries and still have a little time to catch up on my homework.

By October, I was working an average of sixteen hours a week. I didn't want to bring up the subject of money, but finally, in the middle of the month, the old man gave me the raise I had been hoping for. From now on, I would be making fifty cents an hour. He and I were getting along much better, but now that I was making more money, he didn't like to see me sitting around doing nothing. If I had no deliveries, there was always some cleaning to be done. Once the store was clean, I could head downstairs to the storeroom to rearrange the boxes. Mr. Cohen didn't like climbing the stairs because of his leg problems, and if he didn't call me upstairs, I could do most of my homework by closing time.

Those early weeks were relatively easy. The roads were wet, but at least the daylight lasted well into the evening. When the temperature dropped in the late fall, the job became more difficult with every passing day. Some days it took all my concentration just to keep the wheels straight on the slick road surface. No matter how cautious I was, the bike did go out from under me a few times, causing the delivery bags to spill onto the ground. Other than the odd cut or bruise, I was able to keep going, but every day there seemed to be some new problem with the bike. I could only patch the tires so many times before I finally had to buy new inner tubes. Every day I had to tighten the chain, but hitting any big bump would knock it off the sprocket. It only took a few minutes to fix, but then

I had to clean the oil and grease from my hands before appearing at a customer's door. I always hid the problems from Mr. Cohen. He was fair and understanding about many things, but we both knew that without the bike, I could no longer do the job.

The traffic along Parliament and Dundas was bad enough, but nothing could compare to the sheer chaos on Queen Street at five o'clock on a weekday afternoon. Peddling the bike along any of the major arteries was a challenge, but negotiating my way along Queen Street at rush hour could be downright dangerous. The old man didn't like it when I took too long on a delivery, but nothing he said could make me go any faster.

On an average day, I could put roughly ten miles on the bike, travelling from the slightly more affluent neighbourhood west of Parliament all the way east to River Street and, of course, all the apartment buildings that made up Regent Park. Thankfully, I didn't have to make many deliveries to the older part of Regent Park, up near Gerrard Street. Still, I felt uneasy whenever I had to go into those red brick apartment buildings. I never found out who had turned me in to the police, but now I had to assume that the kid I punched must know where I lived. I hadn't seen him since the fight, but I always assumed he and his friends were out there looking for me. When I had a delivery anywhere near Regent Park, I made sure my shirt was untucked. That way, at least, the change pouch I wore around my waist was less visible.

By December, darkness came just after five o'clock, which was right around the time when rush hour traffic reached its peak. Even with a light on my bike, it was difficult to see and be seen as I tried to weave my way through the steady flow of traffic. I had an old pair of woollen mitts, but some afternoons were so cold that I would have to pry my numb fingers from the handlebars. At first I tried thawing my hands under the warm water tap in the basement storeroom, but that only made the pain worse. I thought about quitting many times, but then I would remember Mamie saying she was proud of me, and I knew I couldn't let her down.

Saturday was the busiest day of the week. From noon until closing time, there was rarely a let-up in the deliveries. Because it was the Jewish Sabbath, there were fewer customers in the store, but that only increased the number of orders I had to deliver.

Somehow, through the bad weather and bumpy roads, I managed to keep the bicycle together. But one Friday evening in late December, my luck finally ran out.

My last delivery was complete. All I had to do now was pedal my way back to the store. Maybe I could actually get home a little early for a change.

Normally, I paid attention when crossing the streetcar tracks, but that evening my mind was somewhere else. As the front wheel dropped into the gap between the tracks, I tried to hit the brakes and turn the handlebars, but the sudden jolt sent me and the bike crashing to the ground. My face hit the steel track and my nose began to bleed. Someone helped me over to the sidewalk and sat me down on the curb. When my head began to clear and I thought everything was going to be all right, I looked at my bike, still lying in the middle of the street. The front wheel was bent and twisted. The tire was off the rim and most of the spokes were bent and broken.

I must have looked a proper sight as I made my way down the street, dragging the wreckage with both arms. Every few steps, I had to stop and check my nose, until it finally stopped bleeding. People stared, but I really didn't care. All I could think about was losing my job the moment the old man saw the mess I had made of his bike.

But it was Mr. Cohen who came up with a plan to save my job. He would make the Saturday deliveries in his car, giving me the whole day to get a new wheel and tire and fix the bike, ready for

Monday. I was grateful and relieved to still have a job, but deep down inside, I was more than a little annoyed. Not only would I not get paid for Saturday, but now I would have to use what little money I had to buy a new wheel and tire.

I was making eight dollars a week, and half of that went to Mamie. I was allowed to keep a dollar, and the rest went into a savings account. I certainly didn't like the idea of putting my money in some bank, but I was given no choice. Mamie talked about saving for a rainy day, while all I wanted to do was spend my money on comics and candy, or perhaps even that shiny new BB rifle I'd seen in the Eaton's catalogue.

No thirteen-year-old boy ever wants to admit he was wrong. But now I could see what Mamie had been talking about all along. The rainy day was already here. My meagre savings were about to be wiped out, but at least I had the money to fix the bike and keep my job.

❧

By early spring, we had given up any thoughts of returning to St. Martin's for what remained of the school year. In March, a continuous string of new student teachers began to appear in our class. Mr. Burns was still there, but for most of the day he would sit in the back of the room while the trainee took over the class. Unfortunately for us, many of them were so new and so nervous that they made a complete mess of whatever subject they were supposed to teach.

If someone had a question before or after class, Mr. Burns was never there to answer. When we could manage to ask him, trying to get a straight answer could be very frustrating. But when it was time to take tests, his laziness worked in our favour. Rather than mark them himself, he would have us pass our paper to the person next to us. If the paper you were marking had too many wrong answers, it was easy to change a failure into a passing grade. Still, we had to be careful to change just enough to ensure we didn't raise his suspicions.

Not surprisingly, everyone in the class passed that year. I even managed to achieve an overall grade of above average. Oddly enough, when Harold, Donny, and I compared report cards, we all had different grades, but every word in the remarks column was absolutely identical. I was a little annoyed at first, but then we all laughed. Even if he couldn't be bothered to remember our names, at least we were all moving on to grade eight.

I was nervous that evening when I handed Da my report card. Fred had received his report a few days earlier, and it was as brilliant, as always. No one was prouder than my da when he saw all those perfect scores. At long last, someone in our family was going to make it into high school. After listening to Da's gushing, I knew that there was nothing I could do to top Fred. But I hoped my report was good enough to avoid most of his usual sarcasm.

I could tell by the look on his face that he was not at all impressed by my efforts, but I was long past caring. All I needed was his signature, and then we could go on ignoring each other for the next six months.

I usually arrived home from work just past nine o'clock on Friday nights. The house was always peaceful and quiet at that time in the evening. Michael, the oldest of my brothers still living at home, and his girlfriend, Nora, had just become engaged, so we rarely saw much of him around the house anymore. Johno and his band were playing at the Brass Rail on Yonge Street, so he wouldn't get home until the early morning hours.

Even though school was done for the summer, Fred was busy studying upstairs. Now that he was done with grade eight, he had to take an entrance exam if he wanted to get into Neil McNeil Catholic High School in the fall.

When I got home, Marie and David were usually in their pyjamas and sprawled out on the floor, watching television. Five-year-old Philip would sometimes convince Mamie to let him stay up with the others, but usually by nine thirty he would be fast asleep on the rug and Mamie would have to carry him up the stairs to bed.

Da usually worked the afternoon shift and wouldn't be home until after midnight. When I did manage to catch a glimpse of him, he always looked so tired and worn down. Da was a strong man, but the years of hard work and recurring illness were taking a toll on his health. He was just fifty-five years old, but the deep furrows on his face and his thinning grey hair made him look much older than his years.

Every day when I left for work, Mamie made me promise to be careful riding the bike. She always looked relieved when I came through the door at night. I never told her about the times I fell off the bike or got clipped by a car. That would only add to her worries. As long as I came home safe at night, she didn't need to hear about all my near misses.

With everyone else busy, I had Mamie all to myself on Friday nights. I would sit at the kitchen table while she heated my dinner up on the stove. On cold winter nights she would make me a big mug of tea, and we would sit at the table talking about our day.

Long after I went to bed, I could still hear her puttering around in the kitchen, waiting for Da. When the streetcars stopped running at midnight, he was left with no choice but to walk home from work. No matter what time he came home, Mamie would be there waiting for him with something to eat and a mug of hot tea.

CHAPTER 11

IT IS SUCH a glorious feeling to wake up in the morning and realize that school was over. No need to hop around on the cold floor, trying to get dressed and scribble down some last-minute homework I should have done the night before. Even in the summertime, Mamie would not let us lay about for too long, but just having that extra fifteen or twenty minutes under the covers seemed like luxury. Even a bowl of porridge tasted better when I didn't have to gulp it down before running off to school.

I was a little disappointed when Mr. Cohen told me I couldn't work more hours over the summer. I had hoped I could come in at noon and make all the early deliveries. After all the hours I had spent on that bike, driving through snow and ice and rain, I knew the job would be so much easier in the summer. At first I thought the old man was just being cheap, but then I remembered what he had done last Christmas Eve. Instead of my usual eight dollars, he had handed me an envelope with a Christmas card and fifteen dollars inside. And even though they didn't celebrate Christmas, his wife had made an apple pie for me to take home for the family.

So it wasn't about having to pay me a few extra dollars. The real problem was much worse than that. Ever since the new Rexall drug store had opened up in early May, our deliveries had been in a steady decline. We still had a fair amount of walk-in traffic, but the old man couldn't match Rexall's prices or the sheer variety of items they carried. He believed that his drug store was there to serve the medical needs of his customers. The new store was selling everything from cigarettes to soda pop and candy bars. If Mr. Cohen wanted to survive, he would have to do the same thing.

By July, I was happy just to have a job. Sometimes I could hear the old man mumbling to himself as he filled a delivery order. From what I could tell, he was particularly disgusted with anyone who asked for cigarettes or candy bars to be included in their order. He kept bouncing between English and Polish, but he clearly didn't like what he was doing. "I am a pharmacist, not some damn variety store salesman!"

When he looked my way, I was quick to nod in agreement with whatever he was saying. In reality, I really didn't care what someone ordered. As long as there was something to deliver, my job was safe.

At the start of summer, I was working sixteen hours a week, but as time went on, my hours diminished. When I heard the old man and his wife talking in the back, they weren't the happy conversations I had heard before. Now the talk was serious. She wanted him to give up the store and move before they went broke. He was convinced that things would get better, if only they could hang on for a few more months.

Now that I had all this extra time on my hands, I thought I could see more of my friends. They had dropped by the house from time to time, but I had always been going to or just getting home from work. It would be nice to hang out with Donny and Harold once in a while, I thought. But now I was having a hard time just finding my friends.

I would sometimes see them in line at the movie theatre. I was still barred from the place, so all I could do was wave and keep on going. If I happened to spot Harold's sister waiting in line,

I didn't care about the usher. I would find some excuse to stop, hoping she would talk to me. Jeanette still ignored me at school, but perhaps if she saw me working at a real job, she might look at me in a different light. Try as I might, I couldn't even get her to smile in my direction. Soon the line would begin to move, and all I could do was watch that pretty blond head disappear inside the theatre.

It was another of those hot August days where you could almost see the heat shimmering above the asphalt. Carlton Street was the only place to get some relief from the summer sun. The tall trees on either side of the street spread their branches over the middle of the roadway and created an area of perpetual shade. Walking below the thick canopy of leaves always made me feel like I was moving through a tunnel. In the distance, I could see the edge of Riverdale Park, where the tree line ended and the sunlight returned.

I thought about calling on Donny, but that was never a good idea when his father was around. Kenny Bell wasn't home either, but at least his mother was there to answer the door. Mrs. Bell was a kind and friendly woman, but I was thankful she didn't invite me inside. When last we spoke, Kenny had told me that things had gotten worse for his family. They never had very much in the way of furniture, but now the few good pieces they owned had been sold just to pay the rent.

I must have knocked on Wayne's front door three or four times before he finally answered. I hadn't talked to him since the day we heard about Jimmy's death. I remember how angry I'd felt seeing him shrugging his shoulders and acting like he didn't really care that Jimmy was gone. I'd felt like punching him in the mouth, but that wouldn't have changed anything. After that, I thought it was best if I didn't see him for a while.

Now, as soon as he opened the door, I could tell something was wrong. I had heard his father had lost his job, but it seemed there was more than that going on. We had been talking for about five minutes when his mother called him from the top of the stairs.

His voice grew suddenly loud, and he shouted back at her. "I'll be there in a minute!"

I had always thought it was strange the way Wayne spoke to his mother. His voice always took on a rather nasty tone, yet she never so much as raised her voice to him. Maybe if she had given Wayne a good wallop early on, he wouldn't have turned into the arrogant, self-centred bugger that he had become.

I was beginning to regret ever coming to the door. I could hear them talking from inside the half-open door, and I was thinking it might be best if I just walked away. Then Wayne came storming back to the front door. I had never seen him cry before, but then he told me his parents were getting a divorce. I wanted to say I was sorry, but he slammed the door in my face.

When I walked into the house after work that evening, I could smell the aroma of potatoes and vegetables. There wasn't a dish in the sink or a pot on the stove. Obviously Fred had done both our cleanup jobs, and I was sure he would tell me all about it later.

It was after seven o'clock. I didn't like to worry Mamie, but my last two deliveries had taken longer than expected. Thankfully, she didn't look upset. I think she was just relieved that I had made it home before dark.

"I hope you're hungry," she said. But before I could answer, she was opening the oven door and using the hem of her apron to retrieve a plate full of hot food.

Sitting alone at the kitchen table, I thought about all that had happened that day. It dawned on me that I didn't envy Wayne anymore. Now I just felt sorry for him. Maybe he had a big house and lots of money to spend, but he didn't have a big family he could count on in hard times.

My da and I might never get along, but at least I was surrounded by a family that cared. I had screwed up a lot in the past, and I had no doubt I would screw up even more in the future, but I could take comfort in the knowledge that my family would always be there when I needed them.

❧

It was never fun going back to school after a hot, lazy summer, but that September morning, I think we were all truly grateful that our long treks to and from Our Lady of Lourdes School were finally over.

Everyone seemed anxious that first morning. Most of us arrived early, hoping to get a peek inside the new St. Martin's. The front of the school, on Winchester Street, had not sustained much damage from the fire. Other than some new window frames on the first and second floors, the old part of the school looked the same. The fire had more or less destroyed the classrooms at the back of the building. The exterior wall remained, but the interior structure had been completely gutted and replaced by six new classrooms that jutted straight out from the back of the old school.

On a normal morning there was a lot of chatter in the room as we waited for the teacher to arrive. That morning there was total silence. Every eye was fixed on the door, waiting to see who would enter.

For years now, Sister Alphonse had been the grade-eight teacher as well as the principal of the school. But with the constant influx of new students, she was now far too busy to teach a class. According to the rumours, we were getting a new teacher. After Sister Agnes and then Mr. Burns, practically anyone would have been an improvement.

When Miss Williams walked through the door that first morning, she immediately had one thing going for her. She was gorgeous.

As she strutted to the front of the class, not a boy in the room could take his eyes off of her. She was young and pretty and her clothes looked like something you would see in one of those fashion magazines. She hadn't spoken a single word and already we liked her.

I think we were all hoping for something different from this new teacher, but for the first few hours, our class seemed to be following the same boring routine we all remembered from years past. We went over material we had already done the year before. I guess she was trying to determine where we all stood, but for us, it was a reminder of all those student teachers we'd had to endure back in grade seven.

Our first lesson after lunch was on the subject of health and hygiene. It was an odd term, considering we never actually talked about either our health or our hygiene. Apparently, a few years earlier, the Toronto Catholic schoolboard had decreed that sex education would be taught starting in grade six. But the nuns at St. Martin's weren't about to teach a subject with the word *sex* in it. They could call it whatever they liked, but we all knew what they were talking about. Mr. Burns had touched on the subject once or twice, but his explanations only left us more confused than when we'd started. We had a lot of questions, but never got a straight answer.

That day was different. Maybe Miss Williams looked at all our blank faces and realized that none of us had a clue about sex. We had talked about sex in the schoolyard many times. Some of the boys even claimed that they had done it, but when we pressed them for details, their stories quickly fell apart. Most of us believed that every time you had sex, the girl would have a baby. We just didn't understand how it all happened.

It took us all a few minutes to grasp that we weren't getting the same old double-talk we had heard before. At last here was someone willing to tell us the whole unvarnished truth. Looking around the room, I could see the subject was making a few people uncomfortable. When Miss Williams said the word *penis* and then began to explain about sperm, some of the boys laughed, while most of the girls looked around in shocked disbelief. Nevertheless, when she finally asked if we had any questions, almost every hand in the room when straight up.

We had two or three more classes like that before word went around the school that Miss Williams was about to be fired. Apparently, the mother of one of the girls had complained to Sister Alphonse, and it wasn't long before she called Miss Williams into her office.

When Miss Williams came into class the following morning, we assumed everything was back to normal. She still taught the subject of health and hygiene twice a week, but now Sister Alphonse sat in the back of the room throughout the lesson. Every once in a while, Miss Williams glanced at Sister Alphonse, but the class would go on without interruption.

In the third week of classes, Sister Alphonse spoke up for the first time. One of the girls asked a question about birth control, but Sister Alphonse cut Miss Williams off before she could answer. Sister Alphonse told us to sit quietly while she and Miss Williams went out into the hall. We couldn't hear what they were saying, but after that there was no more talk of birth control. She could talk about abstinence, but all other forms of birth control were expressly forbidden by the Catholic Church and could never be discussed in the classroom.

It is a shame that they couldn't have been more open and honest with us. It didn't happen often, but once in a while a girl in the neighbourhood would be sent away "to visit relatives." We may have been kids, but we all knew what it meant when a belly bump first appeared. Most of the girls would return home months later, but they were never quite the same after giving their baby up for adoption.

Like most kids my age, I looked at school as a necessary evil. It was just something we had to endure until we turned sixteen and were finally free to find a job. But after just a few days in Miss Williams's class, my eyes began to open to the possibility of something better out there, just waiting to be found.

Unlike most of the nuns, Miss Williams was never one to preach or tell us how we should be living our lives. She never talked down to us. From the very outset, her message was simple and clear. "I am here to help you in any way I can," she would say. "Your job is to listen and ask questions when you don't understand. You can fritter away these months in school, or you can give it your best effort. Either way, you will all walk out of here in June. Whether you leave as a success or a failure is completely in your hands."

To this day, I count myself lucky to have been in her class. She could be strict when she needed to be. She might raise her voice, but that was the extent of her discipline. God knows we could try her patience at times, but never once did I see her raise her hand to a student.

Every day she seemed to come up with innovative ideas for teaching old subjects in a new and interesting way. Her methods may have been unorthodox, but there was rarely a dull moment in any of her lessons.

For geography she would line us all up around the walls of the classroom. She would ask us questions about the number of provinces or the names of the Great Lakes or perhaps the capital city of some country in Europe. If you couldn't come up with the proper answer, you had to sit down. The last boy or girl left standing was excused from all homework that night.

For social studies and history we visited Casa Loma and Fort York. We even spent a day sitting in the balcony at Queen's Park to witness a session of Parliament.

I think it is safe to say that for the majority of students in our class, mathematics was the most difficult and boring part of our day. The first time Miss Williams mentioned the subject, a collective groan arose in the room. She gave us a moment to settle down and then put a radio on her desk. She turned the dial until she found the station broadcasting the American League baseball playoffs. While we listened to the game, Miss Williams had us take notes on such things as the team hitting average and fielding percentage and each batter's earned run average. Later, she incorporated all of this statistical information into our next math lesson.

Every morning I would literally run out the door, anxious to get another school day underway. My marks drastically improved in almost every subject, and I even received my first A for an essay I wrote on the Cuban revolution.

When Miss Williams told me I was to read my essay at the school's next Parent-Teacher Association meeting, I was more than a little frightened about the prospect of talking in front of an audience. What I remember most about that night was seeing Mamie sitting near the back of the room. I was extremely nervous, but I knew that if I could just focus on her smiling face, I could get through this without a problem.

The next morning at school, Miss Williams has me stand up while she told the class how well I had done in front of the PTA. At lunchtime, some of the kids jeered me for being the teacher's pet, but there was one good thing that came out of all the attention. Jeanette was no longer ignoring me. For the first time she actually smiled at me when we spoke.

One day, near the end of lunch break, I spotted her coming through the front gate of the school. I tried to make it look like a chance encounter, but in fact I had been standing there for over twenty minutes, just hoping to catch her alone. I hadn't given a lot of thought to what I would say, so I blurted out something about going out for a Coke on Saturday afternoon. By now there were a lot of people starting to converge around the front of the school, waiting for the afternoon bell to ring. After what seemed like an eternity, she finally said she would meet me at the Satellite Restaurant after I finished work on Saturday afternoon.

Every Saturday after that, we went through the same glorious ritual. We always sat in the same booth, near the side wall, where we couldn't be seen by anyone passing by. The waitress was a little impatient at first. The place might have been empty, but she made it clear that if we wanted to stick around, we had to buy more than a ten-cent Coke. I ordered a plate of French fries and hoped that would be enough to keep the waitress at bay for at least a half-hour. I think we were both very nervous about what to say the first time, but soon we were talking about school and our families. When I mentioned Harold, she rolled her eyes. I knew they didn't get along, so I quickly changed the subject. After an hour I could see the waitress looking our way, but I didn't care. I would have gladly sat there the entire day just listening to Jeanette's every word, but as the supper hour drew closer, it was time for both of us to leave.

Walking her home felt so awkward at first. I wanted to hold her hand, but was afraid to try. Then one afternoon, just as we turned onto Winchester Street, she suddenly reached out and took my hand. I looked straight ahead, afraid to say anything that might spoil the moment. I could feel my hand getting sweaty, but I didn't want to let go. As soon as we turned onto her street, she pulled her hand away. Her house was only a few doors down, but this was where our walk had to end. Any farther and there was the possibility we would be seen from her front window. I stood at the corner and hoped she would turn around and smile one last time before disappearing from my sight.

Each time we parted, I promised myself that I would try to kiss her. Maybe with a little more time I would have worked up the nerve to do it. But our relationship was over as suddenly as it began, in just a few short weeks.

Her family had been going through a rough time ever since their father lost his job. When, in late November, Harold mentioned something about moving, I tried to remain calm. I was always very careful around Harold, and as far as I could tell, he didn't know about me and Jeanette. When Jeanette and I met that Saturday, I could see she was upset. She started to cry as she told me the news. Her family would be leaving for Nova Scotia at the end of the month. I thought we would at least talk about it, but the next moment she stood up, ready to walk out the door. She bent down and kissed me on the cheek, and then she was gone.

I tried to talk to her every day at school, but she seemed to be avoiding me. Miss Williams said a few nice words on their last afternoon at school. Some of Jeanette's girlfriends hugged her in the schoolyard, but with Harold right there, I couldn't get near her. The last time I saw her, she was smiling and waving goodbye. I like to think she was waving at me, but before I could wave back, she was swallowed up in a crowd of girls. Just like that, she was gone forever.

I knew it was silly, but when I left work on Saturday afternoon, I felt compelled to drop by the Satellite Restaurant. Only the waitress knew why I had come.

"I'm sorry honey, but she isn't here," she said.

I knew it was true, but still I had to look for myself. The waitress didn't even know our names, yet she seemed concerned. She offered me a free Coke, but once I saw the empty booth, I couldn't stay.

Less than a month after Jeanette left, it seemed everyone at school had forgotten about her. It always made me a little sad to think that, of all the people who knew her, only the waitress and I seemed to care that Jeanette was gone.

CHAPTER 12

THAT CHRISTMAS EVE, in 1961, was the first time Fred and I were allowed to attend midnight Mass. Marie wanted to go, but she was left at home to take care of David and Philip. Sitting in Our Lady of Lourdes Church with Mamie and Da made me feel so mature. We didn't get home until well past one in the morning, but Mamie let me stay up and have some tea and cake.

There wasn't a lot of money to spend on presents that year. There were some colouring books and a toy truck for David and Philip. I was too old for toys, but I was hoping to get the BB gun I had been hinting about for weeks. When I opened my gift, I tried not look disappointed, but it was hard to get excited about a pair of woollen gloves. Mamie said they would be better than mitts and would keep my hands a little warmer as I rode around making deliveries.

In our house, ham with turnips and mashed potatoes was the preferred choice for Christmas dinner. I never really cared for turnips or potatoes when they were served separately, but mashed together and heated in the frying pan, I found them utterly delicious.

Many images of our Christmases in Cabbagetown have faded over the years, but Christmas 1961 will always hold a very special place in my memory. For once my da actually had a few days off work. Now he could relax and get some proper sleep before going back on the night shift.

My big brother Michael had gone away in June to join the army. When he came through the door on Christmas Eve, it was the first time any of us had seen him in months. I couldn't get over how different he looked in his battle dress uniform. Mamie was so happy to see him home at last. From the day he'd left, she had never stopped fretting about him. Michael had spent much of his younger years in and out of hospital with every manner of childhood illness. As he got older, he slowly grew stronger, but for Mamie, the worry would never go away. When he'd left for basic training, he had looked so pale and skinny, but as he stood in the hallway on Christmas Eve, we could all see that army training has done him a world of good.

Rosaleen and Bernard were there with their baby daughter, Linda. Philip was acting a little jealous at the fuss Mamie was making over Linda. He was used to being the centre of attention. Bernard had one of those new movie cameras. After hours of fiddling about, he finally had it set up and ready to go just as Da brought the ham out from the kitchen. The moment Da stepped through the doorway, he was blinded by the big bank of camera lights. He almost fell over the table as he fought to hold on to the big platter of ham while trying to shield his eyes from the bright lights. Mamie screamed at him to careful with her ham. Da pretended to be upset that she was more concerned about a plate of meat than she was about him.

I can never forget all the laughter and joy when Mamie brought out the big bowls of pudding and custard. She warned us to wait until the custard cooled, but we all dug in right away.

After dinner, everyone pitched in to clear away the table and clean up the kitchen. Mamie tried to take over, but we insisted she sit down and rest while the rest of us waded through the mountain of pots, pans, and dishes. When an old song came on the radio, Da swept her up from her chair and began to waltz her around the kitchen floor.

By five o'clock it was getting dark outside and the whole house seemed quiet. Johno and Michael had gone off to visit friends. Philip was still running around and tried to hide when Mamie said it was time to get into his pyjamas. We had not been allowed to turn on the television all day, but now Mamie let me and the younger ones watch TV while she and Da sat in the kitchen, drinking tea and waiting for the telephone to ring.

Early that morning, Da had managed to book a call through the overseas operator. With the time difference, it was already getting on toward midnight back home in Dublin. Mamie wrote to my brother Willy at least once a month, but for Christmas she wanted to actually hear his voice, just to know that he and his new wife, Mona, were doing all right. It was nearly seven o'clock when the overseas operator finally called back to make the connection to Ireland. We all crowded around the phone, hoping to hear something, but there was only time enough for Mamie to talk. The transatlantic lines were always busy at this time of year, and you could never be sure how long the connection would hold. After just a few minutes the line went dead. Even though Mamie was smiling when she hung up, she still had to wipe away her tears with the hem of her apron. Mamie said that Will and Mona were doing just fine, but she told us all to say an extra prayer for them that night before we went to sleep.

Every once in a while, some random thought will trigger a memory that takes me back to that Christmas Day. More than sixty years have passed, but when I close my eyes, I can almost smell the ham cooking in the oven. I can feel the heat of the kitchen as the steam rises from the boiling pots on the stove. I can see Mamie using the edge of her apron to open the oven door and stick a fork in the ham to see if it is ready. The table is set with plates and cups and saucers. There were only a few pieces left from the good set of dishes Mamie brought from Ireland. This was all she had left from her mother and they only came out of the cupboard on special occasions.

I can never be sure if my memories of that day are real or simply wishful thinking on my part. Maybe I'm just trying to idealize that last perfect Christmas our family would ever spend together.

Like an unrelenting tidal wave, the influenza virus came sweeping through Cabbagetown in January 1962. By mid-month there was hardly a house on Dermott Place left untouched. Old Mrs. Baxter, who lived across the street, was the first to go. She was the one who always threatened us with a broom when we made too much noise playing in front of her house. In those early days, none of the kids on our street took the flu seriously. The fact that it could get us out of going to school far outweighed our fear of the illness. But seeing Mrs. Baxter's body being carried out her front door and placed in the back of a hearse made us realize that this epidemic was not to be taken lightly.

David was the first to get sick in our family, but with Mamie there to take care of him, he seemed to get stronger by the day. Just as David was starting to improve, Johno was brought home one afternoon after collapsing at work. From morning to night, Mamie was constantly on the move, up and down the stairs, doing everything she could to help her sons get better.

When we came down for breakfast one morning and found Da standing in the kitchen, we knew something was wrong. Mamie was probably the strongest woman I knew, and if she couldn't get out of bed, this had to be serious.

Da tried to smile, but it was hard for him to hide his concern. "Your mamie came down with a fever during the night and will have to stay in bed for a couple of days. I don't want any of you bothering her. Just let her rest, and I'm sure she will be up and about in no time at all."

Da was not much of a cook, but he did manage to make a pot of porridge before leaving for work. With Michael away in the army and Johno laid up in bed, Da had no choice but to go to work.

I thought we younger kids could all stay home from school, but Da insisted we go. Only Marie was allowed to stay home so she could take care of Mamie until Rosaleen could get there later that day.

A full week went by and still Mamie could not get out of bed. Just a few months earlier, it had seemed like things were finally looking up for our family financially. Now with all the medicine that had to be bought, in addition to the rent and all the usual expenses, we were once again living on the edge. We had nothing but porridge to eat for a few days, but once Da got back on the night shift and Johno was well enough to work, we were able to buy some meat and potatoes and a few vegetables to make a big stew.

At school, the toll the illness was taking among the students and the staff was evident. Each morning when the teachers called the roll, one or two more were students missing from every classroom. Miss Williams tried spreading us out, but our classroom wasn't that big to begin with. If someone sneezed or coughed in class, there was no way to get away from them.

Before the Christmas break, we hadn't seen much of Sister Alphonse. She had spent most of her days in the office. But now every day at lunchtime she roamed the schoolyard. There must have been a hundred or more kids playing outside, yet somehow she seemed to know all our names and what was going on with our families. Even on the coldest days, she would be out there with her heavy woollen shawl pulled tightly around her shoulders. We watched her wander from group to group, sometimes stopping to ask about someone's mother or father, brother or sister. Every day she reminded us to say our prayers so that everything would get better soon.

The illness seemed to take a greater toll on the boys in our class. My pal Donny Lund was sick early on but tried to hide it from the nuns. Having to stay home with his abusive father would only make matters worse for both of them. In the middle of the second week, Donny was finally sent home, leaving only ten boys remaining in the class, including me and Kenny Bell.

Kenny and I would often walk down to Parliament Street together after school. He would pick up his bundle of newspapers on the corner of Carlton, and I would head down to Dundas Street to start work at four o'clock. Kenny was still a very private person, rarely speaking up in class. But in the afternoon, away from school, he was a little more talkative. His father was in a wheelchair now, and his family was barely surviving on welfare. Sister Alphonse still stopped by each month with a parcel of food, but Kenny never wanted to talk about any of that. The only time he seemed happy was when he talked about his plans for the future. He told me he already had a job lined up with the *Toronto Telegram*. He had been delivering the newspaper since he was ten, and once he turned sixteen he intended to get his driver's licence and take over the job of distributing the newspapers all over the city. Everyone knew a person as smart as Kenny could do much better in life than this. Sister Alphonse had tried to convince him to go on to high school, but Kenny didn't want to wait. He would be fifteen when he finished grade eight. He would find some factory work until he was old enough to get his driver's licence and get that job with the *Toronto Telegram*.

One morning Kenny joined the long list of boys missing from our class. His sister confirmed he was sick in bed, but later that day, on my way to the drug store, I saw him standing on the corner, stuffing newspapers into his carry bag. At first glance, he looked fine, but as I drew closer I could see he was far from all right. Even though it was a bitterly cold afternoon, he looked pale and sweaty.

He gave me a half-hearted smile as he struggled to lift the heavy bag onto his shoulders. "At least it's not the weekend paper," he joked. The bag was heavy enough on a weekday, but the weekend paper could easily double the weight.

By the end of January, the worst was over. Slowly but surely, life in our neighbourhood seemed to be returning to normal. Poor Rosaleen was absolutely worn out from juggling all the work in our house as well as taking care of her own husband and baby Linda. Mamie was finally back on her feet, but still weak from her long ordeal. The house had been so quiet for so long that it was nice just to talk normally, without worrying about waking Mamie.

The recovery was a little slower in school, but by the start of February, Kenny was the only one still missing from the classroom. Every afternoon I looked for him when I walked down Carlton Street on my way to the drug store. I thought about knocking on his door, but Kenny never liked anyone seeing inside his house.

Just past eleven o'clock one morning, Sister Alphonse came into our classroom. At first we thought she might be there to listen in on another health and hygiene lesson, but she called Miss Williams off to the side of the room and whispered something to her. It looked like Miss Williams was starting to cry as she turned her back on the class. Sister Alphonse didn't look much better as she turned to face the class. She paused, staring at all the empty desks, trying to collect herself, before giving us the terrible news. Kenny Bell was dead. He had developed pneumonia and had been taken to St. Michael's Hospital the night before, but the illness was too far along for them to save him. Kenny died in the early hours of the morning on February 4, 1962.

Just a few days later, our entire class was marched up to Our Lady of Lourdes for Kenny's funeral Mass. Even with all of his classmates, Miss Williams, and the nuns, there were barely enough people to fill the first three pews. Mr. Bell had to be helped out of his wheelchair and into the pew, next to his wife and two daughters. They never turned around during the Mass, but we could hear their crying as they sat alone in the front row. Kenny's casket rested on a small cloth-covered table, just in front of the altar railing. Mrs. Bell had wanted an open casket, but with so many young people at the service, the priest convinced her to leave it closed.

Father McIsaac did say some nice things about Kenny, although he hardly knew him. Kenny only went to Mass when his mother forced him, and he was always too busy with his newspaper route to show up at any of our baseball games. At the end of the Mass, Father McIsaac encouraged us all to file by the casket and press our hand down on the lid. He said that leaving our fingerprints would be like leaving a part of us to help Kenny find his way to heaven.

After the service, Miss Williams had us all line up outside to watch as the casket was placed in the hearse. It is strange to think where your mind takes you at times like that. Standing there in the cold, all I could think about was my pal Jimmy and how he had died all alone. Even when his ashes were placed in the ground, next to his mother, no one was there to say a prayer for him. It had only been a few months since he died and already his gravesite was forgotten. Kenny's death was a terrible thing, but at least he had a family and friends to remember him.

In the spring, when the snow was gone, Sister Alphonse took a few of us to visit the cemetery. She laid some flowers on Kenny's grave as we all said a prayer for him. Before leaving, we stopped to say a prayer over one more grave. A few days after Kenny died, there was another funeral for one of the girls in grade four. Neither family could afford a proper grave marker, but later on, the parish took up a collection and had a small stone cross placed on each grave.

I have no real idea how many people died from influenza during those long winter months. I do know that the weekly church bulletin listed at least one funeral Mass conducted in Our Lady of Lourdes almost every day. I am sure if one had checked the All Saints Anglican Church on Dundas or the Beth Israel Synagogue on Queen Street, they would have found that the epidemic was equally devastating for every religious group.

Every day when I left for work, Mamie told me to be careful. Mr. Cohen made me wash my hands when I came back from my deliveries. I have to admit I was a little scared whenever I had to deal with a sick customer.

With all the influenza going around, business at the drug store picked up for a month or two. But by March, even the old man had to face the truth. When Mrs. Cohen became ill, he left me alone to run the store while he tended to his wife. I was a little nervous, but fortunately for me, there were few telephone orders to deal with and even fewer customer coming in to the store. It was becoming more and more obvious that the drug store wouldn't be around much longer.

Within a couple of weeks, the downstairs storeroom was empty and there was barely enough stock to fill the shelves. On the last day of March, Mr. Cohen closed the door for the last time. I could see how sad he was when he gave me the news. He let me stay on for a few days to help him clean out the store. The last time I saw them, the old man handed me a brand new ten-dollar bill. Mrs. Cohen, crying, gave me a hug and told me to be a good boy.

I went by the store a few days later, but it was closed up tight. Even the *Cohen's Drug Store* sign above the door was gone. The man next door said they had moved to the north end of the city. I never saw them again, but wherever they were, I hoped they found a little peace and happiness in their lives.

Finally, the end of the school year was upon us. I have to say, I was more than a little surprised to receive such a good report card. I had done extremely well in both English and history. I always had problems with math and science, but thanks to Miss Williams, even those marks had improved somewhat.

For Fred or Marie, an overall grade of 70 percent would have been considered a bit of a letdown, but it was the exact grade I had been hoping for. It was just high enough to satisfy my da, but hopefully low enough to make me ineligible to attend Neil McNeil High School. I would be quite content to go Jarvis Collegiate, where most of my friends were going. I knew Da didn't care where I went in the fall, but as much as I begged and pleaded to go to Jarvis, Mamie just wouldn't give in.

Every morning for the past year, I had watched Fred don his maroon blazer, white shirt, and striped tie and head out the door to begin another ten-hour school day. The seven o'clock streetcar took him south to Queen Street. From there he transferred to a second streetcar, which would take him east to Kingston Road, where he had to catch yet another streetcar all the way over to Victoria Park Avenue. If everything was on schedule and the weather was good, he could expect to arrive at Neil McNeil just before the bell rang at nine o'clock. After six hours of school work and two more hours of travel, he was lucky to reach home by five o'clock in the evening.

If having to wear a uniform and spending endless hours travelling each day weren't enough to test your sanity, there was the added torture of having to deal with all the Catholic priests who ran the school. Needless to say, I wanted absolutely nothing to do with Neil McNeil. Try as I might, Mamie simply wouldn't budge. I was going to a Catholic high school whether I liked it or not.

CHAPTER 13

WHEN I TOOK the entrance exam for Neil McNeil in the summer of 1962, I didn't give it a lot of effort. The test was difficult and I thought I was home free, until the letter arrived from the school. Despite my mediocre effort, I managed to scrape through with the minimum requirement of 60 percent. Maybe they thought some of Fred's genius had rubbed off on me, but for whatever reason, I was accepted into Neil McNeil High School.

If there is one thing I deeply regret about that time, it was my inability to see how great a financial burden my parents were under. I was so busy feeling sorry for myself that I failed to realize just how much money it would cost to make sure Fred and I had a proper education. Our school blazers cost over forty dollars each. It may be difficult to comprehend in this day and age, but back in the 1960s, students had to purchase all their high school textbooks. That expense alone was over a hundred dollars. I could use one or two of Fred's old grade-nine textbooks, but that still left a lot of money to be paid. My da was never one to accept charity, but after discussing it with the principal, he was able to arrange for us to get our books on temporary loan, as long as everything was paid off by the following January.

On my first day of school in September, there were enough new students to fill three separate grade-nine classes. With my less than stellar marks on the entrance test, I was firmly entrenched with all the other bottom-feeders in grade 9C.

It had been more than three years since we left Ireland, but the memory of attending St. Andrew's School was still clearly etched in my mind. Here I was, once again, trapped in an all-boys school, surrounded by Catholic priests. People like Sister Mary Joseph and Father McIsaac back at St. Martin's had done much to quell my fears, but I never felt comfortable in the presence of priests or nuns.

I would have given anything to see one familiar face that first morning at Neil McNeil. All of the new boys were herded into the gymnasium to await the arrival of the principal, Father Troy.

At least I wasn't alone in my first-day jitters. Everyone seemed to be fidgeting about, nervously waiting for something to happen. Based on all the tugging and scratching, most of us were not used to wearing a shirt and tie to school. It was a cool day, but I could feel the beads of sweat forming under my new flannel blazer and pants.

All the time we were waiting, I never took my eye off one priest who kept walking back and forth across the front of the group. If not for his white collar and long black robes, I would have sworn he was a drill sergeant. When someone leaned over to talk to his neighbour, the priest told him, "Shut your gob."

Sitting in that uncomfortable silence in that huge gymnasium reminded me of patiently waiting for the priest to end his sermon at Sunday morning Mass. When the principal entered and took his place on the stage, it was like seeing our parish priest standing in his pulpit. I could hear their words, but I was always aware of the distance between us.

After taking a moment to glance around at his captive audience, Father Troy told us to take our seats. He used his podium like a pulpit as he preached to us about the glories of his school and how fortunate we were just to be there.

It was getting on toward ten o'clock, and Father Troy had been talking for thirty minutes or more. Maybe I was just tired, but I could not have picked a worse time to yawn. I had forgotten about our drill sergeant once Father Troy started talking. In an instant he was right there behind me.

I could feel his hot breath as he leaned down to speak. "Get on your feet, boyo," he hissed in my ear.

The blood rushed to my brain as I sprang to my feet. Father Troy spoke for another ten minutes or so, but to me, standing up in the middle of all those seated boys, it seemed like an eternity.

The remainder of the day was spent running around trying to be in the right place at the right time. The ten minutes we had between classes was barely enough time to find my locker and get whatever textbooks I needed for the next lesson.

Just before the last period of the morning, I had another unfortunate encounter with the dreaded drill sergeant. I had a few minutes to spare as I headed up the stairs to the second floor. I had only taken two or three steps when I heard the familiar voice behind me. "Just where do you think you're going?"

I was a little out of breath as I tried to explain that I didn't want to be late for history class.

"I know where you have to go, but you are not allowed to go up the down staircase. You can only go up the up staircase, at the other end of the hall."

I could see he was becoming annoyed by my inability to comprehend what he was telling me, but all I could do was stand there, I'm sure with a blank look on my face. After a moment, he took me by the arm and pointed down the hall. "See the stairs down there, at the end of the corridor? Go up those stairs."

When I finally reached the right place, the history lesson was already underway. Mr. Herron looked upset by the interruption, but he waved me toward a desk near the back of the room. Thankfully, he didn't ask me why I was late. I still wasn't quite sure what had just happened.

Mr. Herron was probably one of the most arrogant and egotistical people I have ever met, but he was also an excellent history teacher. His method of instruction might have been a little unconventional, but he certainly had an uncanny ability to turn an otherwise dull subject into an exciting, interactive experience. Each of his lessons was like a one-man play in which he took on the persona of each of the characters. For a moment he would speak in the thundering voice of William the Conqueror as he explained his plan for the invasion of England. Suddenly his expression would change, and he would become Harold II, the meek-mannered Saxon, cowering before the new Norman king.

Dealing with a classroom full of boys was never a problem for Mr. Herron. However, talking to him one-on-one could prove extremely difficult. If you approached him with a question before or after class, you rarely got a straight answer. The very fact that you saw fit to bother him with some trivial matter seemed to upset him. Even the most mundane question could draw his look of total contempt. One day I made the mistake of asking him about some point I had missed on the War of the Roses. His response was to have me draw up a diagram outlining the entire royal succession for both the House of York and the House of Lancaster.

Every forty minutes that bell would ring and send the entire class into a frenzy of activity. One moment the hallway would be empty, and in an instant all the doors would open, sending students running in all directions.

I am sure I wasn't the first person to think of it, but after a few days of total bedlam, I began to wonder why we couldn't make the system work better for all concerned. Wouldn't it have been easier if the hundred or more students just stayed in the classroom and let the teachers move around every forty minutes? I thought about bringing it up, but who would listen to a fourteen-year-old kid who had barely managed to pass his entrance exam?

Once I mastered my pesky combination lock, I could at least keep pace with the ebb and flow of traffic. It was such a relief to be among the first to arrive for class. I actually had time to take a deep breath and glance through my books before our first science class was scheduled to begin.

My feeling of calm was short-lived when I saw the teacher walk through the door and take his place at the front of the room. At least we could finally put a name to the priest we all now referred to as the drill sergeant.

Father McCarthy was not a particularly big man. He was tall and thin, with a gaunt face. Maybe it was those long black robes the priests wore, or perhaps it was the bright fluorescent lights in the classroom, but his face always looked pale behind his silver-rimmed glasses.

The first time he asked me a question, I practically jumped out of my seat. Most of the teachers would allow us to remain seated when we were called upon to answer a question, but he insisted that we stand upright and speak clearly. As I stood and rhymed off my answer, I couldn't help but feel a certain amount of satisfaction. But if I was hoping for some words of praise for my brilliant answer, they never came.

"I already know what the textbook says," Father McCarthy said, staring at me over his glasses. "Now tell me what it means in your own words."

All I could do was mumble something about not understanding his question. At last I was allowed to sit down as he turned his attention to one of my smarter classmates.

I had gym right before science. From the moment we entered the locker room for gym class, we had five minutes to change and get out on the floor. Then the gym teacher, Father Sheppard, blew the whistle, and we were off for forty minutes of running around the gym, stopping only long enough to pump out a series of push-ups and sit-ups at the end of each lap.

There was an entire bank of showers in the locker room, but I don't remember ever actually using them. When it came to the choice between smelling clean or showing up late for Father McCarthy's class, there was simply no contest.

The odour produced by thirty sweaty teenage boys in a closed classroom was enough to stop a grown man in his tracks. Of course, the boys all smelled equally bad, so we hardly noticed the problem. Sometimes when Father McCarthy came into the room, he would suddenly stop in the doorway and fan the air with a book or a newspaper. He could open as many windows as he liked, but that smell just wouldn't go away.

The principal of Neil McNeil, Father Troy, seemed like a kind man. Sometimes we would see him roaming the halls between classes. He and I spoke only once, when he stopped me in the hall to ask my name. When I told him, it didn't seem to register at first, but then he remembered. "You must be Fred's little brother."

I nodded, trying not to grimace. When you hear the same question every time your name comes up, it is difficult to maintain a neutral expression. During his first year at Neil McNeil, Fred had attended classes with just about every teacher in the school. Judging by all their positive comments, he had definitely made a lasting impression on everyone he met. They would go on and on about this outstanding student and how he was destined for great things. After a while, I stopped listening. I would smile, but I found it best not to say anything, lest it encouraged them to keep talking.

Fred and I tended to stay out of each other's way during the school day, but in the morning, I could always manage to get under his skin. I liked to take my time getting dressed. By the time I came into the kitchen, he was already fed and anxious to get going. I have to admit that I found a perverse pleasure in my ability to annoy him so easily. Rarely a morning went by when we didn't end up running to catch the streetcar.

One Monday in late September, our normal morning routine was a little different. The day before, Mamie and Da, along with Rosaleen, Bernard, and Aunt Lilly had gone to Buffalo, New York, where all the stores were open on Sunday. They had left early in the morning and they planned to return late that night. On Monday, for once, I was actually up early on a school morning. I knew Mamie was planning to sleep in after getting home so late, but still I was hoping to see her so I could apologize for upsetting her just before they'd left for Buffalo.

It had all started when I heard about their shopping trip. I immediately asked Mamie if I could go. The more she said no, the more I persisted. I wouldn't miss any school, and even though we'd get home so late, I promised she wouldn't hear a single complaint out of me when I had to get up early on Monday. Mamie didn't lose her temper easily, but I could see my constant nagging was beginning to get on her nerves.

Finally, she'd had enough. "You're not going and that's final!"

As I stomped up the stairs, I could still hear her talking to me from the kitchen. "If you want to sulk, I can give you something to sulk about!"

I waited as long as possible on Monday morning, but there was still no sign of movement upstairs when Fred and I headed out the door. I wanted to tell Mamie I was sorry for acting so childish, but that would have to wait until I came home from school.

During the last period before lunch, Father McCarthy came into my English class. We all watched as he made his way to the front of the class and bent down to whisper something to the teacher. They were looking directly at me as they spoke, and I began to feel uneasy. Then Father McCarthy called my name, and the entire class turned to stare as I stood and walked to the front of the room. I tried to stay calm, but I could feel my legs beginning to shake. From the look on Father McCarthy's face, I thought I was in some kind of trouble. He told me to gather all my books and follow him to the principal's office.

The instant I saw Fred standing outside the office door, I knew this was much more than a simple screw-up on my part. The wait seemed endless. I wanted to ask Fred if he knew why we were there, but I was afraid he might say something I wasn't prepared to hear.

To this very day, I cannot fully understand why Father Troy would choose to leave us waiting all that time before finally calling us inside his office. He must have seen how anxious we both were, but still he told us nothing other than to go home, where our brother Michael would be waiting for us.

We hadn't seen much of Michael in the past few months. Camp Borden was only about sixty miles north of Toronto, but the training course he was on kept him busy for weeks on end. When Father Troy told us that Michael was at home, we both knew something was terribly wrong.

It was just past the noon hour, and the Parliament streetcar was practically empty. Fred and I just sat there, hardly daring to look at each other. By the time we reached Carlton Street, I felt like I would burst if I didn't say something. Terrible images kept racing through my mind. The streetcar was still a block away from our stop, but both of us were standing by the exit door, ready to run the moment the door opened.

Michael's fiancée, Nora, stood waiting for us at the front door. She didn't say anything, but I could see that she had been crying. We were barely inside the door when I heard Michael's voice calling us into the living room.

Johno was just putting on his coat and heading out the door as we arrived. Every time I ran into Johno, he would grab me in a headlock and dare me to try and get out of it. Today he didn't say a word or even look at us as he rushed out the door. Nora said he was going to meet Marie and pick up David and Philip from school.

There wasn't a sound anywhere in the house. Nora sat on the arm of Michael's chair, squeezing his hand as tightly as she could. For a moment, Michael just sat staring at the floor, as if he didn't not know what to say or how to say it. Finally the words came spilling out.

There had been a car accident on the Queen Elizabeth Way, the highway connecting Toronto to Buffalo. The accident had happened late at night, somewhere near St. Catharines, Michael told us. He kept talking on and on about how a car had slammed into the side of Bernard's car. He knew what we wanted to hear, but he just couldn't bring himself to say it.

Fred finally asked the question. "Is everyone all right?"

I could see Michael's knuckles turn white as he squeezed Nora's hand tightly before delivering the devastating news. Mamie was dead.

According to the police report, Mamie had been sitting in the back seat and the force of the impact had killed her instantly. Later on we could find some small comfort in knowing that she hadn't suffered, but in that moment, there was simply nothing anyone could say to cushion the blow. I wanted to scream. I wanted to cry, but all I could do was sit there, staring at Michael, hoping to hear a sliver of doubt in his voice.

"Surely there has to be some kind of mistake? Maybe the cops have gotten it wrong," I said desperately.

"No" was all he said. As much as Michael wanted to make me feel better, all he could do was tell me the truth. Mamie was gone, and there was nothing anyone could say or do to change that.

We sat in silence as the seconds ticked by. It is strange the things that cross your mind in a time like that. I stared down at my shoes and thought about how upset Mamie got whenever we tracked dirt through her nice clean house.

I think it was Fred who finally broke the silence with a question. I felt a momentary twinge of guilt for not asking about my da and all the others in the car.

Michael tried to be a little upbeat when he told us that Bernard and Aunt Lilly had suffered only minor cuts and bruises and would be back in Toronto the following day. He allowed us a moment to absorb this tiny piece of good news, but then his expression changed. The situation with Da and Rosaleen was far more serious. Both of them had sustained serious injuries and had been taken to the hospital in St. Catharines. Michael tried to sound hopeful, but the truth was that the doctors simply didn't know if either one of them would pull through.

I am often saddened by some of the choices I made that day, to my great regret. Most people would have chosen to stay close to family in such a time of grief, but all I could think of was getting away. When Marie, David, and Philip came home, I could have stayed in the living room and helped Michael break the news, but instead, I chose to hide away upstairs. I knew the news would be devastating for Marie and David, but at least they were old enough to understand. How could a six-year-old like Philip possibly fathom all that had happened?

I could hear them all crying down in the living room, but still I stayed upstairs, not knowing how to deal with any of this.

Later on, Nora banged on the bedroom door. I told her I wasn't hungry, but she insisted I come down to the kitchen. I didn't know very much about Nora before that day. To me she was just Michael's girlfriend, who I saw around the house from time to time. That day I saw a whole other side to her. She could have left us there to wallow in our own sorrow, but she chose to stay and help us get through it all. For days on end, she didn't stopped cleaning. Rarely an hour went by without a relative or neighbour showing up to offer their condolences. Nora would take them into the kitchen and put on yet another pot of tea. If she wasn't tidying up some mess we had made, she was in the kitchen cooking meals. None of us were hungry, but she insisted that we sit down together at the table.

Our house had always been a place of total chaos at dinnertime. Everyone talked at once while Mamie ran back and forth from the kitchen, trying to get all of us fed before she finally sat down. Now it felt like torture just sitting down for dinner. No one knew what to say. If someone said something funny, we hardly dared to laugh. Even smiling made us feel guilty.

Poor Michael looked so pale and exhausted. He never complained, but I am sure he must have felt a tremendous sense of relief when our brother Willy arrived from Ireland.

After days of waiting, we finally had some good news. Da's condition had stabilized somewhat, but it would be weeks before he was well enough to come home. Rosaleen was finally out of intensive care, but the doctors still weren't sure if she would be able to walk again.

Nora had more or less taken over the running of the house. She could be a little overbearing at times. Every day, she insisted that we all made our beds, washed the dishes, and cleaned up after ourselves. We may have complained, but looking back on it now, I know it was exactly what we needed to keep our minds occupied.

I hated going to bed, knowing how difficult it would be to fall asleep. Eventually I would drift off, only to wake long before dawn. Just for a second or two, I would forget about Mamie. Then I would suddenly remember that she was gone and that I would never get the chance to apologize or even say goodbye. Lying in the dark and quiet, I just wanted morning to come so the house would be noisy again.

The first time we entered the funeral home, I was afraid to see Mamie. In my mind I still saw her sitting at the kitchen table, drinking tea. I was afraid that if I saw her now, that image would disappear forever.

Everyone commented about how peaceful and serene Mamie looked. She was wearing the same dress she had worn last Christmas Day. Mamie didn't have many good clothes, but that dress was her favourite. I could still picture her wearing that dress and hear her laughter as Da twirled her around the kitchen floor after Christmas dinner.

When my turn came to kneel at the casket, I made the sign of the cross and pretended to pray. I told Mamie how much I missed her and how sorry I was for the grief I had caused her, but I just could not pray to a god who would do such a thing to my mother.

A priest from Our Lady of Lourdes came to the house to talk to us all. He kept going on about Mamie being in heaven and how all of this was part of God's plan. I knew he was only trying to offer us some small measure of comfort, but his words just made me angrier. How could he possibly try to justify taking my mother and destroying a family? My mamie was just forty-eight years old when she died. My da was left alone with nine children, five of them still in school. How could anyone believe that this was all part of God's plan?

I would continue to go to Mass on Sunday. I would stand and sit and kneel at all the appropriate times, because that was how we were expected to act. But once I was grown and on my own, I would never willingly set foot in a Catholic church again.

The day of the funeral, nothing was as it should have been. The church was packed with friends and relatives, but with Da and

Rosaleen still in hospital, it didn't seem right. Someone had decided it was best to leave Philip at home. Even though Michael had tried explaining things to him, he was too young to really understand. Long after the funeral was over, he was still asking when Mamie was coming home.

Poor Aunt Kitty could hardly contain her sorrow at the loss of her sister. Uncle Peter held her arm tightly as he tried to guide her toward the altar. I was surprised to see Sister Alphonse and Sister Mary Joseph there for the service. As we waited by the front door of the church, Sister Mary Joseph stopped to squeeze my hand and tell me that we were all in her prayers.

It was a cloudy September morning when we came out of the church, but by the time the procession reached Holy Cross Cemetery, the sun had come out. Somehow it didn't seem right to be burying our mother on a such a bright, sunny day.

It was well into October before Rosaleen and Da were finally released from the hospital. Rosaleen came home first. She was in a wheelchair at first, but after a week or two, she managed to walk with the help of a cane.

When Da stepped out of the car, he looked like a ghost of his former self. His face was scarred and swollen. His cheeks were still covered in small abrasions, and there were black rings under both his eyes. He had difficulty walking the few steps to the front door, but when we tried to help, he insisted on doing it alone.

Our kitchen was far too small to accommodate all of us at the same time, but no one wanted to leave Da's side. He didn't look well at all, but still it felt reassuring to have him home at last. The moment he sat down, Philip was right there, ready to jump into his lap.

I think being home was like a tonic for him. Slowly, over the next few days, he began to look and feel better. Every morning we would creep down the stairs and past the living room, where Da was sleeping on the pullout couch. We never talked about it, but we all knew that without Mamie there beside him, he just couldn't sleep in their bed upstairs.

On a Sunday afternoon in late October, Da, Rosaleen, and our whole family finally stood together beside Mamie's grave in Holy Cross Cemetery. It was too late in the year for grass to grow, but the dirt had been levelled out and the bronze plate had just been added to mark the gravesite. No one spoke. All of us just stood there staring down at the simple inscription: MOLLY BURKE — born 1914 — died 1962.

CHAPTER 14

THE FIRST FEW days back in school seemed like torture. At home I could at least hide away in my room. I didn't want to talk about it, but every teacher in every class would insist on asking how I was doing. Between classes, I tried to get away and avoid those pitying stares in the hallway. At lunchtime, the cafeteria tables were filled with people talking and laughing out loud. I could feel the anger welling up inside of me. How could these people happily go about their daily lives like nothing had happened?

I thought I could find some peace and quiet on the sports field behind the school. At lunchtime, the empty bleachers were the perfect place to get away from all those prying eyes.

When I heard a voice calling my name, I pretended not to hear. Maybe if I just ignored him, he would go away and leave me in peace to eat my sandwich. He didn't. When Father Sheppard came up behind me, I tried to look surprised. I started to stand up, as we were taught to do whenever one of the priests spoke to us, but he insisted I sit back down. I thought if I just smiled and nodded, he might move on. But he sat down beside me, and I knew I was in for yet another drawn-out speech about how sorry he was about Mamie's death. I knew he was only trying to be kind, but the words sounded so hollow to me. He didn't know anything about my mamie. He had never met her. How could he possibly know how it felt to lose her?

But as much as I hated all the pitying comments at school, I dreaded coming home to all that silence.

Da was still quite weak from the accident, but with virtually no money coming into the house, he had little choice but to go back to work on the night shift. Fred and I were usually long gone to school before he came home in the morning. In the evening, everyone walked around the house quietly and whispered so as not to wake him up too early. We sometimes caught a glimpse of him when he got up, but even then he didn't say much to any of us. Marie would warm up whatever we'd had for supper that evening, and he would sit alone in the kitchen, picking away at the food on his plate. If he spoke at all, it was usually to ask about how we were doing in school. I told him everything was fine, and that seemed to satisfy him. Soon enough he would find out that I was failing in almost every subject, but that could wait for another day. He had far too much to worry about right now without me adding to his problems.

Willy had stayed as long as possible, but in order to keep his job with Air Lingus, he'd had to return to Ireland at the end of September. Rosaleen called three or four times every day, but she had her own daughter to take care of, and she still needed a cane to move around. Michael had been given a compassionate release from the army, but there was a mountain of paperwork to complete before he came home for good.

Johno had a lot of difficulty dealing with Mamie's death. He just never talked to anyone. Most evenings he would leave work and head straight downtown to meet up with his band and play into the wee hours of the morning.

Marie was only twelve years old, but already she had more responsibility than a woman twice her age. Before leaving for school in the morning, she had to cook breakfast for David and Philip and get them off to school. After school, she came home to clean the house and start making dinner for all of us. In just a few short weeks, she had gone from being a little sister to more of a housekeeper for all of us.

It didn't take an expert to see that our family was slowly disintegrating right before our eyes. The glue that held us all together was gone, and there was nothing left to hang on to. We were still alive and breathing, but most days it felt like we were just going through the motions of living.

I think we were all relieved when Rosaleen, Bernard, and baby Linda moved into the house in late November. Rosaleen could walk again and Marie was particularly grateful to get out from under all the housework.

Just when it looked like we could finally catch up with the back rent, Da collapsed at work and had to be admitted to the hospital. It would be February before he was allowed to come home again.

One early evening just a week before Christmas, something happened that I still think about to this day. I was so busy lugging the heavy cans of garbage out to the curb that I hardly noticed the car that slowly made its way down the lane and stopped in front of our house. When I turned around, a man climbed out of the driver's seat. "Is this number twelve?" he asked.

It was difficult to see in the semi-darkness, but when the car's interior light came on, I noticed a large stack of toys and parcels piled on the back seat. I thought this must be someone from Da's work. With all that had gone on in the past few weeks, we had completely forgotten about the Christmas party for the city works department. Perhaps they had decided to bring our presents to the house.

It was Michael who answered the door when the man knocked. I couldn't hear what they said, but in less than a minute I heard the front door slam. As the man brushed past me at the bottom of the steps, I saw the long, jagged scar running across the top of his forehead and all the way down the left side of his face. The car was already down at the bottom of the lane when it finally dawned on me. I had just talked to the man who had killed my mother.

Someone bought a scrawny little Christmas tree and stuck it up in the living room. On Christmas morning there were some colouring books and crayons under the tree for David and Philip, but the rest of us knew better than to expect anything. Back in September, there had been people coming to our door with trays of food almost every day. Now it seemed that most of them had moved on with their lives. Most days, there was hardly a knock on the door. All of the food was gone, and there was nothing but a big bag of oatmeal and a sack of potatoes sitting on the kitchen counter. When someone from the Saint Vincent de Paul showed up with a box of food on Christmas Eve, it seemed like a godsend. It was only some canned soup, a box of corn flakes, and a big bag of macaroni, but anything was better than a constant diet of porridge and boiled potatoes.

Rosaleen insisted we all go to Mass on Christmas morning. The past few months had changed her. From morning to night, she never stopped cooking and cleaning. She had always been a very even-tempered person, but in the months following Mamie's death, there were more than enough problems to try anyone's patience. I didn't help matters by complaining about going to Mass. I am ashamed to admit I made my sister cry that Christmas morning.

When she told me I should be grateful for what I had, I just couldn't contain myself. "Mamie is gone and no amount of praying is going to bring her back!"

I had barely finished the sentence when Johno grabbed me by the shirt and threw me against the wall. Only Rosaleen's voice stopped him from putting my head right through the plaster. "If you want to be grateful for something, just look around you," she said. "You should be thanking God that you have a family and you're not alone in the world."

After Mass, we spent most of the day visiting Da in the hospital. We didn't have anything for Christmas dinner at home that year, but Rosaleen wanted to salvage something good from the holiday. After a lot of searching, the only place we could find open was a Chinese restaurant.

Judging by the smile on our waiter's face, we were probably the only customers he'd had that day. Still, it took a little time to make him understand that we all wanted pancakes.

I have no idea what it really was, but the kitchen staff managed to cook up something that resembled pancakes. When we asked for maple syrup, the waiter disappeared into the kitchen for a few moments and then came out with a pot of gravy. Finally he brought us some butter, but by now, the pancakes were so cold that the butter refused to melt.

The whole thing might have been a forgettable experience if not for the fact that we were all laughing from the moment the waiter showed up with the gravy. At least we could find some humour in what was otherwise a sad and sombre Christmas.

It is odd how your outlook on things can change over time. In the fall I dreaded coming home to all the quiet, but now with the house full to overflowing, I couldn't wait to get a quiet moment to myself. I can't speak for the others, but to me it felt like I was trapped in a situation over which I had no control. There were so many people in the house that it was impossible to be alone for even a moment. I could lock myself in the bathroom, but with ten people in the house, there was always someone banging on the door, telling me to hurry up.

When the holidays were over, I could at least find some peace and quiet on the long streetcar ride to and from school. Fred and

I still bickered in the morning, but once we were at school we wouldn't have to see each other for the remainder of the day.

There was, however, one embarrassing situation we both had to face on the first day back at Neil McNeil after the Christmas break. There was still roughly eighty dollars owing on all the textbooks we had gotten back in September. This was one time I was happy to let Fred take the lead while I stood back, trying to hide my embarrassment. We hoped to catch the librarian alone, but as luck would have it, there was already a long line waiting at the counter.

"Name?" the librarian said as she moved toward the file cabinet on the back wall.

Fred tried to whisper the problem to her, but she was already busy flipping through the file of index cards, looking for our account.

"I have no idea what you are talking about," she said, her finger skimming to the bottom of the card. "According to this, your account has been paid in full."

Fred tried to ask for an explanation, but we were pushed aside as she moved to help the next student.

That night Rosaleen confirmed that no one in the family had paid the bill. With no other explanation, we could only assume that the school had made a mistake. Fred and I were willing to forget the whole matter, but Rosaleen insisted that we tell Father Troy about the error. We didn't have a penny to our name, but Rosaleen would never allow any of us to profit from the mistakes of others.

Father Troy told us there was no error. Father McCarthy, the drill sergeant of a priest that no one liked and everyone was afraid of, had paid the debt out of his own pocket. When we tried to thank him later, he seemed quite upset that we knew about it. Still, I thought I detected a hint of a smile as he turned his back and walked away.

As the school year wore on, I could feel myself sinking further and further into a hole from which there was no escape. The very idea of going to school seemed so pointless. The family had barely enough money to pay the rent and buy groceries, and with Da still in hospital, the situation would only get worse. How could the family possibly afford to keep both Fred and me in school for another three years? Fred was a brilliant student and bound for great things, whereas I was near the bottom of my class and no longer willing to even try to get better.

I was expecting more of an argument when I told the family I wanted to quit school. Michael and Rosaleen both tried to talk me out of it, but I wouldn't budge. It would have been nice to have them on my side, but in truth, Da's opinion was the only one that mattered. I was fifteen years old and I would need his signed permission to leave school.

I was quite surprised when he didn't put up more of a fuss. He and I were left alone in his hospital room to discuss it, but within a few minutes, he agreed to sign the papers. At first I was relieved that it had been so easy to convince him, but then I realized that this was really the beginning of the end for the two of us. I was still my father's son, but in that moment, I knew he was finished with me.

If I thought I was going to lay about and do nothing, I was sadly mistaken. I cleaned out my locker at school on a Monday afternoon, and on Tuesday morning I was sitting in the employment office at King and Bay Streets. As I scanned the waiting room, I couldn't help but think that perhaps I had made a huge mistake. There I was, this pimply faced kid surrounded by thirty or forty men and women all looking for some kind of work. They all looked to be decades older than me, and they no doubt had a great deal more experience than I could ever hope to have.

The lady who interviewed me seemed a little surprised by my youthful appearance. I fidgeted as she slowly read through my application. The look on her face wasn't reassuring. I watched as she began flipping through the Rolodex of cards on her desk. Every so often she would stop to read a card and I would lean forward, hoping she'd found something.

When she reached the end of the file, she finally spoke. "Sorry, but I have nothing for you. When you get a driver's licence, come back and see me and maybe I can help you out."

Every morning I would scan the help-wanted column in the newspaper, but most jobs required some experience. I did manage to get a few interviews for some factory work, but when they saw a skinny fifteen-year-old kid standing before them, the answer was always the same. Some were kind enough to talk to me for a few minutes, while others actually laughed in my face. One supervisor gave me a lecture on the need to stay in school, but regardless of who I spoke to, I was usually sent packing within fifteen minutes.

When I spotted the help-wanted ad for National Drug Trading Company, I didn't waste any time getting down to their warehouse near Jarvis and King Streets. According to the ad, the job entailed filling orders for all of the drug stores in the southeastern portion of the city. The man seemed dubious at first, but after a lot of talking, I finally managed to convince him that my experience working in the drug store gave me all the necessary skills he was looking for. The pay started at seventy-five cents an hour, but if I could get through the thirty-day trial period, I would be making a dollar an hour. I worked five and a half days a week and was paid at noon on Saturday.

I will never forget how good it felt that first Saturday when I came home with close to twenty-five dollars in my pocket. With Da still in the hospital, our bills continued to mount up. Mamie's life insurance only covered about half of the funeral expenses. We were a month behind in the rent, and the coal man was threatening not to come back unless we paid him in full for his last delivery. My meagre pay wouldn't solve our problems, but it felt good to know I was able to contribute something to help the family.

When I tried telling Da about my job, he didn't seem even remotely interested. From the moment he had signed the paper releasing me from school, he and I had hardly spoken a word to each other. When he did speak to me, I could hear the disdain in his voice. After a while I found myself making excuses not to go up to the hospital. Anything was better than facing his criticism — or worse still, being completely ignored.

Like anyone starting something new, I had been quite nervous on my first morning on the job. The warehouse was much bigger than I'd expected. The building contained row upon row of metal shelves, each about eight feet high. The sections were laid out alphabetically with all the items you might find in a drug store. Smaller items were neatly stacked on the upper shelves, while the bulkier items, such as toilet paper and cases of cigarettes, were grouped together on a line of pallets set against the side wall. At the back of the building was a small fenced-off area with a locked gate and a large sign saying *Do Not Enter*. All the prescription drugs were kept inside, and only the two resident pharmacists were allowed beyond the fence.

The supervisor stayed with me throughout the morning, but by early afternoon, I was on my own. The sheer volume of items was daunting at first, but once I learned where to find each item, it was just like filling orders back in Mr. Cohen's store, albeit on a much larger scale. It took me all of an hour to fill the first order, but by the end of the week, I could finish most orders in half that time.

When Da was released from the hospital in February, we were all home to meet him as he came through the front door. Philip wrapped his arms around Da's leg and wouldn't let go. Everywhere Da went, Philip was right there beside him.

It had taken a very long time before Philip understood that Mamie was not coming home. When he woke up at night crying, one of us would sit with him until he fell back to sleep. Now that Da was home, Philip never left his side, always afraid that Da might leave again and never come back.

We all told Da how good he looked, but in truth, he was like a shadow of his former self. He was only fifty-six years old, but the stress and strain of the past several months had aged him greatly. The doctors had given him a cane, which he refused to use. Just getting from the front hall to the kitchen table was an effort, but no one was allowed to help.

Rosaleen had spent the morning cooking up all his favourites, but he insisted that a cup of tea was all he needed. He ate a few mouthfuls off his plate, but only enough to satisfy Rosaleen.

After weeks at home, he still couldn't sleep in his bed upstairs. If I woke up during the night, I could hear him wandering around downstairs. In the morning we would find him sleeping on the sofa in the front room. Rosaleen had always been Da's favourite, but even she could not get him to talk about how he was feeling. Over time, his mood only seemed to get darker as he withdrew further and further from everyone.

When Michael and Nora were married in May, it was the first time our entire extended family was together since accident. I am sure Nora's father didn't realize it, but the church he booked for the wedding was the same one used for Mamie's funeral service. It should have been a happy day for all of us, but sitting in that church, it was difficult to think of anything cheerful. I still had the image of Mamie's coffin in front of the altar, where Michael and Nora and the priest now stood. Thankfully, the wedding reception, back at our house, quickly turned into a big Irish hollie, with all of my aunts and uncles singing and dancing long into the night.

After Michael had left the army, he'd kicked around from one part-time job to another. Then he found the kind of job most people only dream about. The day after the wedding, he and Nora left for Nassau, in the Bahamas, where he would start work on the staff of one of the biggest hotels on the island. I was happy for him, but sad at the thought of not having him around to talk to anymore.

I think we all hoped that having our relatives there to celebrate the wedding might finally draw Da out of the gloom that seemed to surround him. Da didn't drink very often, but I saw him take a beer that day as he sat smiling and talking to the uncles and aunts. It had been eight months since Mamie died. Maybe today would be the day when he finally begin to move past the grief.

In the days and weeks following the wedding reception, the house seemed all too quiet. Every evening as I walked home from work, I dreaded the thought of entering that cold house. If I was lucky, Da might be asleep on the couch and we could avoid each other for most of the night. I tried to tell myself I didn't care, but it is a hard thing to deal with when you realize that your father can't stand the sight of you.

His attitude toward me might never improve, but at least he was finally beginning to pay more attention to my younger brothers and sister. Once in a while, I even heard him laugh as he ran around the backyard playing tag with David and Philip. On weekends, he would take Marie and the boys to the zoo or for long walks in the park. Marie might ask me to go along, but when I saw the look on Da's face, I knew I wasn't welcome. When Marie did exceptionally well in her grade-eight exams, he took great pleasure in waving her report card in my face. Sometimes I wished he would just lash out with his fists. I didn't want to fight with him, but at least then his hatred of me would be out in the open.

One Sunday afternoon I was sitting at the kitchen table, reading the newspaper while waiting for the kettle to boil. When Da came in, I asked if I could make him a cup of tea. He brushed right by me and went straight to the stove. He took the kettle off the stove and made an offhand remark about it being too early for tea.

"Are you done with that?" he asked, pointing at the newspaper. Before I could answer, he grabbed the paper from my hand and started to walk away.

It would have ended there if I hadn't jumped up and slammed the kettle back down on the stove. I barely had time to step back before he grabbed me by the neck and threw me down on the floor. Before I knew it, he was pummelling me with both his fists.

Rosaleen begged him to stop, but he didn't let up. It was probably only a minute before he ran out of breath and let me get up off the floor, but it felt much longer. He and I were the same size and I could have fought back, but the thought of raising my hand against my father simply never entered my mind. Even in his weakened state, his fists packed a solid punch. My ears were ringing, but I wouldn't give him the satisfaction of knowing he had hurt me. As a final act of defiance, I turned my back on him and reached into the cupboard for a cup and saucer to make my tea. When I heard his footsteps, I thought he was coming at me again, but all he did was swipe the newspaper from the table and slam the door as he left the kitchen. That would be the last time Da ever laid a hand on me.

Rosaleen tried to tell me that things would get better, but they never did. To him I would always be the disappointing son who would never amount to anything.

In the evening after work I would stay away from home as long as possible. On Friday night I would give most of my pay to Rosaleen, keeping only enough to get me through the week. My Saturday afternoons were spent roaming the downtown. I knew the owner of the pool hall above the Town Tavern at Queen and Yonge Streets. If I helped him clean up the place and take out the garbage, he would let me play billiards for free, long into the evening.

Every bar on Yonge Street was busy on Saturday night, especially the ones that had any kind of a band. When I showed up at the Brass Rail, I was hoping there would be a lineup waiting to get in. I was far too young to get into a bar, but if they were busy out front, I could easily sneak up the alley and use the back door. If I stayed in the dark, next to the fire exit, I could see and hear the band playing on the far side of the room. Johno hadn't been happy for a long time, but playing the drums onstage, he seemed like more of his former self. When the band took a break, he and I might talk for a minute or two. He was glad to see me, but if I asked him for a sip of beer, the answer was always no. I couldn't stick around too long, knowing it would only cause trouble for him if the manager caught me lurking in the shadows.

Rosaleen didn't like me hanging around a pool hall, but she insisted I call her every evening so she knew I was okay. I had to promise to be home by eleven o'clock to avoid any confrontations with my da. As long as I came through the front door and went straight up the stairs, we wouldn't have to see each other. Sometimes I felt like I was living inside a ticking time bomb, ready to explode at any second. Rosaleen was the only one keeping us all together. I might complain about having to call her every day, but I really didn't mind. It was nice to know there was someone thinking about me.

My younger brothers and sister were usually fast asleep by the time I got home. Most nights, I would find Fred pouring over some textbook. Oddly enough, Fred and I had been getting along much better in the past few months. He and I talked from time to time, but there always seemed to be another mountain of homework to keep him up well past midnight.

After the beginning of the new school year, I began to notice a change in Fred's behaviour. The quiet and shy introvert had suddenly become much more outgoing. Every morning he would literally bounce out of bed with a smile on his face. In no time at all, he was dressed and out the door, running to catch the seven o'clock streetcar. As it turned out, Fred had met a nice girl who lived just up the road, on Winchester Street. Every morning they would meet on the Parliament streetcar and sit together on their way to school. They had only known each other for a few weeks, but even I could see the profound effect Marilyn was having on my older brother.

When I was younger, I used to look forward to long, lazy Sunday afternoons. Once Mass was over, there was nothing to do but play outside until Mamie called us in for tea. Now I dreaded waking up on Sunday, knowing this was the one morning of the week when I would be forced to face my father. Any other day, we could go our separate ways, but Rosaleen insisted we all go to Mass together. With any luck, the church would be crowded and I could stand at the back, well-hidden from Da and Rosaleen. Once Communion started, I could easily skip out of it and sneak out the door and have a cigarette. As long as I was back inside before the priest gave his final blessing, no one would ever know the difference.

When Mamie was alive, Sunday dinner had always been a noisy affair. It was important to get to the table quickly and stake out your spot. Soon the pushing and shoving would begin as we each tried to get just a little more elbow room. Mamie didn't mind the bickering, as long as we ate whatever she put in front of us.

Sunday dinner was usually a big pot of freshly made stew. After dinner, Mamie would throw in some potatoes and carrots and a few tablespoons of Bisto powder to give a little beef flavour to the mix. When Da was out of work, Mamie could make a pot of stew last for a week.

I never realized how much I loved those Sunday dinners until they were gone. Rosaleen tried her best to have us all sit down together, but even when everyone was there, it was never the same. Da might sit at the head of the table for a few minutes, but if there was a soccer match on the radio, he would take his plate into the front room to listen. Poor Rosaleen would try to make the best of it. She never said a cross word to our Da, but she was often on the verge of tears.

Maybe it was just me, but Dermott Place now seemed far too quiet on Sunday afternoons. There were still plenty of young kids playing in the street, but when old Mrs. Baxter died from the flu, there was nobody to shout at the kids and threaten them with a broom. I saw my pals Donny and Wayne from time to time, but we were far too old to play games in the street anymore.

I must confess I hadn't thought a lot about Kenny in the many months since we'd visited his grave. I saw his mother in Woolworths one day. I felt so awkward talking to her. Mrs. Bell was a nice lady, but what could I say to a mother who had lost her son? She looked so sad, but still managed to smile as we talked. She told me how sorry she was about Mamie and made me promise to come by her house. I told her I would try, but I think we both knew that would never happen. I knew if I went there, we would talk about Mamie and Kenny, and that would have been just too much to bear.

Donny hardly left his house anymore. Early in the new year, his father had set the couch on fire after passing out with a lit cigarette in his hand. Donny couldn't stop him from drinking, and he was too afraid to leave his father alone for any length of time.

There was a family living in Jimmy's old house, near the bottom of the lane. Sometimes, when I walked past, I could see kids playing and laughing on the porch. I wondered if the new family ever knew about all the sadness that house had seen.

During the spring thaw, a body has been found along the banks of the Humber River. Apparently, the cold temperature had helped preserve the body, and Jimmy's brother, Bill, was able to identify the remains of their long-missing father. After Bill was released from the Don Jail, he had come back to the neighbourhood, trying to find out about his little sister. He spent hours going door to door, but no one knew her whereabouts. She had vanished into the foster system. I don't know if he ever found her, but after a few days of searching, Bill never came back to Dermott Place.

I couldn't help but feel the irony whenever I showed up at Wayne Boland's door. Ever since his father left, he had been telling everyone that he wanted to quit school and find a job. Now here we were almost a year later, and I was the one out there working for a living, while he bragged about how well he was doing in school. He was just about to begin grade ten and was already considering the possibility of going to college once he graduated from high school.

Wayne's father never came home, but he and his mother had adjusted to their new way of life. Mrs. Boland took a job cleaning offices at night. They had to give up the house on Spruce Street, but the upstairs flat they shared near Gerrard and Parliament was large enough to suit their needs.

I must say, I really enjoyed the weekends I spent at Wayne's house. I had almost forgotten how nice it was just to hear people laugh and talk about things other than illness and death. Mrs. Boland had to work late every night, so she was happy her son had some company while she was away.

When Mrs. Boland came home from work around ten at night, that was my cue to start heading home. When she called one Sunday night and said she would be late, I decided to stay just a little longer. To this day, I really don't know why I did it. I knew getting home late would only give Da yet another reason to turn on me. Maybe, in some subconscious way, I was trying provoke him, but in that moment, I just wanted some time to myself before facing another long night in that awful house.

It was long after midnight when I got home. Normally, the front door would be unlocked, but tonight the house was dark and the door was locked. After knocking repeatedly, I finally heard footsteps coming down the hall. I was beginning to regret my decision to stay out late.

When Da opened the door, I tried to give him a half-hearted smile, but he didn't move. It was hard to see his face in the shadows, but I had no doubt that he was angry about the lateness of the hour. I tried to step past him, but he still didn't move.

"Just where do you think you are going at this hour of the night?" His voice sounded strangely calm.

"I just want to go to bed." It was all I could think to say.

He stood in the doorway, still blocking my way. "You can find a bed wherever you like, but you're not coming into this house tonight."

Before I could say anything, he closed the door in my face. For a brief moment, I thought this must be a joke, but when I heard him turn the lock, I knew I was on my own for the night. Still I stood on the doorstep, not knowing what to do next.

We were already well into summer, so thankfully the night was relatively warm. But after thirty minutes of sitting on the front steps, I could feel the dampness crawling up my backside. Every so often I had to stand up and walk around to stretch my legs. By 2:00 a.m. I was beginning to regret not taking a coat when I'd left the house the previous day.

All the while I was sitting there, I kept thinking about Mamie. I still had a vivid image of the two of us sitting alone in the kitchen. I could see how tired she was from looking after us all, but still I just sat there, waiting for her to warm my dinner in the oven. I could have done so much more to help, but I didn't. Sometimes, when I was alone late at night, I liked to look at the little prayer card the priest had given us after the funeral. It was all I had left of Mamie. At the top of the card there was a tiny picture of her, smiling and looking so happy. I found it hard to comprehend that she had been gone for almost a year.

I have no idea when I fell asleep, but when I felt something grab my legs, I sat bolt upright. The sun was already coming up, and for a split second I had no idea where I was or how I got there.

Our neighbour looked a little puzzled, but I made a lame excuse about losing my key and not wanting to wake up the family. I didn't know him very well, but he seemed like a nice enough man. He laughed when I told him the story, but I have no doubt he knew what was really going on. The shared wall between our two houses was thin enough to hear everything that went on.

When I came through the back door, Rosaleen was standing by the stove, stirring a pot of porridge. I think she was about to tell me off, but when she turned and saw me shivering from the dampness, her anger turned to concern. She made me sit and eat some hot porridge. I wanted to say I was sorry for upsetting her, but she was in no mood for talk.

"Hurry up or you'll be late for work," she said.

I still had time to spare, but we both knew the real reason I had to get out of there. Already I could hear the sound of my da's footsteps coming from the hall. When he came through the kitchen door, I braced myself for what was to come. Nothing happened. He went to the stove and poured himself a cup of tea without saying a word. I could hear my brothers and sister moving around upstairs and decided it was best to get out now, before having to face all of them.

When I got up to leave, he finally spoke. "What would your mother think, if she could see you now?"

His words felt like a knife cutting right through me. There was no answer to a question like that. All I could do was get out of there before hearing any more of his hurtful comments.

Rosaleen came out to the hall and shoved a sandwich bag into the pocket of my coat. "For God's sake, be home on time tonight."

Her whispered plea was only meant for me, but Da heard it. Before I could get out the door, I heard them arguing in the kitchen. Rosaleen was a twenty-eight-year-old woman, and for the first time in her life, she actually spoke back to our father. I was glad she was sticking up for me, but very upset with myself for being the cause of all these problems. Later that night, I apologized to Rosaleen and promised I would try to do better.

Sometimes I think my job at the warehouse was the only thing that kept me sane. The men I worked with were older than me, but we all got along very well. Jack Whelan and I became friends almost immediately. He had come all the way from Newfoundland to find work, and now all he talked about was going back some day with lots of money in his pocket. He was just eighteen, but he still called me kid most of the time. It bothered me at first, but whenever I had a problem filling an order, Jack was the one I turned to for help.

Every week or so, we enjoyed the added bonus of free cigarettes. By Thursday or Friday, most of us were close to broke. That was usually when one of the forklifts would "accidently" run into a case of cigarettes. There was never any serious damage, but if the forks happened to puncture one of the cartons inside, the boss would let us divide up the spoils. I was smoking twenty cigarettes a day by then, so I didn't really care if a few were bent or broken. At least I didn't have to go out and spend thirty-six cents on a package of Player's.

The work wasn't all that difficult, and I was grateful to be busy all day. I didn't have time to think about missing Mamie or my troubles with Da. When the boss asked us to work late, some of the guys would grumble, but I jumped at the chance of working every extra hour I could. Anything was better than going home to face the reality of a family falling apart.

CHAPTER 15

IN OUR HOUSE, birthdays came and went without much fuss. When we were very young, Mamie might give us a penny to buy some sweets, but there was never enough money to waste on a cake. When I came downstairs that morning in October, I wasn't expecting a cake and I was too old for a penny bag of sweets, but I had high hopes that someone in the family would remember that today was my sixteenth birthday. But to everyone else, it was just another day. After a few spoonfuls of porridge and a cup of tea, I was out the door and off to work.

I didn't often think about our time back home in Ireland, but as I walked to work that morning, memories of Hogan Place flooded my mind. My pals Al Kennedy and Tony Murphy would have both turned sixteen by now. I could almost picture the three of us standing at the bar in Doolan's, drinking a pint and trying not to grimace from the bitter taste. After all, this wasn't just another birthday. This was the day your father took you to the pub for your first pint of Guinness. Today you were finished with school, and your childhood was at an end. Now it was time to go out and find your place in the working world. This was the day you became a man.

Maybe my family forgot it was my birthday, but my workmates didn't. That evening after work, the guys insisted on taking me out for my first beer. When I looked in a mirror and saw the baby face staring back at me, I was sure I could never pass for a twenty-one-year-old. Jack was too young as well, but at least he had a little stubble on his cheeks to make him look older. When we got to the barroom door I hesitated, but they just pushed me inside.

It took a moment for my eyes to adjust to the dimly lit room. With the lights so low, all I had to do was stay close behind the guys and hope no one would notice me. We took the table in the corner, where I could remain partially hidden in the shadows. I was a little embarrassed when everyone threw a dollar into the centre of the table. I only had two dollars in my pocket, and I needed that to get me through the next few days.

"Don't worry about it, kid. Consider this your birthday present," Jack said as he stuck the dollar bill back into my shirt pocket.

Someone at the table waved his hand toward the bar, and in less than a minute the waiter was right there, placing glass after glass of draft beer on our little table. All the while he was there, I kept my hand up, pretending to scratch my face. I need not have worried. He barely looked in my direction. Once he'd picked up the money and put down eight glasses of draft, he was quickly off to the next table.

I had stolen a few sips of beer before. Back then, like most twelve-year-olds, I had just been trying to show off. I didn't actually enjoy the taste, but it was important to keep a straight face and act like it was something I did all the time.

Now, every eye at the table was on me as I took my first big sip of beer. The taste was as bitter as I remembered, but with them all watching, I forced a smile and smacked my lips like people do when they have finally quenched their thirst. After a few sips, I was starting to get used to the taste. Then one of the guys put a couple of shakes of salt in my glass. After that, the rest went down easy and I was ready for my second. I was just starting my fifth draft when I got a sudden urge to pee. The moment I stood up, I began to feel a little light-headed. Maybe I should have sat back down, but the need to pee far outweighed my fear of being seen. The washroom was all the way over on the far side of the room, but thankfully, no one paid any attention to me.

When I walked back to our table, a little unsteadily, I almost bumped into the waiter. He turned around and looked at me, and I knew the game was up.

He was polite at first. When one of the guys tried to convince him I was twenty-one, he just laughed and told us to leave. But when Jack called him a prick, his attitude changed. There was a little pushing and shoving, and then the bouncer came over and we were all dumped out on the street.

"Ignorant bunch of bastards!" one of my workmates shouted at them, but they were already back inside.

It was very late by now, and most of the guys were ready to head home. Jack and I and one other guy went to the fish and chip shop down near the corner of Dundas and Jarvis. After I'd finished my plate of chips, Jack pulled a mickey of rum from his inside pocket and insisted I take a good swig. I had never tasted anything quite like it before. The smell was bad enough, but then my throat began to burn as I tried to swallow down that first big gulp. They were both laughing at the sight of me, bent over and trying my best not to throw up. One of them tried to egg me into taking another, but that one drink was more than enough for me. As soon as the owner saw the bottle in Jack's hand, he threatened to call the cops if we didn't leave immediately.

I didn't think I was all that drunk, but I was certainly a little wobbly. It was getting close to midnight when I waved goodbye to my friends and started for home. I don't know if it was the beer, the rum, or all the greasy chips I'd eaten, but by the time I reached Parliament Street, I had thrown up everything in my stomach. I pitied the store owner who would have to clean up the mess I made in front of his door. Looking at my reflection in the store window, I tried to wipe away the mess and make myself more presentable. I managed to clean the stain off my shirt and pants, but the bits of vomit on my shoes would have to wait until the dizziness went away.

The cool night air helped clear my head, but my stomach was still churning when I reached the back door of our house. I could see light from an upstairs window, but the kitchen was dark and empty. If I was really quiet, I could sneak up to bed without anyone seeing me. I no longer cared if anyone remembered my birthday. All I wanted to do was bury my head in a pillow and maybe then the room would stop spinning.

Even in the dark I knew that kitchen like the back of my hand, yet somehow I managed to bump into a chair as I felt my way across the floor. That's when the lights snapped on and I saw Da standing in the doorway. I could see the disgust on his face as he looked me up and down. "Just look at the state of ya. You should be bloody well ashamed of yourself."

I don't know why I smiled, but it just seemed funny. He had hurt me with his words and fists so many times, but not anymore. I had been brought up to believe that you must never speak back to your father. A smile was not an act of defiance, but somehow I had to show him that he couldn't intimidate me any longer. It had taken me sixteen years to realize that, regardless of what I said or did, he was never going to like me.

When he walked toward me, I didn't try to move. He could hit me as hard as he liked and I wouldn't even raise a hand to defend myself. Maybe it was false courage brought on by the alcohol, but in the moment, I had to show him that I wasn't afraid of him anymore.

Standing in the middle of the kitchen, I waited for the blow to land. But he just stared at me. Whenever Da was angry, he came at me with a fury, ready to let fly with both fists. This time, his demeanour was altogether different. His voice sounded calm as he spoke. "You're sixteen now and it's time for you to go. You can sleep here tonight, but you will pack up your things and be out of this house by the time I get home in the morning."

Maybe I should have spoken up right then, but I was dumbfounded. All I could do was watch him put on his coat and head for the front door. He paused in the hall, and I thought perhaps it had all been some sort of a joke, meant to scare me.

"Don't be here when I get home" were the final words he said before closing the door and heading off to work.

When Rosaleen came into the kitchen, I was bent over the sink, trying not to puke. I didn't have to explain what was going on. She had heard the whole thing from the top of the stairs. I could see she was in a terrible state. Whispering so as not to wake the rest of the family upstairs, she kept telling me that it would be all right, but we both knew that wasn't true. I felt sick to my stomach and my head was splitting, but still the anger welled up inside me. I was angry at Da for his cruelty, angry at myself for my own stupidity, and God help me, I was even angry with Mamie for not being there when I needed her most. The moment the words came out of my mouth, I cursed myself. I could only pray that Mamie would forgive me for thinking such terrible things.

When the sun came up, Rosaleen and I were still sitting at the kitchen table. I was so tired, but I didn't want to lie down, for fear I wouldn't wake up before Da came in the door from work. Rosaleen and I had talked through the night, but in the end, we both knew there was nothing to be done. The atmosphere in our house was like a poison vapour, seeping into every crack and crevice and enveloping everyone it touched. Rosaleen was the only one who could stop it. She couldn't help me, but without her there, the entire family would surely fall to pieces.

❧

I was thankful to have a job to go to that morning. At least I had the next eight hours to think about what to do in the coming days. Rosaleen had given me her last five dollars and stuffed some sandwiches and an apple in a grocery bag, along with my socks and underwear. It is sad to think that everything I had in the world could fit inside one large brown paper bag. When one of the guys saw me coming into the break room with a bag under my arm, he made some joke about me having a lunch big enough for three people.

Fortunately, it was one of our busier mornings and no one had the time to slow down and talk. At lunchtime, I managed to get Wayne on the phone and arrange to stay at his house until I got paid on Friday. I was a little surprised that Wayne and his mother didn't ask more questions. Considering all the times I had shown up at their door unannounced, I guess they already knew how bad things were between me and my da.

It was kind of Mrs. Boland to let me stay even though their flat was barely big enough for the two of them. I had to sleep on the floor, but she gave me an old piece of carpet to put underneath me to keep the dampness away. I only stayed there for three nights, but I will always be thankful to Wayne and his mother for giving me the time I needed to figure out what to do next.

I wasn't planning to tell anyone at work about my plight, but after watching me mope around for days, Jack asked me what was going on. I had this idea that perhaps we could get a place together and split the rent, but he was already living with relatives. When I came into the lunchroom the next morning, he was already there, with the newspaper spread across the table. Together we scanned the classifieds section, looking for rooms for rent. There were quite a few, but we only circled the ones close to the downtown core. I tried to pretend I knew what I was doing, but in reality I didn't have a clue. I was so relieved when Jack said he would help me check a few places after work.

All the rooms look basically the same to me. There was a bed, a dresser, a table, a lamp, and one or two chairs. Thank God Jack was there to ask all the right questions. By the time we were finished, I knew all about mattresses, blankets, sheets, pots and pans, and all the other things I would need on a daily basis. Jack told me that the most important thing to look for was cleanliness. The room might look clean, but he pulled back the blankets to check for any stains on the mattress. How many people shared the washroom in the hall, and how often was it cleaned? Were any meals included in the rent, and what were the rules about cooking in the room?

It was late in the evening by the time we'd looked at most of the boarding houses in the neighbourhood. Thankfully, we finally found a room that seemed to be a good fit, a boarding house near the bottom of Sherbourne Street. The landlady was quite leery of me at first. All of her tenants were older men, and she wasn't convinced that someone so young could pay the rent. After a lengthy negotiation, she finally agreed to let me stay under two conditions: each week's rent would have to be paid in advance, and if the rent was even one day late, I would be evicted immediately.

I moved in on Saturday afternoon, after work. The room was quite small, but at least I could walk to work and save the streetcar fare. The rent had started out at thirty dollars a week for full room and board, but Jack had talked the landlady down to twenty for the room only. I wouldn't be getting any meals, but I could cook in my room if I had my own hot plate.

With my remaining money, I was able to pick up a few cans of vegetable soup, a pound of bologna, a loaf of bread, and some sugar and milk to put in my tea. The tea bags I bought didn't taste as good as loose leaf, but at least there were no leftover bits to skim from the top of the cup. On Saturday night, I might treat myself to an order of fish and chips, but for the rest of the week I had to get by with toast in the morning, a bologna sandwich to take to work, and a saucepan of soup and some crushed-up crackers for dinner. I managed to pick up a two-burner hot plate and an old metal bread box from a second-hand store. After a couple of weeks, I learned a few tricks for finding bargains. Soup was ten cents a can, but if I could find some dented cans, the store owner would sell them to me for half-price. If I couldn't find any that were damaged, I would wait until the clerk was otherwise occupied. A couple of hard taps on the edge of the shelf was usually enough to save me from paying full price.

When I turned out the lights on my first night in my new room, I heard the familiar sound of tapping coming from the linoleum floor. I wasn't sure if it was mice or rats, but I put anything edible inside the bread box, just to be on the safe side.

The landlady gave me clean sheets once a month, but as far as cleaning and washing were concerned, I was on my own. All together, there were four of us sharing a washroom on the second floor. There was only a sink and one of those old-fashioned toilets with a tank suspended high on the wall. When the chain was pulled, the pipes would rattle and the sound of flushing could be heard all over the house. The first time I flushed the toilet in the middle of the night, I was sure I'd woken the whole house. After that, I picked an old coffee can out of the garbage and used it during the night. It was the same thing we had done when I was younger, only now I had to make sure it was empty and hidden behind the dresser before I left for work in the morning.

Our landlady was not the most pleasant woman to deal with. Her abrupt manner reminded me of Sister Agnes, back at St. Martin's. She didn't wear a black habit or carry a cane, but I never doubted that she was the one in charge. Either we followed her rules or we were out on our ear.

She certainly knew all the ways to squeeze every last penny from her tenants. I could use the shower in the basement once a week. Anymore than that would cost me a dollar each time. The front parlour was locked during the day, but for fifty cents I could watch television from seven to ten at night. The telephone in the hall had a lock on the dial, but for ten cents she would remove it — and then stand there to make sure I didn't make a long-distance call.

Even though it had been days since Da threw me out of the house, it didn't really sink in until that first night in the boarding house. When I closed the door, it dawned on me that for the first time in my life, I was truly alone. Sleep had never come easy for me, but that night seemed endless. I finally dozed off after midnight, only to jump awake at the slightest sound. Like every old house, this one had its own unique set of creaks and groans. I wouldn't notice them during the day, but late in the evening, when the air was cool, I could hear the pipes rattle and the wooden floors groan. It was like the house was contracting its limbs as it slowly settled down for the night.

Almost a week passed before I met any of the other tenants in the house. During the work week, I might catch a glimpse of one of them in the hall. Sometimes I regretted not having the money to pay for meals. In the morning I would make some toast on the hot plate. But it wasn't so much the food I missed in the morning. After another long night alone, I just wanted to talk to someone — even a simple good morning from a stranger to break the silence. The kitchen and dining room were at the back of the house, but when I came down the stairs for work, I could smell the coffee and hear the other tenants talking over breakfast. On the weekends, when most of the tenants didn't have to work, the dining room was the noisiest place in the house. I overheard them complaining about the food, but if they wanted to eat, they had to get there before the landlady closed the dining room at eight o'clock sharp. Missing breakfast would mean waiting until dinner was served at six o'clock in the evening.

Early one Saturday morning, my next-door neighbour knocked on my door. We had nodded at each other in the hallway, but we had never spoken. When he asked me downstairs for coffee, I didn't want to seem unfriendly, but I knew the landlady would not be pleased to see one of her non-paying tenants sitting in her dining room. As soon as we walked in, I could feel her watching my every move. It was just after seven o'clock, and already the table was crowded with men. Some of them nodded hallo as we sat down, but most were too busy eating. The landlady placed a stack of toast in the middle of the table, only to see every slice disappear in a matter of seconds. The smell of hot coffee and buttered toast was enough to make my mouth water.

I was surprised when the landlady put a cup of coffee down in front of me. She gave me a half-hearted smile when I said thank you. When someone offered me a piece of toast, the look on her face told me to say no. I was hungry enough to eat a loaf of bread, but I would have to settle for a cigarette to go along with my coffee.

Once all the tenants had their fill, there was time to talk. It seemed that everyone smoked in those days, and soon a thick haze hung over the table. Someone made a crack about me only having a coffee and cigarette. He called it a "whore's breakfast," and almost everyone laughed. His remark only upset the landlady, who made it quite clear that she wouldn't tolerate any bad language in her house.

I didn't go down to the dining room very often, but now that I'd had a chance to meet everyone, I didn't feel quite so alone. The landlady would not allow alcohol in the house, but that didn't prevent some of the guys from sneaking it into their rooms. Everyone was busy working during the week, but on Saturday nights we all got together for a beer and some talk in one of the rooms. I was too young to even go into the beer store, but the guys didn't mind giving me a beer, as long as I brought along an extra pack of cigarettes for all to share. I am sure the landlady had some idea of what was going on, but as long as we kept our voices down and the windows wide open to release the smoke, she never said a word.

Now it made me laugh to think how frightened I had been during my first few days in the house. As it turned out, most of these men were not much different from me. Some were married, but most were single. All of them were from somewhere else. None of them really wanted to be in Toronto, but this was where you came to find work. I hadn't been alone long enough to give a lot of thought to the future, but listening to them talk, I knew there had to be something better than this. Whether single or married, they all seemed to think that their current situation was only temporary. It was something they had to endure until they could go back to whatever life they had left behind. Some of the men had spent years in that boarding house, yet they still hung on to the dream of going home someday. I would laugh right along with them as they talked of their homes and families. At least for a little while, I didn't have to think about all the things I had left behind.

My next-door neighbour, Ron, seemed to be the leader of the pack. He wasn't the biggest or even the oldest, but whenever thing got too loud and boisterous, he was the one to step in and quiet everyone down. Sometimes our little get-together would last late into the night, but eventually someone would decide it was time to go to bed. There were always a few protests as we all returned to our rooms, but slowly the house would begin to settle down. As I lay there in the dark, the night noises didn't bother me anymore. I would never stop missing my brothers and sisters, but now that I had people to talk to, the nights didn't seem so long and sleep came much easier.

Now that I felt comfortable in my new surroundings, the days and nights seemed to fly by. I worked until five o'clock during the week, and sometimes much later if there were extra orders to fill. Saturday, I would be off at one o'clock. Once I had paid my rent and picked up some food for the week, the afternoon was more or less over. If I had a little time to spare, I could hurry down to the library on Gerrard and pick up a few books to read during the coming week. Back in grade eight, Miss Williams got me interested in reading the classics. It seemed like such a long time ago now. By the time school ended, I had read most of the books written by Mark Twain and Robert Louis Stevenson. Once I'd read *The Old Man and the Sea*, I was hooked on the novels of Ernest Hemingway.

Sunday was the only day of the week when I truly dreaded waking up in the morning. If I had somehow forgotten what day it was, there were plenty of church bells to remind me that this was the day to be in church. St. Michael's Cathedral was all the way over on Bond Street, but the sound of the bells seemed to bounce off the buildings and echo throughout the downtown. Once the bells from Our Lady of Lourdes and Sacred Heart chimed in, sleep became impossible. From eight o'clock until noon, the streets were filled with the constant noise of traffic and people coming to and leaving from every church in Cabbagetown. Then, suddenly, everything just stopped. Once church was over, it was like the entire city shutdown for the rest of the day.

The landlady didn't like when I did laundry in the bathroom sink, but if I waited until she went out for morning Mass, I could get all my dirty socks and underwear washed and hung up to dry before she got back. If I spread it out on a chair and kept it near the heating vent, most of my laundry would be dry by Sunday night.

I could read my books and do some laundry, but it was never enough to fill the endless hours. Sometimes I would just sit staring out the window, wondering what was going to become of me. The people walking by on the street all seemed to be in a hurry to get somewhere. They had a purpose in their step, while all I could do was sit there and watch life passing me by. I wasn't a boy anymore, but I didn't feel like a man either. It felt like I was trapped between two worlds. I couldn't seem to let go of the past when all I could see was a bleak and empty future.

On Sunday afternoons, I just had to get away from that boarding house. Yonge Street would be teeming with people and cars during the week, but on Sunday, when everything was closed up tight, I could have the whole sidewalk to myself. I didn't have anywhere to go, but if I could wear myself out walking, maybe I could fall asleep that night.

If the weather was good and I really wanted to stretch my legs, I could head down Yonge Street all the way to Queen and Bay. It would take more than an hour, but it was fascinating to see how the area had changed in just a few short years. Standing on the corner, I could see the old city hall and the courthouse. The stately old brownstone building took up the entire block on the north side of Queen Street. If I arrived at the right time, I could listen to the bell in the clock tower strike the hour, just as it had done for close to sixty-five years.

Look slightly to the west, I could see the new city hall beginning to take shape. Construction had started in the latter part of 1961, and now two massive concave structures were beginning to rise high above the street. Soon these twin high-rise buildings would dwarf everything in the area.

When the weather turned cold and I wanted to be inside, I would wander north to Yorkville. Even on a Sunday afternoon, the coffee houses were open, and with any luck I could find a game of chess. I had learned the game only so I would have an excuse to stay inside one of those tiny cafés on cold afternoons. A cup of coffee cost fifty cents, but if I took small sips, I could make it last throughout the afternoon.

No matter the time of day, there was always an odd assortment of people hanging around the coffee houses in Yorkville. Most were in their twenties or thirties, and listening to them talk, I could tell they were well-educated. The majority seemed to take a dim view of how the country was being run. Any mention of the Diefenbaker government led to a lively debate that could go on for the entire afternoon. I had always thought that politics was boring, but listening to all the differing opinions certainly opened my mind to a world I knew so little about.

If I timed it right, I wouldn't get back to my room until well after six o'clock. Sunday dinner would be over by then, and I wouldn't have to smell the food and hear all the supper noises coming from the dining room. Those long Sunday walks always made me hungry, so I didn't relish the thought of smelling meat and mashed potatoes when all I could look forward to was another night of canned soup and crushed crackers. At least I had my tea and a decent book to read. With any luck, I would fall asleep by midnight and put an end to another long, lonely Sunday.

CHAPTER 16

WHEN THE WEATHER turned cold in late December, Rosaleen stopped by my work to bring me my heavy coat, some socks, and the gloves Mamie had given to me that Christmas when I was working at the drug store. I hadn't thought it was much of a gift at the time, but now they were special. It was the last gift I had from Mamie, and they reminded me of a time when my life was so much simpler.

Da had forbidden all my younger siblings from speaking to me, but Rosaleen said they all missed me just the same. It would be a long time before I saw any the others, but Rosaleen came by every couple of weeks to make sure I was all right. We only talked for a few minutes, but she always left me with a bag of sandwiches and biscuits. I tried to tell myself to save some for later, but within a day they would all be gone.

I appreciated everything Rosaleen gave me, but the socks couldn't have come at a better time. I was down to my last two pairs and they were already falling apart. When I looked in the mirror, I could see that my clothes looked quite worn and I had lost a few pounds, but all in all, I felt good.

The only real problem I had was my feet. My canvas running shoes were good enough in the fall, but when the winter rain and snow came, they leaked like a sieve. If the sidewalk was slushy on the way to work, my feet would be cold and wet all day. When I got back to the boarding house in the evening, it was a relief to finally take off my wet shoes and socks. The landlady turned down the heat at night, but if I left them on the floor vent, they might be dry by morning. I even tried putting my socks on the hot plate while I got dressed in the morning. I turned my back for only a minute and suddenly smoke was rising from my socks and the smell of burning wool filled the air. I turned off the burner, but the landlady was already up the stairs and banging on my door. Thankfully, she didn't actually come into the room, but she did threaten to throw me out if I ever did it again. The whole thing was rather embarrassing, but at least when I put on the socks, my feet were toasty warm for a little while.

Most nights, I would wake up with a tingling pain in my toes. My second pair of socks had holes in the toes, but wrapping a towel around my feet kept them warm and helped me get back to sleep. After Rosaleen brought me new socks, I would have two dry pairs to wear at night even if I got one pair wet during the day. My feet were still red and swollen, but the tingling pain in my toes finally went away. It would not be until January that I would be able to afford to buy a decent pair of second-hand boots.

The closer we came to Christmas, the more depressed I became. Early on, I'd had this notion in my head that maybe my da would relent and let me come home for the holidays. When I spoke to Rosaleen on Christmas Eve, I realized nothing had changed.

My workmates were happy to be off for Christmas and Boxing Day, but I needed to find some way to fill all those empty hours. Even the coffee houses in Yorkville would be closed up tight for the holidays.

Thankfully, I managed to get to the library on Gerrard Street just before they closed early on Christmas Eve. I knew my way around the library by now, and it only took me a minute to find what I was looking for. Reading Hemingway's *A Farewell to Arms* was not the way I envisioned spending Christmas, but at least I had something to help take my mind off my family for the next few days.

On the way back to the boarding house, I finally decided to take the landlady up on her offer of Christmas dinner. Three dollars for a plate of corn beef and cabbage seemed like a lot of money to me, but it would be better than eating soup and crackers alone in my room on Christmas Day.

I was just settling down to start the book when Ron and a couple of the guys came banging on my door. I could tell they had been drinking most of the afternoon, and now they wanted to go out for fish and chips before the shop closed up for Christmas Eve. I only had a few dollars left to get me through the holidays, but it was the excuse I needed to get out of my room.

Ron didn't seem all that drunk, but the other two were taking forever to get going down the street. One of them had a flask of whiskey under his coat and kept stopping to take a swig. He offered me some, but after my first experience with the hard stuff, I had decided it was best if I stuck with beer.

I wasn't really hungry until we were a block away and I got my first whiff of fish and chips. Suddenly, all I could think about was devouring a big bag of chips smothered in salt and vinegar. I was hoping Samantha would be working behind the counter that night. If the boss wasn't around, she always gave me an extra big order of chips. She was much older than I was, but we seemed to have a lot in common. She had been twenty years old when she immigrated from Scotland in the late fifties. I don't think she had many friends, and hearing her talk, I could tell she still missed her family. She often said I reminded her of the brother she hadn't seen in many years.

It was just after six when we got to the shop, but there was still a customer inside waiting for his order, so we thought we had made it, but the door was locked. I saw Samantha working near the back and tried knocking on the glass to get her attention. I think she wanted to let us in, but her boss, behind the counter, waved us away. The smart thing would have been to just walk away, but my drunken friends were having none of that. Soon they were both banging on the glass and rattling the door handle, hoping the owner would see how desperate we were for something to eat.

Maybe if the owner had stayed behind the counter, they would have given up, but when he came out holding a baseball bat, matters quickly got worse. "Get the fuck out of here or else I'll give you some of this," he yelled at us through the window.

The guys were so angry by now that they just kept rattling the door and banged even louder. One of them must have pulled too hard, because he ripped the handle right off the door. The owner went back behind the counter and picked up the telephone to call the police. The moment he mentioned the word *cops*, we knew it was time to get out of there in a hurry. Ron and I tried walking away fast, but one of our drunken friends decided that if he couldn't get food, at least he could keep the door handle.

We were a couple of blocks up Jarvis when the police car pulled up beside us. We might have thought the whole thing was funny, but our laughter ended when one of the officers ordered us all up against the wall. We might have been able to talk our way out of it if the guys had just kept their mouths shut. Judging by their demeanour, I don't think the two officers were that interested in locking us up over something so trivial as breaking a door handle. Ron and I tried to explain what had happened and promised we would pay for the damage. Unfortunately, when one of the officers tried to take the handle, our drunken friend called him an asshole and refused to give it up. About ten minutes later, the paddy wagon showed up and we were all handcuffed and taken off to jail.

It took a while to complete the paperwork and search each one of us. I didn't know why they had to take our belts and shoelaces. By nine o'clock that night, we were all placed in a cell at 52 Division on Queen Street West.

If I thought the smell inside the paddy wagon was bad, it was nothing compared to the odour that permeated every inch of the cell block at the back of the station. The stench of urine and vomit was almost overwhelming. There were only three cells, and two of them were full already. As soon as the guard opened the door to the cell block, the jeering began. Some of the inmates were laughing at us, while others were cursing and screaming at the guards, demanding to be set free. It felt like we had entered an insane asylum. When the guard put the four of us in the last empty cell, I actually felt somewhat relieved. I was still scared, but at least I didn't have to share a cell with any of those lunatics.

Just when I thought things couldn't get any worse, the desk sergeant seemed to take an almost sadistic pleasure in giving us even more bad news. "You should make yourselves comfortable," he said. "You're going to be here until the twenty-seventh of December, when the court reopens after the holidays."

My friends were all laughing and joking about getting a free Christmas dinner in jail. I tried to smile and show the guys that I was just as tough as they were, but when the guard slammed the cell door shut and dimmed the lights, I was overwhelmed with fear and anxiety. I could handle the three days in jail, but if I didn't show up for work on the twenty-seventh, I was bound to lose my job and maybe even my room at the boarding house.

They had confiscated our watches, so it was impossible to know what time it was. There wasn't much in the cell other than a metal toilet bowl and a series of wooden slabs protruding from the wall.

They left us with a blanket each, and soon I could hear snoring as two of the guys fell into a drunken sleep. I wrapped myself in a blanket, but I was far too anxious and afraid to even lie down.

Ron was never much of a talker, but I was grateful to hear his reassuring voice in the dark. "Don't worry, kid. It'll be over before you know it."

It always galled me when the guys called me kid. Any other time, I would have come back with some smart remark, but sitting there staring at the iron bars, I just wanted this all to be over.

I can't be sure, but I think it must have been after eleven o'clock when I heard the key rattling in the iron door of our cell. The lights came on, and our jailer shouted at us all to stand up. Ron and I were still wide awake, but it took a lot of shaking to get the others on their feet. Once my eyes adjusted to the light, I could see a second person standing in the open door. It was the owner of the fish and chip shop, and judging by the look on his face, he wasn't at all pleased to be standing in a jail on Christmas Eve.

"Is this the four of them?" The guard told us to step forward so the man could get a better look.

"That's them," he said.

I thought he was only there to identify us, but then the guard said, "Mr. Stancous here has agreed to drop the charges as long as you pay for a new lock."

I realized that we were about to be set free. The other two were still a little bleary, but Ron and I said yes immediately.

As soon as we were back on the street, I was able to catch Mr. Stancous as he was getting into his car. I could see he was in a hurry to get out of there, but I told him how thankful I was and that we would pay him as soon as we had the money.

I didn't know Mr. Stancous, but in all the times I had seen him in his fish and chip shop, I had never seen him smile. Now he smiled when he said, "It's not me you should be thanking. It was

Samantha who convinced me that no one should have to spend Christmas in jail."

I couldn't think of anything to say.

"Have a merry Christmas and stay out of trouble," he said, and then he drove away.

The landlady didn't like any noise in the house after ten o'clock at night. The guys used to joke about how the old bat could hear a pin drop from twenty yards away. By the time we made it back to the boarding house, it was two in the morning, but somehow we were all able to get back to our rooms without waking a soul. For days I had been dreading the thought of being alone for the holidays. Now, I couldn't wait to get back in my room and close the door behind me. It was still just a cold and empty room, but it was far better than spending Christmas behind bars.

By the start of the new year, I was beginning to find some peace within myself. I had been on my own for three months, and once I'd finally rid myself of the notion of ever going home, I just stopped being afraid all the time.

In January 1964, the warehouse was operating at full capacity. From morning to night, the orders just kept on coming. Every week we were getting hours of overtime just to keep up. All that extra pay meant I no longer had to live on soup and crackers. For fifteen dollars more a week, I could finally afford to have dinner in the dining room each night. The meals weren't very good, but at least I didn't have to go to bed hungry anymore.

The work could be quite dull and repetitive, but whenever the receptionist came into the warehouse, she grabbed our attention. From the moment Sharon walked through the door from the office, we just couldn't take our eyes off of her. The other women in the front office called her a floozy, but the guys loved to watch her strutting across the floor with her backside swaying under her tight skirt. She was a little on the plump side, but that only made her breasts look bigger. The buttons on her blouse always looked like they were about to pop open. She never hurried her steps, making sure that every man in the place got a good look at her. Judging by her sly smile, I'm sure she knew exactly what she was doing.

I managed to make a little small talk with her one morning when I was sent to the office. She said something about liking my Irish accent, but I hardly heard her words. I was too busy looking down the front of her blouse as she leaned over her desk. When the boss stuck his head out the door, I knew it was time to get back to work.

When the catering truck showed up that afternoon, there was the usual mad scramble to get a coffee and a have a smoke before our fifteen-minute break was over. The women usually stayed inside, but that afternoon we all watched as Sharon came out to the loading dock and headed straight to where I was sitting. When she sat down on the platform, her skirt rode up so high, I practically swallowed my cigarette. I wanted to say something clever, but nothing came to me.

"Can I have one of your cigarettes?" she asked.

I was keenly aware that every man in the yard was watching as I fumbled around, trying to dig my cigarettes and matches out of my pocket. My hand shook as I tried to light her cigarette, but when she leaned in and cupped her hands around mine, the softness of her skin and the smell of her perfume were almost overwhelming. I only wished it could have lasted a little longer, but already the foreman was ordering us back to work.

The guys didn't help my confidence by giving me a hard time all afternoon. I knew they were only kidding when they called her a man-eater. At least Jack didn't laugh, but he did warn me to be careful around her. Of course, I wasn't listening. I was too busy fantasizing about being in bed with her. As with most sixteen-year-old boys, sex was never far from my mind. If I could just get her alone, maybe my daydreams would finally come true.

In the days ahead, I could hardly wait for the afternoon break, when she would smile and sit next to me for a few minutes. I would have a Coke and a sandwich waiting for her so she didn't have to waste what little time we had together by standing in line. Sometimes she would brush her hand across my leg and lean in so close that I could feel her breast against my arm.

When I finally worked up the nerve to ask her out, I thought I was prepared for any answer she might give me, but I never expected she would actually laugh in my face. "You're sweet to ask," she said, "but I already have a steady boyfriend, and I would never go out with anyone from work."

I don't know why I apologized, but I did. For once I was actually glad to hear the foreman yelling at us to get back inside.

Thankfully the weather turned cold enough to keep her inside for a few days. In spite of my disappointment, I still missed talking to her. She would always wave at me when I saw her in the warehouse, but when I came out for the afternoon break, she was already sitting and eating a sandwich with someone else. Sharon's newfound friend seemed like a nice guy. Every afternoon, I would see him heading for the bathroom, trying to smarten himself up before he headed for the loading dock. All the guys tried to warn him, but just like me, he would have to spend a lot of money on sandwiches and Coke before he learned the truth about sweet, young Sharon.

I don't remember who mentioned it first, but by the beginning of February, there was a rumour floating around that the warehouse might be closing. The foreman kept denying it, but by mid-month, the number of orders being filled was steadily decreasing, and there was no stock coming in to refill the shelves.

I don't think anyone was surprised when the foreman came into the lunchroom and announced that the warehouse would be closing by the end of the summer. Apparently, the company's other warehouse, up near Dufferin and Lawrence, was being expanded and modernized to take over the job of filling orders for the entire city.

Some of the more senior people would remain to close out the old warehouse. The rest of us could finish out this month, but after that, we were done. The news was disheartening, to say the least, but at least I had a couple of weeks to look for a new job.

Every morning I would scan the newspaper, looking for any kind of factory work. It was not easy to look for a new job when I was supposed to be at the warehouse from eight in the morning until five in the afternoon. Thankfully, the foreman understood the problem and was willing to let me go a little early in the day. I had a couple of promising leads, but everywhere I went, they wanted someone older, bigger, or stronger. When a manager looked across his desk, all he saw was some skinny kid who looked like he belonged in school, not on a factory floor. Even if I managed to pique someone's interest, the moment they asked about a driver's licence, I was done.

Rosaleen still dropped by from time to time, but I could see the strain of taking care of her own baby along with our brothers and sister was taking a toll on her health. She had always been a kind and gentle person, but after months of worry and fatigue, she could barely smile anymore. I never wanted to lie to my sister, but I knew I couldn't add to her worries. I told her I still had a job and would be moving to the new warehouse at the end of the month. To compound my lie, I told her I was looking for a new boarding house and, although it was too far away to visit, I promised to call her every few weeks.

Each time I left work for an interview, I was losing more pay. Soon, I could no longer afford the boarding house meals and had to go back to a diet of soup and crackers every night. I cut back as much as I could, but all I was really doing was postponing the inevitable. When rent came due at the end of March, I was out of work and had just five dollars left in my pocket. I was hoping that when the landlady saw me out looking for work every day, she might let me stay longer, but as she had so often said, she was running a business, not a charity. I could stay for the weekend, but after that I had to go.

CHAPTER 17

ON THE FIRST Monday in April, I packed my few bits of clothes into a canvas bag. I knew the blankets didn't belong to me, but I was sure to need one for the cold nights ahead, so I stuffed one in my bag. I didn't need the frying pan or the pot or any of the dishes or cutlery I had managed to accumulate, so I took them all out to the alley and threw them in the dumpster. At least I had the satisfaction of not leaving anything behind for that nasty woman. The hot plate was the only thing of value I still owned. It was awkward to carry around under my arm, but it would be worth it if I could get a couple of dollars for it from the pawn shop.

Standing alone on the street, I felt the fear welling up inside me. All the self-confidence I had built up in the past few months simply vanished. In the six months I had been on my own, I had held on to a faint hope that somehow things would get better. Now it took all I had to stop trembling and try to focus my thoughts on just getting through this one day. There was time enough to think about tomorrow later.

My mind kept going to all those desperate men I saw wandering the streets of Cabbagetown each and every day. On my way to work, I would see them begging for money on the corner. In the evening they lined the street in front of the shelter, hoping to find a bed for the night. If I walked down Yonge Street later at night, I would see men sleeping on the air vents, trying to catch the warm air billowing up from the subway below. Most had been on the street for years, yet somehow they kept surviving. I had no idea how to live on the street, but somehow I had to find a way to survive the days and weeks ahead.

All day long I just wandered around, too afraid to stop and talk to anyone. At least I had some cigarettes to smoke to help keep my mind off food. The few dollars I had hidden in my sock was meant to last as long as possible, but by nightfall, I was so hungry I couldn't resist buying a hot dog from a street vendor. I still felt an emptiness in the pit of my stomach, but I had to resist the urge to buy more food.

When the night finally came I was dog-tired, but I knew I had to keep moving. It had been a mild day, but when the sun went down and the winds picked up over Lake Ontario, the night air became damp and chilly. After midnight I finally found a doorway that offered some protection from the wind. I curled up into a ball with my stolen blanket pulled around me. As I lay there shivering, I prayed for morning to come. I tried to close my eyes and think about those warm summer days when the whole family had been together on Kew Beach. The sand had been so hot under our feet, we'd had to run into the water to cool them down. Mamie had been there, handing out sandwiches and telling me to put on a shirt before I got a sunburn.

I tried not to think about Da. I had cursed his name so many times in the days and weeks after he threw me out of the house that now it was hard to think of him without getting angry. It took me a long time to realize that all that pent-up rage was only making me feel worse. I couldn't change the past, and if I was ever going to feel better about myself, I had to clear my mind of all those hateful thoughts.

I have no idea what time it was when I felt a hand shaking me awake. For a moment, I thought I was having that same old terrible dream where a shadowy figure was standing over me, ready to strike me down. When I opened my eyes and saw the man leaning over me, I instantly drew my arms up to cover my head from any blows that might come. I think my sudden move startled him, as he backed away from me. I was wide awake now, my guard up in case he might still come at me.

"You haven't been on the street very long, have ya?" he said.

As I tried to stand up, I wanted to say something to stop him laughing at me, but all I could think about was the pain and stiffness I felt in every joint. Once I stepped out of the shadows of the doorway and he got a good look at me, he stopped laughing. He picked my blanket up off the ground, and I grabbed it out of his hands, thinking he was trying to steal it.

"Relax, kid. I don't want your blanket, but if you're gonna sleep on the ground, you have to put some newspaper or cardboard under ya to keep the dampness down."

I didn't get it at first, but when I felt my damp blanket, I understood.

Now that I could see him in the light of the street lamp, he didn't seem all that intimidating. His tattered old coat hung below his knees, and a woollen toque was pulled down over his ears. Judging from his thin, wrinkled face and the grey stubble on his chin, he looked to be well past his prime. When he asked me for a smoke, I was happy to give it to him. I just wanted him to stay with me until the sun came up. As long as he kept talking, I didn't have to think about the hunger in my belly and the stiffness in my bones.

He smoked half the cigarette, then stubbed it out and stuck the butt in his pocket. I thought he was going to leave, but he stood there staring at me as I jumped about trying to get some feeling back in my legs.

"Are you hungry, kid?"

I was shivering so much I could barely get the words out. In that moment, I would have given up my soul for some hot food and a cup of tea, but I could only nod my head. He was laughing again, but I didn't care.

"Okay," he said. "You're going to have to do a little hard work, but it will be worth it in the end."

By the time I'd packed up my meagre belongings and stuffed the wet blanket into my bag, I had to run to catch up to him. We hardly spoke, but as the first signs of daylight approached, he started moving even faster. When we reached King Street, he finally slowed down and told me where we were going.

The St. Lawrence Market was just south of King Street, on Jarvis. The market opened every morning at seven, but if we got there around dawn on a Tuesday or Thursday, when the new produce was delivered, there was a good chance we could find some work unloading the trucks and getting everything ready for sale.

My new-found friend was right about the hard work. That first hour was spent lugging fifty-pound bags of potatoes from the back of a truck and stacking them on a wooden pallet. Fortunately, there was a forklift there to carry them to the stand inside the market. The baskets of apples were a little lighter and easier to handle, but they had to be carried, one at a time, all the way down to the fruit stand near the end of the aisle. It was already past six when the final trucked backed into the loading dock. They didn't have to tell us what was onboard. As soon as they opened the cargo door, we were hit by the strong odour of fish. They gave us each an apron to wear, but by the time we'd finished, we smelled like we had been dipped in a can of sardines.

One of the vendors gave me a couple of bruised apples to stick in my bag, but when the supervisor called us all together, I was hoping to get at least a few dollars for all the hard work. When he handed us each a paper ticket, I thought it was some kind of a joke. There were eight of us working that morning, but other than me, they all seemed pleased to have a ticket in their hands. I stared at this little ticket stub that looked like something you'd get at a movie theatre.

One of the guys started laughing at me when he saw my confusion. "Don't look so glum, kid. This will get you the best breakfast you've ever had," he said, waving his ticket stub in my face.

Thankfully, we didn't have far to walk. The restaurant was just around the corner, on King Street, but rather than go in the front door, the eight of us were told to go around back. I guess the owner didn't want us smelling up his restaurant, but there was a table set up for us near the back of the kitchen. The waiter didn't look too pleased to be serving our ragtag group. He took our tickets and slapped down a plate of scrambled eggs in front of each of us. Then he placed a big jug of coffee and a stack of bread in the middle of the table. All of it was gone in an instant. No one talked. We just kept eating. That arrogant little shit of a waiter made it quite clear that we had to eat in a hurry and be out of there before any of the paying customers saw us.

I wish I knew the name of the man who saved me from the hunger and cold that morning. The other men disappeared after our hasty breakfast, but he and I stayed together for the rest of the morning. He wasn't unkind, but I sensed that he preferred being alone. Every time he looked ready to leave, I ask him another question, hoping he would stay just a little longer. By noon, we had walked all the way over to the edge of Chinatown, near Spadina Avenue and Queen Street. He showed me a tiny shop where I could get some leftover food if I came just before they closed at midnight. We sat on the curb, sharing my last cigarette, and then he was gone. I hoped to see him again, but that was the last time I ever laid eyes on him.

The days and weeks ahead were not easy, but thanks to my nameless friend, I did learn a few little tricks to help me survive on the streets of Cabbagetown. To clean up or use the toilet, it was always best to head for the department stores along Yonge Street. With so many customers to deal with, the staff were too busy to notice some scruffy kid heading for the washroom. It was best to pick the stall farthest from the door, where I could take my time doing my business and not be seen when someone came in. After I was done, I would listen for the sound of footsteps. Once the coast was clear, I could wash my face and neck and run a wet comb through my tangled hair. It didn't do much to improve my appearance, but after a long night on the street, it was good to feel the warm water putting a little life back into my tired body. If I went to the Harbour Light Mission on a Saturday afternoon, I could have a shower, but during the week, the sink in the department store washroom would have to do.

When the bars closed after midnight, they stacked their empty bottles outside the back door, ready for pickup the next morning. If you knew your way around the alleys behind Yonge Street, it was easy to fill a bag with empty bottles to cash in for a dollar or two.

I tried to hang on to what little money I had, but on rainy days, I headed straight for the Rio Theatre, near Yonge and College. I didn't like spending fifty cents for admission, but on a wet afternoon, sitting in a warm theatre watching the same two movies over and over again was a lot better than wandering the streets, trying to find shelter.

It didn't matter what movie was playing. The heat inside the theatre would put me to sleep in no time at all. My friend from the market had warned me about the perverts who hung around the Rio, but the first time I felt a hand on my leg, I froze. I stared at the screen, hoping he would leave me alone. When his hand started moving up toward my crotch, I was terrified, but I knew exactly what I had to do. I swung my arm around and hit him with all the force I could muster. I couldn't make out his face in the darkness, but as soon as the back of my fist struck his nose, he pulled his hand away from my leg. I was ready to lash out again, but he jumped up and headed down the aisle, holding his hand over his nose. It would happen again, in the park and even at the homeless shelter, but once they saw I could defend myself, they left me alone.

I hated to leave the warmth of the movie theatre, especially if it was raining outside, but if I wanted a bed for the night, it was best to be at the men's mission by seven in the evening. There were only fifty beds in the place, and when the doors finally opened at nine, you had better be prepared for the pushing and shoving as you fought your way forward in the line.

If I managed to get a bed, I was still in for a long restless night. The mattress was covered in a rubberized sheet to protect against vomit and urine stains. There was nothing else on the bed other than a single woollen blanket. They insisted we take off our boots, but keeping our clothes on was the only way to ensure they wouldn't be stolen in the middle of the night. I used my canvas bag as a pillow. It wasn't very comfortable to sleep on, but if I kept it tucked under my head, I had less chance of being robbed.

All night long a steady line of men, coughing and wheezing and gagging, headed for the washroom. By the time they woke us all at seven, the smell in the building was almost overwhelming. It was hard to hold back the urge to pee during the night, but it was not a good idea to go to the toilet in the dark. If I could hang on until morning, at least I could see the floor and avoid the puddles of urine and the splatters of feces and vomit around the toilet bowl.

As bad as it was, it was better than sleeping outside on a rainy night. Before they put us out in the early morning, they always gave us a bowl of porridge and a mug of coffee. It almost made me smile to think of how I used to turn up my nose at this grey pasty stuff. Now I gobbled down every spoonful and would have taken more, if they had given it to me.

Many nights, I couldn't get a place in the shelter. If I didn't want to spend a cold night sleeping on the cement sidewalk, there was only one other alternative.

Whenever I entered Allan Gardens, I was reminded of the time Jimmy and I had gone there in search of his father. By day, it looked like any one of the many small parks you could find throughout the city. It was only its proximity to the downtown that made it different. Once the sun went down, it became a refuge for all the homeless who had nowhere else to go.

The night people in Allan Gardens tended to be older men who generally kept to themselves. It took a lot to gain their trust, but after I'd been on the street a few weeks, they began to look at me as one of their own. Even then, I had to be very careful when I came to the park looking for a place to sleep. Johnny Forty Coats was long gone, but now there were many other men who ruled their own little section of the park. There were many benches and picnic tables, but picking the wrong place to sleep could get you beaten or stabbed. Out on the street these men were just faceless bums, lost in the crowd, but in the park they were a force to be reckoned with. When you entered their domain, you'd best follow the rules if you wanted to make it through the night.

These were tough old men who knew how to survive in even the harshest of times. Most were ragged and dirty, their blackened fingers and blotchy skin evidence of exposure to the elements and years of alcohol or drug abuse. They were always wary of strangers, but once they knew you were not a threat, they would open up enough to allow you a glimpse into their world.

Some nights it was just too cold to sleep. In the early morning hours, all I could do was keep moving around, trying to stop the shivering, as I watched the sky and waited for the sun to come up. If we could find some dry wood to burn, we would light a fire in one of the forty-five-gallon drums the city put out for garbage cans.

Everyone crowded around it, trying to get close to the heat while making sure the light was hidden from any police cars that might be cruising the surrounding streets. A few of the men had bottles hidden under their coats. They would take a swig when they thought nobody was looking. If they knew you well, they might offer you a drink. The first time I was offered a swig, I had no idea what it was, but the burning sensation in my throat made me feel warm for a little while. Thankfully, someone had warned me to take only a small sip. Take a big gulp of another man's bottle and you could find yourself lying in a bloody heap, somewhere out there in the dark.

The cops rarely entered the park at night, but as soon as the sun rose, it was time to move on. Anyone foolish enough to be sleeping on a bench in the daylight, when the cops came through to clear the park of what they called undesirable people, could expect to deal with the business end of a nightstick.

During my first few weeks on the street, I kept my promise to call my Rosaleen. Sometimes I thought my brothers and sisters had forgotten all about me. Still, it was nice to hear that the younger ones were all doing well in school. Fred was in grade eleven now, and Marie was just starting high school. Johno loved playing the bars every night, but it paid next to nothing. With Da in and out of hospital, Johno had to leave the band and find a full-time job. Michael would be coming back from the Bahamas sometime in the summer. Rosaleen made me promise to come and see him when he returned, but I knew I never would.

The news about Da was never good. He had spent a week in the hospital with pneumonia, and now he was home, still too weak to return to work. According to Rosaleen, it didn't look like he would ever be well enough to return to his job with the city.

Every time Rosaleen talked about Da, it was hard to control the sarcasm in my voice. I knew she was on my side, but despite that, she refused to listen to any negative comments I made about Da. When she told me how sick he was, I tried to pretend I didn't care, but deep down inside, I still worried about him. Sometimes when I closed my eyes late at night, I could see him in those long-ago times, when he would come up the stairs after the late shift and make us kids laugh as we wrestled around on the bed.

Whenever Rosaleen asked about my job in the new factory, I tried to sound cheerful and positive, but after so many weeks, it became harder and harder to maintain the charade. When she asked too many questions, I tried to change the subject, but I could tell she was beginning to see through all my lies. When we talked at the end of June, I finally told her the whole truth. She said that she would talk to Da again, but we both knew that it wouldn't change anything. She made me promise to call back, but when I hung up, I knew this would be the last time we spoke. It was time to stop deluding myself with false hope and to face reality. I was never going home again.

Through May and June it never seemed to stop raining. By day, all I could do was wander from one place to another, always in search of food and a dry spot where I could sit and rest. I wasn't doing any harm, but within a few minutes, there was always someone there telling me to move along.

Most nights, it was too wet to build a fire in the park. There was never an empty bench, but there were plenty of trees where I could hunker down under the branches and hope to find some sleep before the new dawn arrived. Sometimes in that moment between sleep and wakefulness, I could hear Mamie's voice calling me to come downstairs for something to eat. For that split second, it seemed so real. Then I opened my eyes, and it was gone. When the sun rose above the horizon, it was time to leave the park and start the cycle all over again.

The jeans I wore were all I had left of the clothes I'd packed back in April. Everything else was so filthy and worn out, it barely kept me warm anymore. One Saturday morning, I got to the men's mission early enough to get in line for a hot shower. Afterward, I was able to find an overcoat, a shirt, and a pair of socks in the donation bin. It wasn't much, but for the first time in many days, I actually felt alive.

When summer arrived to take away the dampness, I thought things would get better. One morning in early July, I was wandering the back alleys, looking for empty bottles, when suddenly I felt my stomach begin to churn. I hadn't felt well all morning, but I thought it was just the hunger. If I could only get enough money to buy a chocolate bar, I knew I'd be fine. Then the dizziness hit me, and I had to grab the wall before I fell over. I felt something rising in my throat, and just as I bent forward, the vomit came spewing out of me. I was still a little dizzy, but with my stomach now empty, it seemed like the worst was over. It was a warm, dry summer morning, yet I felt a chill running through my body. I thought if I could get to the Rio Theatre and stay off my feet for a few hours, I was sure to feel better.

The next thing I remember was being jarred awake by the sound of an explosion. I was frightened for a moment, but then I realized the noise was coming from the war movie playing on the screen. I had no idea how long I had been asleep, but when I got back outside, it was already getting dark. I had a headache, but that was probably from the chocolate bar I had eaten earlier. I was still very hungry, but I took that as a good sign that my stomach had settled down.

It was too late to get into the homeless shelter, but thankfully, it was a warm night. If I hurried, I could get to Allan Gardens before all the good sleeping spots were taken.

Warm summer nights always brought more street people into the park. All of my usual sleeping spots were gone by the time I arrived, but there was a huge hothouse near the corner of the park. It took a little prodding around in the dark, but I managed to find a flat area next to the outer walls. The grass was damp, but if I kept my back up against the wall, some of the residual heat from the building would keep me warm during the night.

Sometime in the night, I was awakened by a commotion. Just as I opened my eyes, I could hear someone cursing. Before I could move, hands grabbed my coat and dragged me across the ground. All I could see in the dark was a large, imposing figure standing over me. Every time I tried to get up, he kicked at me and screamed, and then threw me back down. I managed to deflect a kick from my face, but his boot glanced off my ear and the side of my head. I blocked the blows to my head with my arms, but he just kept kicking me in the chest and stomach. His words didn't make a lot of sense, but the message was clear. This was his sleeping spot, and any bastard who tried to steal it was in for the beating of his life.

I have no doubt that he would have kicked me to death if someone hadn't finally pulled him away from me. I should have retrieved my blanket, but I just wanted to get away from this lunatic before he came back to finish me off.

The days that followed were some of the worst I can remember. With every breath, pain shot through my ribs. Every bone in my body hurt, but if I laid down for too long, it was difficult to get moving again. I couldn't work at the market, but I did manage to scrounge some bread and a few pieces of fruit to keep me going through those long days and nights. I knew I needed to rest, but I was too afraid to go near the park, or even to the homeless shelter. Every face I saw appeared hostile. I has this uncontrollable fear that everyone was out to hurt me. My paranoia kept telling me it wasn't safe to be around these desperate men. I had gotten away once, but next time one of them might actually kill me.

Through all of that, I don't believe I ever really understood how truly desperate my life had become. For days, I just wandered from place to place, never really caring about anything except finding something to eat and somewhere I could rest and feel safe. I stopped only when heat and exhaustion forced me to rest. If I could just get off my feet and sit in the shade for a few minutes, I would think, I would be ready to move on. The shops were always busy during the day, and sure enough, it wasn't long before a shop owner came out and demanded I get away from his doorway.

It was during this time that I saw Samantha, the waitress from the fish and chip shop, coming up the steps from the King Street subway station. Hoping that she would remember me from all the times we had talked in the shop, I said hallo and waved. She looked right at me and then started walking faster. I thought if I could catch up to her, she might recognize me, but she just kept speeding up. I was still following her when I caught a glimpse of myself in a store window. When I saw the pathetic figure staring back at me, I understood why she'd run away. I had been wandering around in a daze for so long, I didn't realize how filthy I had become. There was dried blood on the side of my face, and my cheek was still bruised and swollen. I barely recognized myself through all the dirt and grime. I didn't blame Samantha for running away. To her, I was just another one of those smelly old bums she saw every day on the streets of Cabbagetown.

That night, I found refuge in a back alley behind the bus station on Bay Street. After midnight, the rain began to fall. It started slowly, but in the predawn hours it became a steady, unrelenting downpour. The cardboard I had over me protected me at first, but as the night wore on, I could feel the rain seeping in around me. I should have gotten up and moved around, but as I lay there on the cold, wet ground and the numbness slowly took over my body, I felt only a strange calm. Every part of me was soaking wet, yet

I didn't feel cold. Something inside told me it was time to stop fighting and just let myself go. The cold and the rain didn't matter anymore. All I had to do was close my eyes and let sleep take me to a place where I wouldn't have to feel pain or hunger or loneliness ever again.

Maybe it was divine intervention or maybe it was simple good luck, but if that garbage truck hadn't entered the alley in the early morning hours, I wouldn't be alive to tell my story. The sound of screeching brakes frightened me awake and brought me back to reality. The truck would have run right over me if the driver hadn't seen movement in the beam of his headlights.

He sounded anxious as he pulled away the cardboard and helped me to my feet. "Don't you know you could be run over, lying there like that!"

I guess I should have been grateful, but in that moment, I really didn't care what he thought. Now that I was up and moving, the numbness was gone and my whole body shivered in the freezing cold. Any thoughts of giving up were gone. I had to get away from this dark place and get some warmth back into my body.

The rain stopped just after dawn, and by seven the bus station was just starting to come to life. With the constant flow of passengers through the terminal, it was easy enough to get inside and find some heat in the crowded waiting room. I kept moving around in the hope that no one would notice me. After an hour, my clothes were still damp, but I could feel the stiffness leaving my body.

By noon, the streets and sidewalks were dry from the hot summer sun. I couldn't do anything about my bruised face or the soreness in my ribs, but I thought if I could just get inside the shelter and clean myself up, maybe I would start to feel better.

I thought I had gotten over my fears, but standing in line with all those men still felt very unnerving. I could sense my panic building as the crowd continued to close in around me. When the door finally opened and the shoving began, I had to fight an overwhelming urge to just run away.

It had taken hours of waiting, but when I finally felt that hot water cascading over my weary body, it was worth it. I wanted to wash away the stink of the street and try to feel human again.

Later, when the Salvation Army lady saw the bloodstains on my collar, she let me pick through the clothes bin. I was hoping to find a heavier coat or some socks, but they were always the first things to go. I couldn't find any clothes, but thankfully I still had my canvas bag with Mamie's picture stowed away safely inside. I was nervous about spending the night surrounded by all these men, but if I wanted something to eat, I would have to stay there until the morning.

❧

I can't pinpoint exactly when it happened, but one day I just decided I was fed up with being hungry all the time. It had taken some time to get over the aches and pains and feel well enough to work at the St. Lawrence Market, but getting breakfast twice a week and the odd bowl of porridge at the shelter was never enough to keep me going through all those empty days. From dawn to dusk, all I could think about was food. When darkness came, I was so exhausted that I could sleep almost anywhere. Those few hours of rest were the only time I could escape the hunger in my belly.

I had always told myself I would never beg for money, but when you haven't had anything to eat in a couple of days, you soon forget your pride. I thought it would be easy to stand on the corner of Queen and Yonge with my hand out, asking for money.

As it turned out, this and every other intersection along Yonge Street was already staked out by beggars, and they didn't take kindly to anyone trying to invade their space. When a big guy grabbed me and pushed me against the wall, I thought I was in for another beating. But at the last second, he dropped his fist and let me loose. Luckily for me, it was someone I had met in the shelter. I didn't know his name, but he had given me some helpful advice the first night we met. I guess he saw me as some young, naive kid who didn't have a clue about anything. He was never much of a talker, but he did teach me how to avoid the bullies in line and how to safeguard my stuff while I slept.

I might have avoided a beating that day, but I was still hungry and penniless. If I couldn't beg, I knew there was only one other way to make a little money. I had stolen my fair share of apples and oranges and dozens of empty bottles, but if I wanted to end my hunger, I had to steal something that would get me more than a few measly pennies.

As I entered the ground floor in Eaton's, I could feel myself shaking. I knew exactly what I wanted to steal, but first I had to calm myself down.

I was familiar with the layout of the place, and if all went according to plan, I could grab what I needed and be out the door in five minutes. There was always a security guard on duty, so I waited until I saw him moving down the floor before I made my move toward the jewellery counter. The moment the saleswoman turned her back, I snatched a watch from the rack and jammed it into my pocket. The door was just steps away, but I told myself not to run. Once I was back on the street, I walked faster and faster until I reached the pawnshop near the corner of Church and Queen.

The man behind the counter didn't say a word as he inspected the watch. Maybe I should have kept my mouth shut, but instead I gave him this long-winded story about the watch being mine and how I needed to sell it to get my bus fare home.

"I'll give you four dollars for it," he finally said.

I thought it was worth a little more, but judging by the look on his face, this was not the time to haggle.

I thought he actually believed my story, but just as he was handing me the money, he smiled. "The next time you need bus fare, kid, make sure you bring me a more expensive watch."

Sitting in the fish and chip shop, it was hard not to cram every morsel straight down my throat. It was the best meal I had ever eaten. I didn't care who was watching — I couldn't get it into me fast enough. When it was all gone, I even licked the greasy wrapping paper. I had been hoping my friend Samantha might be there so I could explain our encounter, but the lady behind the counter told me Samantha had moved on to another job.

Over the next couple of weeks, I alternated between Eaton's and Simpson's. After a few successful robberies, I began to feel a little more brazen. Then I tried to snatch one of the more expensive watches from the Eaton's store. Just as I had it in my hand inside the showcase, I heard someone shout. The security guard was coming toward me. I dropped the watch and ran out of there as fast as my legs would carry me. Once I was well away from the store, I could finally relax and take a deep breath. After such a close call, I knew I had to stay away from the big stores for a while.

For hours I had the jitters, and I kept getting the urge to look over my shoulder. By early evening, I decided it was best to get off the street and spend the night in the shelter. On warm summer nights like this, I preferred sleeping in Allan Gardens, but I still couldn't find the nerve to go back there.

Just as the line began to move forward, I felt a tap on my shoulder. Startled, I turned and saw one of the guys I knew from working at the market. He kept looking around as he leaned in and whispered in my ear. He told me that someone had been there earlier, asking about me. I could see he was concerned about losing his place in line, and before I could question him, he was already on the move. "Don't worry. Nobody told him anything," he yelled back, just before disappearing inside.

Maybe it was just paranoia, but I immediately knew it must have something to do with the failed robbery. I was sure the guard had recognized me and now there was someone out there looking for me. People were pushing me toward the shelter door, but I couldn't go in. If he came back, I would be trapped inside, with nowhere to run. I stepped out of line, knowing what I had to do. It is hard to think straight when you are frightened, but if I wanted to avoid the cops, the only safe place to spend the night was Allan Gardens.

It was twilight when I reached the park. At first, I stayed on the fringes, scared that I might run into my attacker. I had intended to stay awake, but by midnight I was too tired to stay on my feet. I just wanted to rest my back against a tree for a few minutes, but when I woke up, I could feel a chill from the damp grass beneath me. The park was still dark, but there was already a sliver of light in the eastern sky. Not far away, a man stood over a barrel, trying to start a fire. As the fire slowly grew, more and more men came out of the darkness and found a spot near the flames. I stayed back in the shadows at first, not wanting to push too close until I could be sure there were no hostile faces in the crowd. I recognized most of the men in the firelight. No one talked at this time of the morning. Most were just waking up and wanted to get the chill out of their bones before the cops arrived after sun-up and chased everyone from the park.

After sunrise, I spotted a man I knew named Billy standing across the barrel from me. The moment he saw me, he came rushing over and grabbed me by the arm. Billy could be quite lucid and friendly most of the time. What little money he had would have been better spent on food, but whenever I ran into him in a downtown alley, he always had a bottle of Lonesome Charlie tucked under his coat. He would get upset if someone refused to take a drink. I didn't care much for the bitter taste of his cheap red wine, but I always took a small sip just to please him. He and I would talk about places he had been and people he knew. I don't know if it was the drink or some bad memory he had dredged up from his past, but suddenly, out of the blue, he would become agitated and his words became a kind of gibberish only he could understand. I would try to say something to calm him down, but it was like he had retreated inside his head and didn't see me anymore.

Billy was never a violent person, but I was startled that morning when he pulled me away from the crowd. I wanted to stay near the warmth of the fire, but when I saw the look in his eyes, I knew it was best to just go with him.

Once we were far enough away, he finally spoke. "You better get out of here soon. There was a man here looking for you yesterday, and he said he was coming back today."

I tried to get more information out of him, but he just kept tell me to get away before the man came back.

I'd had such high hopes when I woke up that morning. All I wanted to do was warm up by the fire for a few minutes and then head down to the market. With a little luck, I would find some work and have a belly full of coffee and eggs by the end of the morning.

Now I couldn't go anywhere near the market. I didn't know why this stranger was hounding me, but he seemed to know my every move.

By the time the sun had fully risen, I was well away from the park and heading toward the corner of Church and Carlton Streets. Maple Leaf Gardens was quiet during the day, but they always left one side door open for employees. There was a large washroom just inside the hallway, and if I was careful not to make noise, I could take my time and clean away all of yesterday's dirt. I knew I had lost weight in the four months I had been on the street, but I didn't really know how much until I took off my shirt and saw the outline of every rib pressing again my skin. There were still some faint bruises on my chest, but at least it no longer hurt to take a deep breath.

I knew that the cleaners didn't get to this end of the building until mid-morning. I had lots of time to think, but even after I was back outside, I still couldn't decide what to do next. The streets were busy now, and every passing glance from a stranger seemed like a threat. I quickly realized that I had to get off the main streets and find an alley where I could stay hidden in the shadows for the next few days. Maybe the stranger might finally give up the search and leave me in peace.

I managed to find enough empty bottles to buy a chocolate bar, but it did nothing to fill my empty belly. After two days without food, the hunger became too much. I had stayed away from Eaton's for as long as I could, but the pain in my stomach convinced me it was time to go back and try it again.

I was concerned when I saw that the crowd inside Eaton's was unusually small for a Friday afternoon, but once I was inside the main door, I knew I had to go through with it. The need to have food in my belly far outweighed my fear of being caught.

All told, I had managed to lift five watches and two necklaces during my little crime spree, but this sixth watch proved to be my undoing. I was only ten feet from the door when I felt a hand grab the back of my collar and throw me to the ground.

Even after the security guard had handcuffed me and taken me into an office, I had a faint hope that I might be able to talk my way out of it. I tried to elicit some sympathy by telling him how hungry I was. I could see my sad little story was beginning to get through to him. If I'd had just five more minutes, I was sure I could have convinced him to let me off with a warning. But then a second security guard appeared in the doorway, and I knew I was doomed. It was the same guard who had chased me from the store just a week earlier.

By nightfall, I was once again in a cell at 52 Division. It may sound strange, but sitting there in the cell, I felt a sense of relief. At least I was warm and dry, and the sergeant had promised we would get a mug of coffee and some bread before we were taken to court in the morning.

There were only two other people in the cell block when I arrived, but by midnight the place was starting to fill up. The desk sergeant made a joke about how Friday nights always brought out the crazies. Most people were paid on Friday, and once the bars closed at 1:00 a.m., there were enough troublemakers to fill every cell in the station.

The next morning, I was handcuffed to a rather large bearded man who stank of alcohol. I tried to keep up with my big hairy partner, but every time he tugged on the handcuffs, I could feel myself being dragged along like a rag doll. I didn't feel all that scared until they shut the door of the van, leaving us with only a sliver of light from a wire-mesh window on the side wall of the van. As we sped along Queen Street, fear and anxiety were building up inside me.

Spending a night in 52 Division was one thing, but if the stories I'd heard were true, there was a strong possibility I would spend the next week or two in the most dangerous jail in the city. Shoplifting was considered a minor offence. Most people could expect to be given a fine, or possibly some probation to be served at home. For those of us who didn't have money or a home to go to, the sentence could be much worse. Once the judge took a good look at me and realized I was just another homeless vagrant, I could expect to spend a week to ten days in the Don Jail.

I remembered all the times my pals and I had passed by the Don Jail as we explored along the banks of the Don River. Harold Garvy used to try to scare me and Donny with stories about the ghost that roamed the grounds at night. Harold said they were the restless spirits of the thirty-four men who had been hanged there over the years. The last hangings took place in December 1962. Those two executions at the Don Jail would mark the last time capital punishment was ever used in Canada.

Many of the men I talked to in the park or at the shelter had their own frightening stories about their time spent in the Don Jail. There were bullies on every cell block who would take everything you had and would gladly cut your throat if you tried to refuse. Any new inmate could expect to be harassed and beaten in their first few days, just to make sure they knew their place.

When we reached out destination, we were all thrown forward as the van make a sharp turn and descended down a steep ramp. Once the big iron gate had closed behind us, the van door was opened and we emerged to find ourselves in an underground parking lot. From there, we were marched into a huge holding cell directly below the courthouse.

There must have been thirty or more of us, all jammed together in that big cell. As soon as they removed our handcuffs, a lineup of men formed, all waiting to use the single metal toilet bolted to the wall. Most didn't even bother to aim for the bowl, leaving pools of urine all over the floor. There was only one bench along the back wall, and every time someone got up, there was a scuffle to see who would be next to sit down. The guards generally ignored it all, but when a fight broke out, two of the guards came storming in wielding nightsticks and beat both men down to the ground.

It was mid-morning when a guard finally called my name. I was escorted up a narrow staircase and into a small enclosure in the middle of the courtroom.

All morning long, I had hoped that no one in our family had found out about my arrest. If they knew I was a homeless beggar and a thief, it would prove that my da had been right all along. Still, in spite of that, I was very disappointed when I looked around that crowded courtroom and didn't see a single friendly face.

I was somewhat relieved to learn I would have someone from legal aid to speak for me. However, my confidence quickly evaporated when my lawyer had to ask my name and then took a few minutes to find my paperwork buried among a tall stack of files.

By the time he found the pertinent documents, the court clerk was already calling the court to order. My lawyer had just enough time to lean over and tell me that he was trying to get me probation, but there was a problem. I realized that all my fears were about to come true. Without an address or any kind of character witness to speak up for me, I was about to be sent to the Don Jail. When the lawyer said he would try to keep my sentence down to ten days, I began shaking so bad, I thought I was going to faint right there in the box. He tried to calm me down, but the judge kept shouting at him to hurry up.

Then I looked toward the main door and saw my brother Michael coming into the courtroom. With him came one tiny glimmer of hope.

The whole frightening experience took just thirty minutes, but to me it seemed to take an eternity for the judge to make up his mind. He finally sentenced me to thirty days' probation, but only on the condition that I stay in Michael's house. I just wanted to get out of there as quickly as I could, but before the judge released me, he promised me I would see the inside of the Don Jail if he ever saw me inside his courtroom again.

It took over an hour to sort out all the paperwork with the court clerk, but it is hard to describe how good it felt to walk out of that door and take a deep breath of fresh air.

Just as Michael and I reached Albert Street, behind the courthouse, a police van came roaring up the ramp and turned toward

Queen Street. Some of the men I had been with that morning were probably in that van and heading for the Don Jail. If Michael hadn't shown up when he did, I would have been right there with them. As I stood watching the black van disappear around the corner, I vowed to myself that I would never again do anything that might put me behind bars.

CHAPTER 18

NORA AND MICHAEL had a tiny basement apartment near Dufferin and Eglinton. The moment Nora opened the door, I began to apologize for troubling them. Judging by the look on her face, I must have looked a terrible sight. I hadn't had a proper wash in many days, and even though I had cleaned my face and combed my hair, I could still smell my own stink under all my filthy clothes.

Instead of standing back away from me, Nora gave me a big hug and began to cry. "Don't you worry about a thing," she said. "I am just glad that Michael found you at last."

There had never been a stranger out to get me. Only my fear and paranoia had kept me on the run. It had been Michael out there searching for me all along. It had been Michael who rescued me from drowning all those years ago, and now here he was, ready to save my life once again.

When I woke up on the couch the following day, it was already well past noon. It took me a minute or so to get my bearings. I was still half-asleep when I remembered that all of my clothes were gone. While I was in the shower the night before, Nora had thrown all my clothes down the incinerator and had left me an old bathrobe to put on. But where was my wallet? My first instinct was to run into the hallway to try to retrieve the one thing that meant so much to me. Then I spotted the wallet, still lying on the chair. They could burn every filthy rag I owned, just as long as I still had that old wallet with Mamie's picture safely inside.

On the armchair next to me, I found some of Michael's old clothes, along with a note saying they had gone to work and should be home at six that evening. Michael had always been much thinner than me, but I had lost so much weight in the past few months that his old clothes hung on me like an oversized blanket. Even with a belt cinched tight around my waist, I could barely keep my pants from falling down.

I tried to make myself useful by straightening up the mess I had made in the living room and scrubbing away the grey ring I had left around the bathtub. The kitchen was still a mess from all the food I had eaten the night before. As I dried the plates and cups, I couldn't help but remember all those times Fred and I had argued in the kitchen over that very task. Now I would have given everything just to have those times back again.

Those first few days I spent at Michael and Nora's place, I felt safer than I had in months. When I spoke to Rosaleen on the telephone, I could hear the relief in her voice. It would be a long time before I saw my other brothers and my sisters again, but it was nice to know that I was still in their thoughts. Whenever someone mentioned Da, it was hard to hide the bitterness in my voice. Still, when Fred told me that Da asked about me from time to time, I could pretend I didn't care, but deep down inside I still hoped that I could go back to Dermott Place someday.

Sometimes, late at night after Nora had gone to bed, Michael and I would sit drinking tea in the kitchen. He was never one to talk a lot, but if I got him on the subject of the military, he could go on for hours. He had been given his release from the army shortly after Mamie died, but there was no doubt that he still missed the life he had left behind. I had never given much thought to joining the military, but our late-night talks began to make me think that perhaps it was time to leave all the ghosts of Cabbagetown behind and find something worthwhile to do with my life.

The seed was firmly planted in the back of my mind. It was nice to think about the possibilities, but any real change would have to wait a few months, until I turned seventeen. Right now, I had a more pressing problem. It was time to stop being a charity case and start looking for some kind of work.

Unfortunately, there wasn't much in the way of factories or big stores in that area of the city. I did manage to find a moving company that was hiring, but when they found out about my past, I was escorted out the door. I could have falsified the application, but that would have only made things worse.

Finally, after a week of rejections, my luck took a turn for the better. After reading a want ad in the newspaper, I left the apartment at 6:00 a.m. and took a bus and a street car east, all the way to Don Mills Road. From there, it was just a short walk to the Robin Hood Flour Mill.

The manager was hesitant to hire me once I told him the truth. At least he didn't throw me out right away, and as long as he would listen, I just kept talking. It took a lot to convince him, but finally he agreed to give me a one-month trial. At eleven o'clock that same night, I was back at the flour mill, ready to start my first shift. Technically, I was in breach of my probation, but I assumed that as long as I was off the street and actually working, any judge would understand.

I could tell the foreman wasn't particularly thrilled to see me. I found out later that he didn't get along with the manager who had hired me. The foreman was a stocky man who looked to be in his forties. If I was hoping for some words of encouragement from him, I was in for a shock. He didn't mince words. "I don't really care what anyone told you, but in here I'm the boss," he said. "I will give you exactly one week to prove to me that you can do the job. If I see you slacking off, even for a minute, I will personally kick your ass straight out the door!"

After he saw that I was sufficiently intimidated, he threw me a set of white coveralls to put on. I had barely gotten them buttoned up when he yelled at me to follow him around the mill floor. It took about thirty minutes to complete the tour of the two-storey building. All the time he kept shouting and pointing at various bits of equipment and giving me instructions on how each piece worked. I tried to stay right on his heels just to hear what he was saying, but with all the noise from the machines, it was practically impossible to follow his words. If I asked a question, he seemed annoyed by the interruption.

The flour mill seemed huge to me, but there were only six of us working the 11:00 p.m. to 7:00 a.m. shift, including me and the foreman. The other four men had the job of filling fifty-pound bags of flour and wheeling them into a railway car that sat open against the loading dock at the side of the building. I was greatly relieved when the foreman left to do other things. At first all I had to do was watch the process. Thankfully, the four men on the line were a good deal more helpful than the foreman. After watching for a while, I finally had the opportunity to try my hand at filling a few bags.

I quickly discovered that the task was not as easy as it looked. Once I placed one of the big paper sacks over the nozzle, I simply pulled down on the lever and the flour poured through the chute and into the waiting bag. The trick was to let go of the lever at just the right moment to ensure the flour stopped flowing in time. The sack was designed to hold exactly fifty pounds of flour, but after my first few attempts, I was surrounded by white mounds of flour that had overflowed onto the floor. I had probably wasted at least a hundred pounds of flour by the time I figured out the precise moment to let go of the lever.

Once the bag was full, I had to manhandle it over to the next machine, where a string was sewn across the top to seal the bag. When we had twenty bags loaded onto the trolley, it was a simple matter of wheeling them out to the loading dock and stacking them, row upon row, inside the railway car.

By the time we had our lunch break at 3:00 a.m., I was beginning to feel more sure of myself. I was still making mistakes, but given a day or two, I knew I could master all the intricacies of these machines.

I hoped my efforts would be enough to satisfy the foreman, but when he came into the lunchroom, he immediately began shouting at the two men sitting across the table from me. It seemed their efforts to teach me the bagging process had put us well behind our nightly quota. The foreman kept up his tirade for fifteen minutes, until one of the guys had finally had enough.

"You can take your job and shove it up your arse!" Without another word, he stomped out of the building, still wearing his white coveralls.

I assumed that any second now, the foreman would turn his attention on me. I was expecting anger, but when the foreman finally spoke, all I heard was panic in his voice. "I hope you're a quick learner, because if you want to keep your job, I need two hundred bags filled by morning."

I don't think I have ever heard anyone swear quite as much as he did that night. He cursed everything, including the guy who'd quit and the machines for working so slow, but most of his venom was directed toward me. Every time I overfilled a bag, his curses only became louder.

Now I'd had enough. "Goddamn it," I screamed. "I'm doing the best I can!"

My little outburst was enough to quiet him down for a minute or two, but soon he started all over again. By seven in the morning

I was completely surrounded by mounds of spilled flour, but at least we had achieved our two-hundred-bag quota.

When I looked in the mirror, I hardly recognized myself. A fine white powder covered me from head to toe. My face was streaked with long narrow bands where the sweat had washed away the caked-on flour.

I washed and changed as quickly as possible. I hadn't seen the foreman since the end of the shift, when he took off into the office. I had this crazy idea that if I could just get out of there before he came back, he wouldn't have a chance to fire me this morning. If he fired me at the start of the next shift, I would at least have the entire day to think about everything I would say to that son of a bitch the next time I faced him.

I was only a few feet from the door when I heard his voice calling my name. I pretended not to hear, but suddenly he was right there beside me. I braced myself, ready for the next onslaught of abuse.

"Listen," he said. "I know things didn't go well tonight, but under the circumstances, I think you did a pretty good job."

In the three months I worked at the mill, those were the kindest words he ever spoke to me. He was probably the most obtuse and ignorant person I ever had the misfortune to work for, but once I learned to read his moods, I just did my job and stayed out of his way.

Aside from the pay of $1.25 an hour, the job had one other great benefit. Loading and lifting all those bags of flour was hard work, and as the weeks went by, I slowly began to build up my strength and endurance.

For the first time in a very long time, I was actually beginning to feel like myself again. The job had given me a new sense of self-worth, but still, I could not see myself slugging around fifty-pound bags of flour for the rest of my life. The long bus and streetcar rides to and from work gave me ample time to think about what lay ahead for me. If I was going to take control of my future, I had to stop dwelling on the past. By the first week of October, my mind was made up. I was about to turn seventeen and it was time to move on.

The subway ride north seemed to take forever. I tried to take deep breaths and relax, but it was very hard to do when I knew that the next hour or so could decide my entire future. I must have checked my pocket a dozen times, but as I stood in front of the recruiting centre at Yonge and St. Clair, I just had to make sure those two key pieces of paper were still there.

When I approached the sergeant behind the counter and told him I wanted to join the army, he barely looked up from what he was doing. He had the bored look of a man who had been forced to ask the same questions many hundreds of times. I thought my criminal record would be a major obstacle, but the letter stating I had completed probation was all they required. However, when I handed him my Irish birth certificate, I could see that it was a problem.

"I am sorry," he said, "but only British subjects and Canadian citizens are eligible to join."

Every ounce of hope drained from my body. On any other day, I might have walked out of there feeling like a failure, but by sheer luck, the officer in charge happened to walk by and overhear what the sergeant had said. I could see the sergeant didn't like being corrected, but thank God the officer was there to take a closer look at my birth certificate and set him straight. As it turned out, I was just barely eligible to meet that requirement. Ireland had become a republic in 1948, and because I was born in October 1947, I was still considered a British subject.

Just as I was beginning to think that I had actually made it through the vetting process, the officer told me there was one final hurdle: a seventeen-year-old could join the army, but only with his parent's permission.

The streetcar ride to Parliament and Carlton gave me plenty of time to consider what I wanted to say. Michael had told Da why I was coming, but I had no idea how he would react. Would he talk to me or even acknowledge my existence? I picked a time when I knew my brothers and sister would be at school and he would be alone in the house.

When I knocked, he opened the door almost immediately. Before I could say anything, he caught me completely off guard by smiling and inviting me inside.

I was shocked to see how thin and frail he had become. He had always been so proud of the watch Mamie had given him more than twenty years earlier. It was a beautiful timepiece with a gold flex band that had fit perfectly around his wrist. Now when he reached up to take a teacup from the kitchen cabinet, I noticed how the watch slid freely along his arm, almost to his elbow. Even his breathing sounded laboured as he plodded about the kitchen, trying to find a pot to put on the stove.

It dawned on me that it had been exactly one year to the day since he had thrown me out of the house. He seemed so different now. Maybe it was just wishful thinking on my part, but his smile and demeanour seemed to say that he was genuinely glad to see me.

He took only a moment to glance over the consent form before signing it and pushing it back across the table. "Do you have time for a cup of tea?" he asked, still smiling.

"No," I said, not knowing why I felt so uncomfortable. "I'm sorry, but I have to get going."

I had so many things I wanted to say, yet I couldn't find the words to ask the one burning question that had plagued me for the past year. Of all his nine children, why was I the one he detested so much?

The last image I have of my da was him sitting alone at the kitchen table, drinking his tea as I walked out the front door.

In the weeks and months that followed, I often thought about that day in the kitchen. So much was left unsaid, but maybe it was better that way. I liked to think that for the first time in my life, he was proud of me. Maybe there was still time for us to repair our relationship.

I thought that once the permission form was signed, I was ready to go, but as I soon found out, the paperwork had only just begun. The next morning, I was sent to Sunnybrook Hospital, where I underwent a whole series of physical and mental tests, all designed to make sure I were fit to serve in the army. Once I'd passed all those requirements, there was another full day of filling in paperwork, swearing oaths, and getting fingerprinted and photographed. Then I was finally handed a train ticket for London, Ontario, where I would begin my six months of basic training.

The train would depart at 6:00 p.m. the following day. It didn't take long for me to pack up my few belongings, but before heading for Union Station, I needed to say a final goodbye to Mamie and let her know that I was going to be all right.

I got off the bus on Yonge Street past noon, just outside the gates of Holy Cross Cemetery. It has been two years since Mamie died, but already the bronze plaque on her grave was beginning to sink down into the grass. It was a nice sunny day, but a cool October breeze blew across the open ground. Soon the flowers would wilt and the trees would begin to shed, making it more difficult to find the grave marker among the scattered leaves.

I never gave much thought to what happens in the afterlife, but I hoped that if I pressed my hand against her nameplate and spoke out loud, maybe somehow she would know that my life was back on track and she need not worry about me anymore. I took her picture from my wallet, so she could see that no matter where I was in the world, she would be right there with me.

When the train pulled away from the station that evening, I couldn't help feeling a little apprehensive about what lay ahead. The train began to move west just as the sun was beginning to set. Once we cleared the station, we picked up speed. The other passengers didn't like it when I opened the window to the cool night air, but I had to get one more look at Cabbagetown before it disappeared in the twilight.

As we reached the outskirts of London, the overhead lights came on and most of the passengers began to stir and gather up their belongings. By the time the conductor came through to announce our arrival, most of them were already standing in the aisle, anxious to get off the train and get on their way home. For them, this was the end of their journey, but for me it was just the first leg in a journey that would take the next forty-three years to complete.

EPILOGUE

January 1969

An unrelenting rain had been pelting the camp all morning. I should have been used to the weather by now. I didn't miss those cold Canadian winters, but after four years in Germany, even a little snow would have been preferable to the constant rain. Today had started out as just another typical winter's day in northern Europe, but by noon, it would become a date I would never forget.

When a soldier was told to report to the padre, he could be sure the news was not good. I actually felt sorry for the padre. It couldn't have been easy to always be the bearer of bad news. His facial features were appropriately sad when he sat me down.

Da had been diagnosed with cancer back in the spring of 1968, but according to Rosaleen's letters, his condition had remained stable for months. Just before Christmas he began to deteriorate rapidly, and the doctors discovered that the cancer had moved into his lungs.

Shortly before midnight on the twentieth of January, Da had died in his sleep.

Somehow I always thought I would have one more chance to make things right between us. In her letters Rosaleen told me that Da often asked about me. We hadn't spoken in over four years, but it was reassuring to know that he was thinking about me from time to time. I thought about writing to him many times, but there was so much I wanted to say, I knew it was best to wait until we could speak face to face. Now it was too late.

The weekly flight from Düsseldorf had departed the day before, so my only option was to try to reach the Canadian air force base in Marville, France. After forty hours and numerous transfers at every major rail centre in Germany, Luxembourg, and France, I made it to the airport with little time to spare.

It had been a very long time since I had voluntarily stepped inside a Catholic church, but that didn't stop me from saying an earnest prayer for my da. I no longer believed in the power of prayer, but I knew that Da did, and that's all that really mattered.

The doctors said that cancer killed my da, but I have always believed that there are illnesses that cannot be seen or treated by medical science. Cancer took his body, but all his spirit and zest for life had left him the night Mamie died on the highway in 1962.

Back in the summer of 1966, the family had finally moved out of the old house on Dermott Place. The new house, near Bathurst and Lawrence, was a lot more modern, but the neighbourhood didn't seem to have any of the character you could find only in a place like Cabbagetown.

Standing in the living room after the funeral, I felt strangely out of place. My brothers and Marie were talking about people and places I knew nothing about. There had been a lot of change in the five years I had been away. I was still very much a part of the family, but listening to their conversations, I quickly realized how different our lives had become. In the decades to follow, I would return from time to time and would always be welcomed with open arms, but I could never be part of their daily lives anymore.

Although it was a sad occasion, it was still wonderful to have us all together again, even if it was only for one day. Rosaleen scurried about with a tray of sandwiches and the ever-present pot of tea. I couldn't get over how much Marie had changed. When I left she was a skinny little girl and now she was a young woman.

Fred and Marilyn had married, and within the next year they would each be receiving a bachelor's degree in education from the University of Toronto. David was still the shy and quiet one, but although he was just turning fifteen, he was already the tallest of all the boys in the family. Philip, just twelve years old, didn't like it when we referred to him as the baby. Still, I think he enjoyed the fuss we all made of him as the youngest in the family.

Our brother Will had been delayed coming from Ireland, but he managed get to Toronto just hours before the funeral. Michael was managing a limousine company in the west end of the city, and he and Nora were busy making plans to visit Will and Mona in Dublin that coming summer.

Johno had gone his own way for a while, but now he was back to his old self. When I met his girlfriend, Alice, I could tell right away that they were perfect together. They planned to get married the next year. I would miss most of the family weddings in the coming years, but thankfully, I made it back to Canada just in time to be the best man at their wedding.

I loved talking to Aunt Kitty, but it also made me a little sad. My mother and her sister had not only looked alike, but they had shared many of the same mannerisms. Just seeing her reminded me of how much I missed Mamie. Aunt Kitty kept squeezing my hand and telling me I was too skinny. I told her I was fine, but she didn't believe the army was feeding me enough.

My last full day in Canada was spent wandering the streets and lanes of Cabbagetown. I stood gazing at our old house at the top of

Dermott Place. What had once been a home full of life and noisy kids now sat empty and abandoned.

There weren't any kids playing in the street that day, but if I closed my eyes, I could still picture a warm summer afternoon and all my pals running up and down the lane, playing street hockey. Jimmy and Kenny were there, running and laughing and shouting when one of us scored a goal. Old Mrs. Baxter was standing on her front porch, waving her broom and giving us hell until we moved the game farther down the street. It was getting on past six o'clock, and I could hear Mamie calling me from the top of the lane. It was time to go home for tea.

When I opened my eyes, all my pals were gone. It was a cold January day, and the laneway was covered in snow. I could dream all I wanted, but Jimmy and Kenny were gone, and those warm summer days spent playing in the lane were never coming back.

When I rang the bell at Wayne's flat on Gerrard Street, a stranger answered the door. The woman wasn't very friendly at first, but once she realized I wasn't a bill collector, she told me what little she knew about the previous tenants. Wayne's mother had passed away in the winter of 1967. Wayne had sold most of the furniture to pay for the funeral. He had stayed alone in the flat for a few weeks, but when the landlord came looking for back rent, Wayne had just disappeared into the night. According to rumours, he had left the city in search of his father.

When I strolled up Winchester Avenue past St. Martin's, it was nice to see that at least one place hadn't changed. It was afternoon recess and the schoolyard was full of screaming kids. One of the nuns was waving her finger in some boy's face. I didn't know the nun, but I could picture Sister Mary Joseph standing in the schoolyard, chastising Donny and Harold for picking on me that January day back in 1960.

I knew Sister Alphonse had retired and was living in a convent somewhere north of the city. Any thoughts I'd had about going inside the school to say hallo had been quickly erased when Marie told me that Sister Agnes was now the principal.

Over the years I thought about going back there many times, but my military life always seemed to get in the way. When I did return in the late nineties, St. Martin's was in the process of closing. The influx of new immigrants had slowed to a trickle, and there weren't enough students to keep the school going. In 2002 the school did reopen as an adult learning centre, but all of the nuns were long gone.

Just when I was losing hope of seeing anyone I knew, there was Donny Lund, smiling as he opened his front door. He hadn't changed very much. He had grown taller, but he still had the pale complexion and skinny frame I remembered.

He and I spent an hour catching up as we walked through Riverdale Park. The zoo was closed for the winter, but we could still smell the distinct aroma of all the wild animals inside. Within the next two years, it would shut down for good. Construction of a new zoo was already underway near the eastern edge of Toronto.

The park was always quiet at this time of year, but the hills leading into the valley were crowded with screaming kids. It had snowed the night before and now the conditions were perfect for tobogganing down the slopes. We stood there briefly, watching the cars in the distance as they sped along the Don Valley Parkway. Donny laughed when I reminded him about our little trip along the river bank looking for muskrat. We could still see and smell the waters of the Don as it flowed south along the valley floor, but the chain-link fence guarding the roadway made it almost impossible to reach the river bank.

I hesitated to mention Donny's father, but when the subject did come up, he actually sounded happy. His father had been too sick to work for the past couple of years. Donny was working in a factory down near the lakeshore. He had always talked about going back to school to learn a trade, but with his father sick, all of Donny's dreams would have to wait for better times.

His father still drank and even fought with Donny sometimes, but through it all, Donny never stopped caring about his old man. He cooked and cleaned and brought him medicine, all in the hope that his father would get better someday. As we walked along Carlton Street, I told him I hoped that everything would turn out okay.

He just smiled and shrugged. "What else can I do?" he said. "He may not be the best father in the world, but he's all I've got."

Donny and I lost track of each other over the years, but I always hoped that he found some measure of happiness. I never met anyone who deserved it more.

As I waved goodbye to Donny and stepped onto the streetcar, I couldn't help but feel a twinge of sadness. In the four and a half years I had been away, I'd always considered Cabbagetown to be my home. Now I could see that the memories I'd held on to for all those years were no longer real. The streets and alleys, even the old houses in the laneway, were all still there, but the Cabbagetown I remembered was gone forever.

I no longer felt a sense of belonging to my old neighbourhood. I remembered a line from a Thomas Wolfe novel I had read years earlier. I hadn't really understood it at the time, but now I knew what he meant when he said, "You can't go home again."

ABOUT THE AUTHOR

TERRY BURKE WAS born in Dublin, Ireland, in the tenements, near the River Liffey. He immigrated to Canada with his parents and eight brothers and sisters in the late 1950s, and they settled in the Toronto neighbourhood of Cabbagetown.

At seventeen, Terry joined the Canadian Forces and spent forty-three years serving all over Canada, as well as numerous tours in Europe and the Middle East. He retired in 2007 with the rank of Captain. Since retiring, he has written numerous articles for *Esprit de Corps* magazine and two previous books, *Cold War Soldier* and *Under the Blue Beret*, about his time in the armed forces.

Terry met his wife of fifty-three years, Brigitte, while serving with NATO in northern Germany. They live in London, Ontario.